SO-AZU-902

World-Class Selling

New Sales Competencies

Brian W. Lambert, Tim Ohai,
and Eric M. Kerkhoff

ASTD
PRESS
Alexandria, Virginia

© 2009 the American Society for Training & Development

All rights reserved. Printed in the United States of America.

13   12   11   10   09   1   2   3   4   5   6   7   8

No part of this publication may be reproduced, distributed, or transmitted in any form or by any means, including photocopying, recording, or other electronic or mechanical methods, without the prior written permission of the publisher, except in the case of brief quotations embodied in critical reviews and certain other noncommercial uses permitted by copyright law. For permission requests, please go to www.copyright.com, or contact Copyright Clearance Center (CCC), 222 Rosewood Drive, Danvers, MA 01923 (telephone: 978.750.8400, fax: 978.646.8600).

ASTD Press is an internationally renowned source of insightful and practical information on workplace learning and performance topics, including training basics, evaluation and return on investment, instructional systems development, e-learning, leadership, and career development.

Ordering information: Books published by ASTD Press can be purchased by visiting ASTD's website at store.astd .org or by calling 800.628.2783 or 703.683.8100.

Licensing information: Organizations may license the results of *World-Class Selling: New Sales Competencies*. For more information on licensing the model and results of this study, contact ASTD at 1640 King Street, Box 1443, Alexandria, VA 22313; 703.683.8100; or www.astd.org.

Library of Congress Control Number: 2009922406

ISBN-10: 1-56286-558-7
ISBN-13: 978-1-56286-558-0

ASTD Press Editorial Staff:

Director: Dean Smith
Manager, Acquisitions and Author Relations: Mark Morrow
Editorial Manager: Jacqueline Edlund-Braun
Senior Associate Editor: Tora Estep
Associate Editor: Maureen Soyars
Editorial Assistant: Georgina Del Priore

Copyeditor: Ann Bruen
Indexer: April Davis
Interior Design and Production: Kathleen Schaner
Cover Design: Steve Fife
Cover Illustration: Fotolia

Printed by Victor Graphics, Inc., Baltimore, Maryland, www.victorgraphics.com.

Contents

Foreword

Today's global economy and business climate can be summed up in one word: change. As business leaders work to increase profits, maximize shareholder value, and grow the business amid change and economic uncertainty, they rely on their sales function to move the organization forward. This means that everyone in the sales function must be in the right jobs and equipped with the right skills to perform effectively for the organization.

What does it take to have the right sales force with the right skills? It starts with understanding what a sales professional must know and be able to do to be successful for an organization or client. In other words, knowing what competencies are necessary for sales success will help organizations recruit, build, and manage their sales talent more effectively, now and in the future.

For more than 20 years, the American Society for Training & Development has created competency models that define the standards of excellence for the learning profession. The ASTD 2008 World-Class Sales Competency Model is an example of the growing importance of the sales function within organizations. The model provides a framework for the competencies that sales professionals need today and will need in the future. Having a defined set of competencies is a hallmark of a true profession.

To form a new, competency-based approach to sales training and development, ASTD commissioned the 2008 World-Class Sales Competency Study. This report is the culmination of that work. Building on ASTD's competency research from the past three decades as well as work by Productivity Dynamics, Growth & Associates, and a blue-ribbon panel of experts, this report will help guide sales training and development into the future.

This report and the model within it take a systems view. The report describes how stakeholders within the sales organization can improve the collaborative strength of the whole and unveils a new competency model that defines selling—including training and development—within the context of the roles sales team members play and the processes they follow. It is much bigger than the traditional definition of sales training for people who work toward sales quotas. Rather, it relies on a view of selling as a system, an interrelated set of functions that constitutes a shared performance culture driving toward a mutually beneficial exchange of value. It also takes into account the barriers that salespeople encounter on their way to excellent performance, as well as the trends influencing changes in the profession and their implications.

By adopting a systematic, strategic, and competency-based approach to sales training and development, organizations can tear down those barriers. Aligning business needs and revenue goals with sales training and development efforts and performance improvements can significantly increase the return-on-investment that companies obtain from their investments in sales training.

Tony Bingham
ASTD President and CEO

Preface

Now is an exciting time to be in the sales field. As the profession continues to evolve, sales professionals will find that their work is frequently redefined as organizations rethink their business strategies and objectives in the face of economic uncertainty, new opportunities, and constant change. And while these challenges may affect many organizations regardless of industry or geography, one thing is certain: Having a competent and confident sales force can help an organization grow and achieve a competitive advantage.

The tactics of professional selling are well defined. Any bookstore features shelves full of volumes on identifying opportunities, defining cost of ownership, negotiating, using closing techniques, managing time, and exerting influence. A well-documented and well-defined competency model does not seek to replace those books, training methodologies, or practices. What a well-defined competency model can do is provide functional and commonly accepted expectations about what people need to know and do to be successful in the sales profession. It is a framework, rather than a technique. More important, the well-researched ASTD World-Class Sales Competency Model provides global insight into and standards for the critical human link required for world-class selling.

The outcomes of this research study are groundbreaking; the implications are far-reaching and relevant to a broad audience. Because the study defines sales competencies, as well as key actions and outputs required for all sales professionals, it can benefit sales managers, salespeople, sales trainers, sales coaches, sales consultants, sales operations team members, academics, and sales recruiters. The results of the study also provide numerous benefits to workplace learning and performance (WLP) professionals. WLP professionals are those individuals who are called upon by organizations to manage employee learning, training, and development; measure its impact on performance; and demonstrate business results based on improved performance.

To paraphrase John Coné, former chief learning officer for Dell, WLP professionals are more than just developers of people; they are enablers of outcomes and instruments for change. They help people grow, learn, and realize potential that, in turn, helps organizations perform at a higher level. The importance of their work stretches beyond individuals and organizations, beyond economies, and beyond cultures and borders.

Coné wrote this in his foreword to *Mapping the Future: New Workplace Learning and Performance Competencies* (Bernthal, et al., 2004). That book was the result of ASTD's 2004 Competency Study, a rigorous, disciplined approach to defining exactly what members of the WLP profession must know and be able to do to be successful. ASTD developed a comprehensive competency model that helps individuals and organizations to identify gaps in skills and knowledge. This model helps to close those gaps through training, development, and other efforts. Now, ASTD has done the same for the sales profession by building the World-Class Sales Competency Model.

Faced with the reality of rapidly changing skill needs, the efficiency of technology-enabled learning, and an increasing shortage of skilled labor across many industries, business leaders understand that they must train and develop their employees or risk the organization's potential growth and sales success. *World-Class Selling: New Sales Competencies* is a great place to start.

To your sales success,

Brian Lambert, PhD
Director, Sales Training Drivers
ASTD

Reza Sisakhti, PhD
Director, Learning Practice
Productivity Dynamics, Inc.

Executive Summary

Sales is dead. Or rather, sales as we know it is dying. Much in the same way that old-fashioned bookkeeping gave way to finance and accounting and old-fashioned advertising was transformed into marketing, the old concept of sales is fading away and something new is emerging. Many call the new idea *professional selling,* yet even that term potentially limits the concept. It is not just about the transaction, or multiple transactions anymore.

Old-fashioned sales measured quota performance as the only indicator of true selling success, which is a bit like judging a doctor solely by the number of operations he or she performs. By contrast, professional selling gauges success not on whether quotas were met, but on the long-term capacity and competence the organization develops to manage the buyer-seller relationship and subsequently to generate revenue.

Old-fashioned sales focused on managing time and activities without relying on others to help. This is like expecting a doctor to handle testing, billing, diagnosing, prescribing, and administrative duties. The old approach to sales created a complicated and overwhelming set of tasks, requiring salespeople to understand psychology, sociology, finance, marketing, selling, law, economics, purchasing, and management. It created an atmosphere that is more competitive than collaborative—a system that competed with itself for survival. It is no wonder that old-fashioned sales is dying.

For professional selling to fully emerge, a competency-based approach is required. Having a defined set of competencies is a hallmark of a true profession, and the practice of creating and supporting a competency model is a key role of a professional association dedicated to making the world work better.

For the past 20 years, the American Society for Training & Development (ASTD) has created competency models that define standards of excellence. The ASTD 2008 World-Class Sales Competency Study is another milestone on that journey. It provides a framework for the competencies that sales professionals need today and will need in the future.

The study culminates in this report, which unveils the ASTD World-Class Sales Competency Model. This report defines a competency-based approach to sales training and development that can drive sales and help attain business outcomes. Equipping all sales team members, not only those who carry quotas, with the skills they need for success puts the learning function in a leadership position. Together with sales managers, vice presidents, and chief executive officers (CEOs), sales training and development professionals can use the action plan in this report to assess potential gaps, set goals, implement learning solutions, and measure organizational results.

The ASTD World-Class Sales Competency Model sets expectations that apply to all sales professionals regardless of vertical market, country of origin, or sales methodology. From the CEO to frontline sales representative, these tools help the entire organization understand the discipline of professional selling. More important, it defines minimum expectations for sales team members and supports their professional development within the context of a professional sales system.

This book provides a continuous improvement approach to the sales profession by defining what selling is and—equally critical—what it is not. This understanding is necessary as the profession continues to forge new ground while balancing on the leading edge of the global economy. An organization's ability to understand and leverage this framework while transferring these professional expectations to application is crucial to its success.

The purpose of this report is to

- ▲ identify trends and drivers with the greatest impact on the current and future practice of the sales profession
- ▲ describe a competency model that is comprehensive, inspiring, and future oriented
- ▲ provide a foundation for competency-based applications, deliverables, and outputs.

Four Trends Shaping the Profession

This landmark report was created with the participation of more than 2,000 ASTD members and other practitioners who helped define the current and future state of the sales profession in the global marketplace. They also identified key trends—economic, social, and technological—that are shaping the profession. The following four trends are driving change in the marketplace and will have significant implications for sales team members.

Globalization

The globalization of the marketplace is increasing the pressure to perform in all business areas. Salespeople are often the front line of a company's presence in a new country, but can face potential language, cultural, and geographic challenges that require specialized knowledge to overcome. These dynamics create teaming requirements that can strain communications and information flow across departmental boundaries and slow down the solution definition process. Sales team members must understand logistical implications as well as cultural differences within the buyer-seller relationship to sustain long-term relationships.

Competition

As organizations seek to expand, intense and often brutal competition can be a fact of business life. To meet revenue goals while penetrating customer organizations and maintaining solid customer relationships, decision making must become flat and frontline sales managers must be empowered to make decisions, maintain momentum in the sales process, and acquire the right resources in support of the sale. Sales teams must have (and sales training teams must develop) strategy-building capabilities to cultivate increased capacity for more customer-centered relationships and adapt responses to opportunities, requirement changes, and competitive threats as they emerge.

Technology

The field of professional selling has been buffeted by technology in multiple ways. Today, both buyer and seller have begun to leverage technology to help manage all but the most routine buyer-seller activities and purchases.

Buyers arm themselves with information through the wide variety of technology and tools available, long before the sales call ever occurs. Online marketing materials and product information helps buyers understand their options. More buyers have access to highly technical buying consultants, sophisticated decision-making support tools, and real-time access to customer reviews of products and services. Technology also has helped buyers hold fewer inventories, manage just-in-time inventory, and embrace systematic purchasing.

Sales team technology is increasingly sophisticated, and salespeople must become skilled at using the handheld devices, mobile computing, instant messaging, and social networking applications that have revolutionized how salespeople sell.

Selling is taking place in new venues and channels. For example, the "click to talk live" feature of many websites blends customer service with telesales in a call-center environment. Selling is also becoming the responsibility of nontraditional sales roles, and companies are cross-training installation, service, product development, and other staff in sales techniques.

Demographics

For the first time in history, sales managers may find themselves managing members of three or four distinct generations in the workplace. In industrialized markets, these diverse workers bring differing approaches to their work, their learning, and the ways in which they respond to management and hierarchy.

The United States and many other industrialized nations are also facing the imminent retirement of hundreds of thousands of skilled, knowledgeable workers. Despite the fact that technology has rendered many jobs obsolete, the need for skilled salespeople remains great; and, while most other professions can rely on a steady supply of potential employees from high school, college, or workforce-development programs, the sales profession lacks a comparable system to generate new talent. Over the past five years, colleges and universities have begun to offer courses in professional selling, but not nearly enough to meet the need.

Implications of These Trends: Changes in Buyers' Expectations

Buyer expectations are rapidly changing. As they become more knowledgeable and informed, they expect the same from their salespeople. They expect sellers to be stakeholders in the buying organization's—as well as the selling organization's—success and to work as partners to find advantageous business solutions. Increased competition means that buyers have many more choices and can be more discriminating and demanding. Further, the requirements of a rigid bottom line and brutal competition have driven the commoditization of many products.

The buyer-seller relationship contract has irrevocably changed. Here is how:

Increased responsibility on the part of the salesperson. Salespeople are under increased pressure to attain not only the goals of the selling organization, but the goals of the buying organization as well. Salespeople are learning that they must be willing to accept responsibility for ensuring the success of both the buyer and the seller, as defined by each party.

Sales managers should recognize that their products, which they thought were sufficiently different from other competitors, may be viewed as commodities by many buyers who cannot make the connection between the problems they have, the outcomes they wish to attain, and the potential solution being offered.

Increased need for relationship selling. Salespeople also are continuing to transition from transactional selling to consultative selling. More firms are striving to become trusted advisors to their customers. As a result, salespeople are focusing on developing deeper relationships and personal networks inside their target companies as well as within the specific industry.

Such salesperson skills as listening, analyzing, problem solving, and questioning help buyers navigate the complexity of the solution and the plethora of available information. Communication skills such as active listening can help sellers identify root problems and hidden obstacles that affect the buyer's business success. Building rapport, demonstrating patience, and exercising astute timing contribute to building the foundation for a trusting relationship.

Increased seller responsiveness. A keen focus on monthly or quarterly results forces many sales professionals into a commodity-selling situation that is very transactional. However, sales team members must maintain professionalism with buyers who may not have the same timeframe or who may have strong negotiating skills. The salesperson must stay focused on delivering value to the buyer based on mutually agreed-upon goals and objectives. This requires taking the client's best interest into account while providing a relevant solution to the business issues at hand. At the same time, salespeople need to balance revenue implications with ethical and legal considerations.

Truly productive sales environments. Changing times have brought a decreased emphasis on quotas as more firms examine the profitability of specific sales and of service to the individual customer. More sophisticated productivity measures are surfacing as organizations attempt to shift or replace direct selling with lower-cost sales channels, such as telemarketing, direct mail, or email marketing—with little or no success.

More important, because of the increased complexity of the selling environment, organizations are working hard to ensure their sales team stays focused on the most appropriate use of time. These challenges place an increased expectation upon those who deliver sales training—and rightfully so. Learning organizations and sales team members are uniquely positioned to work together to achieve revenue growth goals, improve salesperson competency, and achieve world-class sales performance.

The Power of Alignment

To create and sustain an environment for world-class sales performance, the training and development of sales teams must be holistic, all-encompassing, and proactive. There must be a paradigm shift in thinking. Sales training must evolve quickly and deliberately from an occasional activity by sales managers to an intentional effort that is directly tied to business strategy and measured according to business outcomes. Sales professionals must be knowledgeable, dedicated, and guided by a competency-based approach to develop and hone their skills.

A quantum shift to a competency-based approach will help sales trainers align their efforts with the real needs of the business and the roles that salespeople play. Sales trainers will be more effective in helping their organizations attain business outcomes and results by focusing on sales team member knowledge, skills, and abilities that are closely linked to workplace demands. Sales training and development staff will be able to work proactively with hiring managers to select new employees who demonstrate the predetermined competencies and expertise required for success in each position. These competencies then become part of the performance management system that monitors and evaluates each employee's performance on the job. Finally, these competencies will lay out clearly what each worker needs for possible promotions and the assumption of new roles and responsibilities.

Alignment Balances Competence and Capacity

An organization often will build its sales team to support revenue generation. Frequently, leaders will work hard to build a sustainable model that helps optimize the customer experience. Sales team member efforts support customer service actions, and sales managers interact with leadership teams in other departments. The efforts of the leadership team to create and sustain revenue generation activities are therefore directly affected by how well everyone in the organization works together to support revenue generation, no matter their role. It is every person's job to support the mission of the organization; every employee should understand his or her potential impact on the overall sales effort. Organizations can ensure that understanding by aligning sales *capacity* with sales *competence.*

Sales capacity. Sales capacity is an easy concept to understand, but a difficult one to execute. It rests on the premise that the more sales capacity an organization has, the easier it is to sell products and solutions. Conversely, the less sales capacity that exists, the harder it will be. Sales capacity can be measured by leadership position, market share, and customer loyalty. Solid performance in these areas is built upon an organization's business strategy, processes, tools, and innovation. Sales capacity can "create space" for sales professionals to occupy and allows them to produce the desired outputs. Without sales capacity, even the highest performing sales professional will have difficulty achieving results.

Sales competence. Sales competence comprises the knowledge, skills, and abilities of salespeople. By understanding what it takes to achieve sales competence, organizations can effectively address the challenge of executing higher-level strategies with tactical finesse and successful revenue generation. More important, sales competence helps organizations focus on what customers want and need despite rapid changes in the market. *World-Class Selling: New Sales Competencies* contains the validated definition of world-class sales competence and provides a solid foundation for sales excellence.

A Model for Today and the Future

A model for this dynamic and complex profession must paint a picture of the current reality and also point toward the future; things are moving too fast to do otherwise. It must also encompass the sometimes conflicting perspectives of those who focus on immediate results with those who take a long-term view.

This report paints a picture of what to expect over the next few years. It is an image that begs the need for a new competency model—a model that spells success for sales organizations now and in the years to come. Because the profession spans a range of expert areas of focus, the model (see figure 1) is broad enough to cover all sales jobs, but it is not so broad that it can be applied to jobs outside the sales profession. It is also specific enough to outline real requirements for most jobs in the sales profession.

Figure 1. The ASTD World-Class Sales Competency Model

© 2009. ASTD. All rights reserved.

This competency model also serves as an excellent resource for professional growth and development. It is comprehensive enough to guide career development at all levels of the profession, and it covers a wide spectrum of roles—both those that are directly responsible for revenue generation, and those that support them. The model includes three layers of knowledge and skill areas: roles, areas of professional expertise, and foundational competencies.

Roles

Most people will relate to the ASTD World-Class Sales Competency Model based on the role(s) that they play. Roles are not the same as job titles; they are much more fluid, depending on the application or activity. While there may be a loose formal association between roles and job titles, roles are the "hats" that people wear within the sales profession, despite specific job titles.

The sales roles are:

Consultant. Leverages expertise and resources to build strong advisory relationships. Suggests best courses of action based on data and helps with rational decision making. Guides the decision making of others, including internal or external customers. Recognizes product, service, or solution opportunities for bringing parties together to accomplish a mutually beneficial relationship. Acts as the point person in negotiating transactions, fulfilling documented agreements, and building the relationships that are essential to long-term partnering.

Strategist. In response to challenges or opportunities, envisions ways of operating or achieving goals that do not currently exist. Articulates the vision in a way that facilitates its transformation to an operational reality. Applies or leads the application of innovative ideas and systems to create a business or organizational advantage.

Developer. Creates business, organizational, or operational solutions or performance improvement initiatives by designing, developing, and delivering specific processes, systems, tools, events, or products intended to add value. Creates or contributes to plans, specifications, or designs that guide individual, product, or process development activities.

Manager. Exercises direction and supervision of an organization or department. Controls and allocates resources and budgetary expenditures, enforces accountabilities and compliance with work-related policies and procedures.

Analyst. Collects, synthesizes, deconstructs, and reconfigures information (for example, ideas, facts, raw data) to provide insight to others.

Administrator. Performs procedure-based activities that are often scheduled on a regular basis or require documentation. Typically involved with activities that require compliance with established processes, practices, or operational rules.

Using their roles as the entry point, sales team members can identify which areas of expertise they need to develop and which foundational competencies will compose those areas.

Areas of Expertise

Areas of expertise (AOEs) contain the specific technical and professional skills and knowledge required for success within a professional sales role. To be proficient in an AOE, a person must display a blend of the appropriate foundational competencies and a blend of unique technical or professional skills and knowledge found in the AOEs. An individual may have expertise in one or more of the following areas.

Building sales infrastructure. Defines requirements essential for creating an efficient and unified sales environment, including necessary processes, procedures, tools, and systems; works with experts and stakeholders to design and implement appropriate solutions (for example, tool or system experts, organization development experts); tests systems against desired outcomes and resolves issues; maintains process, tool, or system usability and integrity; identifies and proposes innovations to advance sales force productivity; manages reporting and administrative support as required; creates and leads sales capacity planning efforts; and implements solutions with minimal disruption to sales team productivity.

Coaching for sales results. Engages sales personnel in individual or group coaching; draws out the best performance of the individual or group through observation, motivation, and developmental feedback; leverages best practices and selling standards as learning tools; provides on-the-job reinforcement and corrective feedback; models appropriate and expected behaviors; develops or encourages relationships to directly grow sales talent; develops or hones sales-related subject-matter expertise; identifies areas of performer excellence and maximizes development in these areas; identifies areas for improvement and addresses related obstacles; develops coaching strategies for both individuals and teams; and ensures that the salesperson's best performance is linked to sales results.

Creating and closing opportunities. Continuously scans for prospects to achieve new sales, expand account control, and populate account pipeline; leverages customer referrals and targets new leads; follows up on leads and assesses prospect readiness to buy; performs necessary interest-building calls; builds and drives simple or complex opportunities by generating and nurturing internal and external stakeholder interest; manages sales cycle progress; conducts or orchestrates business or technical qualifications; acquires the technical expertise required for well-targeted solution design, business case justification, and subsequent negotiations; drives or manages the resources necessary for effective negotiations, including the alignment of expert input within the negotiation strategy, and asks for the business; and effectively addresses any objections or concerns, closes unique transactions, and achieves a mutually beneficial win for the buyer and seller.

Defining and positioning solutions. Drives the technical component of opportunity qualification; translates business requirements to solution requirements; shapes solutions to capitalize on seller or partner solution advantage; coordinates the additional technical expertise required for building complex solutions; creates solutions that clearly address and align with customer business needs; conducts effective technical presentations at all appropriate levels within the client's organization; supports the sizing, scoping, and identification of delivery or deployment resources essential for accurate costing; ensures the accuracy and feasibility of all proposals and solution-oriented communications to the customer; and supports internal acceptance of proposed solutions and monitors post-sale customer satisfaction.

Delivering sales training. Understands the challenges and demands of the selling environment and leverages that insight in preparation of sales training events; seeks out nontraining-related issues and creates separation between what can be targeted through training initiatives and what cannot; prepares for instruction by reviewing materials; supplements training events with real-world examples and relevant experiences; reviews training sequencing and clarifies module organization and events or activities; sets expectations and defines expected learning outcomes; delivers instruction and stimulates discussion; orchestrates interactive events that transfer knowledge or skill (for example, break-out groups, small group discussions); develops and manages learning attendance and performance feedback systems; manages and controls training environment within specified parameters; matches training delivery to individual salesperson learning styles; and tests and scores achievement of learning outcomes.

Designing compensation. Researches industry sales compensation metrics and best practices; collaborates with others to ensure that the end-to-end compensation environment motivates and rewards the right sales behaviors and contributes to overall sales growth; ensures that the sales behaviors targeted for reward link to the overall sales and marketing strategy; ensures the company has the information and metrics necessary for accurate and on-time revenue credit and compensation pay-out; determines and proposes sales group or aggregate competitive compensation models; ensures compensation models balance the business interests of the company with the needs of a well-motivated sales force and the realities they face; identifies areas of conflict between sales behaviors and compensation; introduces and explains new compensation processes or calculations to the sales force; and serves as the functional representative to the sales team for resolving compensation-related issues and processing exception requests.

Developing sales force capability. Assesses capability gaps and identifies strategies and solutions to overcome them; determines new sales performance requirements associated with business strategies; identifies learning solutions required for new product or service launches, or new sales force requirements; creates and updates sales competency profiles by meeting with relevant sales stakeholders, increasing awareness of sales context and following sound competency-based approaches to planning and development of capability; drives a competency-based approach to planning and developing capability based on a solid understanding of critical levers that will most likely increase sales results; designs and develops learning solutions essential for skill and knowledge acquisition within unique sales cultures (for example, courses, curricula, mentoring, coaching, on the job resources); utilizes rapid design delivery methods where appropriate (for example, virtual, collaborative, platform, stand-alone); manages program rollouts in the most effective manner; and measures and evaluates the impact of learning solutions.

Maintaining accounts. Actively manages account or customer portfolio; conducts account performance data analysis; generates reports essential for determining account status (for example, credit analysis, account performance assessment, contract renewal scheduling); focuses individual activities on selling priorities while determining best strategies for handling accounts (for example, renew, drop, expand selling); fulfills and troubleshoots orders, including contract formalization, resolving fulfillment bottlenecks, and troubleshooting off-shore fulfillment challenges; ensures compliance with service-level agreement terms; and provides contract administration and tracking centered on contract renewals, contract expansion opportunities, and contract terms requiring renegotiation.

Managing within the sales ecosystem. Synthesizes team data for reporting purposes (for example, sales forecasts, team progress, delivery, project results); monitors individual metrics achievement (for example, project completion, progress against goal, quota performance, technical coverage, margin); monitors budgets and controls expenditures; ensures activity meets demand (for example, sales funnel activity, project management activity, technology, margin protection); determines functional or organizational structure (for example, territory alignment, workgroup alignment, team organization); conducts recruitment, hiring, promotion, termination, and career development activities; conducts performance reviews, facilitates individual development planning, and offers career development guidance; manages expectations and individual team member responsibilities; ensures optimum collaboration links among functional areas; works with peers and upper management to optimally align workload, divide labor, and allocate resources; sponsors sales force capability assessments and incorporates findings into development planning; leverages technology to improve results and operations; conducts business analysis to align business goals with team performance; and drives and manages sales-specific actions related to product or service launch and rollout.

Protecting accounts. Gathers account intelligence and maintains current understanding of customer's business; develops and monitors sales plans; monitors and communicates sales forecasts and pipeline activities to ensure accuracy; develops expanded relationships with customers to achieve trusted advisor status and entry into business planning activities; screens account activities and protects customers from unnecessary sales or marketing activities; monitors competitive growth in accounts and builds strategies for countering competitive messages; where warranted, determines account transition readiness to sales farming and maintains customer trust during and following this transition; and ensures customer satisfaction as well as delivery or deployment alignment with contractual terms and conditions.

Recruiting sales talent. Ensures job descriptions are accurate and include the information essential for recruiting the salespeople with the right level of knowledge, skills, abilities, and other attributes for the position; sets and aligns performance and financial expectations with sales management as well as potential candidates to establish clear recruitment parameters; orchestrates individual and professional networks, agencies, and other resources and tools required for sourcing, identifying, and selecting the most appropriate matches; conducts interviews with sales candidates; knows sales compensation plan elements and relays appropriate levels of information regarding compensation to candidates at appropriate time; maintains sensitivity to individual personalities, negotiation styles, and worldviews unique to the sales or sales support environment; contributes to effective candidate interviewing through participation in sales simulation exercises and structured behavioral interviews or other methods; provides process oversight; negotiates effectively to bring key stakeholders together and achieve a win-win deal for both the sales organization and the candidate; and facilitates sales on-boarding to ensure the mutual benefit of all recruitment stakeholders (sales organization, new hire, and recruiter).

Setting sales strategy. Engineers world-class selling performance by helping the organization expand its understanding of a professional selling systems view; establishes long-term sales pursuit and business partnering philosophies with team and colleagues; balances short-term requirements with long-term results; recognizes and advances innovative sales practices and sales team configuration strategies; promotes integrated sales automation tools and processes; develops sales territory and organizational alignments; establishes interface processes and working relationships with key business stakeholders at the executive level to build mind-share across all functions (for example, marketing, engineering, supply chain peers); and leads and evaluates change management programs that continuously improve sales performance.

Supporting indirect selling. Conducts joint planning and marketing activities at all levels within partner organizations; conducts appropriate opportunity-targeting, inventory clearance, and sales pursuit activities; builds partner business relationships essential to the maintenance of partner trust and preference; collaborates effectively with partners to present a unified position to customers; protects partner interests and ensures internal compliance with partner obligations; educates partners on products or services and motivates partner interest selling; and, where warranted, participates as a team selling member in building customer confidence in partners.

Competencies

Competencies are the basic building blocks of a competency model. They form the foundation of the pyramid that is graphically represented in the model. More important, they represent the common competencies required of all sales professionals regardless of job title.

Competencies are the clusters of skills, knowledge, abilities, and behaviors required for job success. Sales professionals can use the ASTD World-Class Sales Competency Model to guide the training and development of salespeople.

Competencies also have many applications for organizations and individuals. Organizations can use competencies to define selection criteria for new hires or transfers and to guide their training and development. Individuals can use competencies as a roadmap to their own success on the job.

The results of the ASTD 2008 World-Class Sales Competency Study identified 29 foundational competencies common to all sales team members. Those competencies cluster into four categories, logical groupings that facilitate definition and assessment.

The competency clusters are:

Partnering competencies. These competencies enable the effective creation and leveraging of relationships within the sales context and facilitate sales interactions. This cluster includes

- ▲ Aligning to customers—aligns perspective to the customer's to ensure that the concerns of the customer are understood and addressed and overall customer satisfaction is achieved.
- ▲ Building relationships—builds and nurtures solid relationships to advance stakeholder satisfaction and professional influence in the stakeholder's organization.
- ▲ Communicating effectively—ensures that all communications are clear, focused, and based on a solid understanding of needs, using whatever medium is most appropriate.

▲ Negotiating positions—seeks to align the interests of all relevant stakeholders to create mutually beneficial agreements.

▲ Setting expectations—establishes shared expectations to minimize surprises and align stakeholders within a common understanding.

▲ Spanning boundaries—understands how interpersonal or organizational boundaries can affect success while actively managing these boundaries for the good of an initiative.

Insight competencies. These competencies enable the development of robust analysis and synthesis skills. They permit salespeople to use information effectively and efficiently. This cluster includes

▲ Analyzing capacity—assesses and weighs competing requirements against available resources to minimize risk, ensure quality deliverables, and balance capabilities with capacity.

▲ Building a business case—builds the business case that is essential for justifying the investments required to advance a solution.

▲ Evaluating customer experiences—assesses the effectiveness and positive impact of solutions and communicates the results to stakeholders.

▲ Gathering intelligence—systemically acquires need information and data for effective decision making, planning, relationship building, and the well-informed execution of responsibilities.

▲ Identifying options—determines the best course of action based on systematic assessment of what is possible in the situation.

▲ Prioritizing stakeholder needs—assesses stakeholder needs in terms of their critical importance and uses this ranking to prioritize actions.

▲ Understanding business context—develops a sound understanding of the business operations and priorities that serve as the context for work.

Solution competencies. These competencies enable the effective development of strategies and support for the resulting solutions. This cluster includes

▲ Articulating value—clearly links solutions to the challenges they are meant to solve or the opportunities they are meant to actualize, and confirms the validity of the solution with stakeholders.

▲ Facilitating change—retains an optimistic and adaptive perspective in the face of change and focuses on the positive innovations where change initiatives are being implemented.

▲ Formalizing commitment—ensures all commitments are formalized in sufficient detail to guide implementation of agreed-upon solutions.

▲ Leveraging success—leverages the positive impact of an action, solution, or outcome to advance or expand the level of partnership.

▲ Managing projects—applies basic project management methods to ensure the successful progress of critical tasks.

▲ Resolving issues—works with others to resolve or escalate solutions to problems quickly.

Effectiveness competencies. These competencies enable the demonstration and development of personal effectiveness and responsibility. This cluster includes

▲ Accelerating learning—uses conventional and innovative approaches to quickly gain and maintain the knowledge and skills necessary for effective job performance.

▲ Aligning to sales processes—understands the key phases of selling and how personal responsibilities affect effective execution.

▲ Building business skill—demonstrates business understanding to develop solutions relevant to business success.

▲ Embracing diversity—values diversity and effectively leverages the insights and experiences of others to achieve goals and establish a stimulating, productive work environment.

▲ Executing plans—organizes tasks and resources in a manner that coordinates resources efficiently, maximizes productivity, and communicates expectations and results to stakeholders.

▲ Solving problems—creatively brings new or alternative perspectives forward for consideration to overcome difficulty or uncertainty.

▲ Making ethical decisions—adheres to ethical standards of personal conduct and business rules when making decisions or executing tasks.

▲ Managing knowledge—actively captures and communicates essential information with the goal of advancing objectives or sharing best practices.

▲ Maximizing personal time—ensures time and effort align with priorities and provides for the most efficient use of resources.

▲ Using technology—demonstrates comfort with technology and uses technical innovations to advance the efficiency and effectiveness of work processes, procedures, and outputs.

Assessing Your Organization's Readiness for Change

The typical sales organization conducts activities across the spectrum of marketing, selling, and fulfillment. Sales teams often are given goals that are loosely defined and difficult to measure, such as:

▲ drive revenue for the selling organization

▲ create and maintain successful client relationships

▲ build trust and loyalty with every client interaction

▲ capture more market share for the selling organization

▲ align the functional areas of selling to the vision and strategy of the selling organization

▲ maximize sales process efficiency

▲ maintain visibility and accountability through technology.

A solid understanding of professional selling competencies and an intentional process for developing those competencies can help salespeople set, understand, and exceed these goals, thus driving revenue and improving performance in your world-class sales organization. But this is easier said than done. If your organization is like many others around the world, you have probably witnessed several shifts in how your organization approaches markets and buyers. These shifts make goal attainment much more difficult. For example, your organization's selling efforts likely have shifted

▲ from an *ad-hoc* selling approach to a *process-centric* selling approach

▲ from a focus on a *single-transaction decision* to a focus on *how buyers make specific decisions* about value

▲ from *product* or *service selling* to *solution-oriented* or *consultative selling*

▲ from an understanding of the *transaction experience* to an understanding of the *customer experience*

▲ from *hiring to fill a position* to *hiring for talent*

▲ from *opportunistic revenue results* to *strategic revenue generation.*

All of these shifts require a balance between capacity and competence. While many managers strive for balance, success will depend on where your organization is and where it wants to go. So where should you start? The ASTD sales effectiveness levels can help you assess your organization's critical work-related outputs and how well these outputs support your sales goals. Each of the five levels builds upon the previous ones and is critical to striking the right balance between competence and capacity (see figure 2).

The levels are sales science, sales process, sales relationship, sales technology, and sales competence. As your organization progresses through the five levels, your understanding of the keys to world-class sales effectiveness will become clearer and more sophisticated. Assessing your organization against the sales effectiveness levels will help you understand how well your organization balances capacity and competence to achieve desired results.

Conclusion

The ASTD World-Class Sales Competency Model provides a common language and framework for selling competence that defines the sales field—for today and for years to come.

Figure 2. The ASTD Sales Effectiveness Levels

The model's broad perspective ensures its lasting value. It defines the way people operate within the sales system, whether they are directly responsible for revenue generation or support those who are, rather than speaking from a narrow, transaction-based approach. It assumes—and celebrates—the fact that anyone who works within the sales team is a part of its success and, as such, deserves intentional, focused professional development to ensure individual success.

Although many sales organizations include workplace learning and performance professionals, not all do. The ASTD World-Class Sales Competency Model can help the people in your organization responsible for sales training—whatever their job title—speak a common language, pursue the same goals, and realize a shared vision of excellence that is world class.

Introduction

A Strategic Roadmap for Sales Training and Development

With the publication of the whitepaper "Selling with Competence: How Sales Teams Succeed" in Spring 2008, ASTD, the world's largest association dedicated to workplace learning and performance, began to leverage its expertise and resources to improve people development and performance in sales organizations. Why? Because organizations around the world employ millions of people in the sales profession who create, sustain, and deliver results for their employers. CEOs and senior leaders know that they must have a long-term vision and build a world-class sales organization, but few understand exactly how to do so. ASTD research conducted in 2007 shows that much of the worldwide annual expenditure on sales training—estimated to be as much as $15 billion each year in the United States alone—is wasted. Sales training, in its current form, consists mostly of just-in-time, on-the-job skill development that does not address the root of sales team performance problems.

To build a world-class sales organization, companies must build a sales team with a solid understanding of the requisite knowledge, skills, and abilities that drive sales results. With a solid foundation of individual competencies, developed and reinforced through education, training, and coaching, salespeople can deliver stellar business results for their companies and for themselves.

A Note About the Organization of This Book

This book has been written with three primary audiences in mind. To find the content that is most appropriate for your needs, look for the icon that best describes you. Sections with no icon apply to all three audiences.

Sales Trainer

As a sales trainer, you are experienced in training and development and identifying performance gaps to achieve business goals. You may have some work experience in the sales profession, or you may be strictly a workplace learning and performance professional. Whether you need some grounding in adult learning and competency model development, or a quick education on the evolution and methods of the sales profession, the majority of the book's content will be relevant for you.

Sales Manager

As a sales manager, you have considerable experience in the sales profession. You are adept at managing people in pursuit of revenue goals. However, you may have little or no background in adult learning principles and competency model development and how these can be leveraged to improve performance. The sections of the book that explain the field of workplace learning and performance will be highly relevant for you and provide you with a solid understanding of how to leverage the ASTD World-Class Sales Competency Model.

Sales Executive

As a sales executive (for example, vice president of sales or chief sales officer), you have considerable experience in sales and business management. You may manage a number of sales teams and be responsible for setting strategy and generating results. You have overall authority for the performance of the sales team and view the sales process from a strategic perspective. The sections of the book that explain how to align the sales process with a competency framework and how to assess your organization's readiness for change will be especially valuable for you.

Workplace Learning and Performance: A Primer

Workplace learning and performance (WLP) hinges on the belief that the performance of people is key to business success. WLP professionals strive to maximize the potential of people through training and development, talent management, and performance improvement so that their organizations can succeed in today's global economy.

One of the basic building blocks of WLP is the idea of *competence*. Merriam-Webster defines *competent* as "having requisite or adequate ability or qualities." Competency modeling is the formal practice of determining what it takes to be competent in a certain job, job family, or occupation, and then showing people how to get there. The research to determine this is called a "competency study," and its end result is a "competency model." A competency model often is represented in graphic form and depicts the knowledge, skills, and abilities necessary to do the job. Represented as a triangle or pyramid with three parts, the ASTD competency model shows how competencies—knowledge, skills, and abilities—are needed along with areas of expertise to perform certain roles in an organization.

> *[In today's market,] training professionals will likely find their budgets receiving intense scrutiny. Concurrent with pressure to reduce costs is the requirement for companies to ensure their employees have the necessary skills, not only to compete effectively, but to ensure organizational survival. A critical way to both assess and build skills is through competency models.*

—Marjorie Derven, "Lessons Learned: Using Competency Models to Target Training Needs," *T+D* magazine, December 2008

The ASTD Approach to Competency Modeling

Why did we create the model the way we did?

A competency model can be developed in several ways. ASTD purposefully involved experts from around the world to ensure the model's applicability in multinational organizations. ASTD also created a model that assumes an output-driven stance, which focuses attention on the outputs, or desired results, of the sales profession. Outputs are what successful performers produce or provide as a service to others. Because professional selling is results focused, the output-driven approach makes sense here.

The model also is designed to be occupation specific, which has several advantages for organizations:

- ▲ Competencies are defined in the occupation's language.
- ▲ The model is descriptive of an entire occupation, not just a niche or a specialty.
- ▲ It incorporates expert input that is broadly representative.
- ▲ The results are easier to defend in court (Dubois and Rothwell, 2000).
- ▲ The model can be adapted or customized to specific organizational needs.

On the last point, there are several types of models that an organization can choose to use. Organizations can build a model from scratch, purchase an off-the-shelf model, or use a hybrid or customized model by tailoring a model that already exists. There are many rules of thumb to guide which approach is right for an organization. For more information, see *The Competency Toolkit,* by Dubois and Rothwell (2000), available from HRD Press.

The ASTD World-Class Sales Competency Model is the only widely available occupation-specific model for sales team members. It considers those who are directly responsible for revenue generation, as well as those who consult with, train, develop, and support them. Highly customizable to any kind of sales organization, the model provides structure while leaving room for unique characteristics or unusual requirements. The occupation-based model, focused intensely on the knowledge, skills, and abilities of all within the sales organization, embraces consultants as well as internal and external sales representatives at various levels of the organization. The model incorporates the basic tenets of workplace learning and performance and can be used by WLP professionals and those for whom sales training is only one part of a demanding job.

Methodology Overview

To create the ASTD World-Class Sales Competency Model, analysts began by conducting a thorough literature review. From there, the team moved to a validation process that ultimately produced the final model. Figure I-1 illustrates the development process used to create the model. A complete explanation of this process is included in Appendix D.

During phases 1 and 2, content was drawn from a review of previous ASTD studies, more than 100 academic and practitioner articles, existing publicly available occupation-specific competency models, expert input, and more than 120 subject matter experts (see Appendix F for a full list of the individuals who contributed to this study).

In phase 3, more than 2,000 people within the sales profession responded to a survey and rated the importance of the competencies, areas of expertise, and roles to their current jobs. All of the components that appear in the final model were considered moderately important to essential.

In this report, the authors have attempted to balance readability with scientific detail. Extensive details about the survey ratings, averages, and frequencies can be found in Appendix E. The executive summary covers the high-level findings and trends.

The ASTD World-Class Sales Competency Model

Sales training and development professionals focus on providing dramatic results through

- ▲ improving salesperson performance
- ▲ balancing individual and organizational needs
- ▲ building knowledge within the organization
- ▲ maximizing return on the company's investments.

Figure I-1. Process Used to Create the World-Class Sales Competency Model

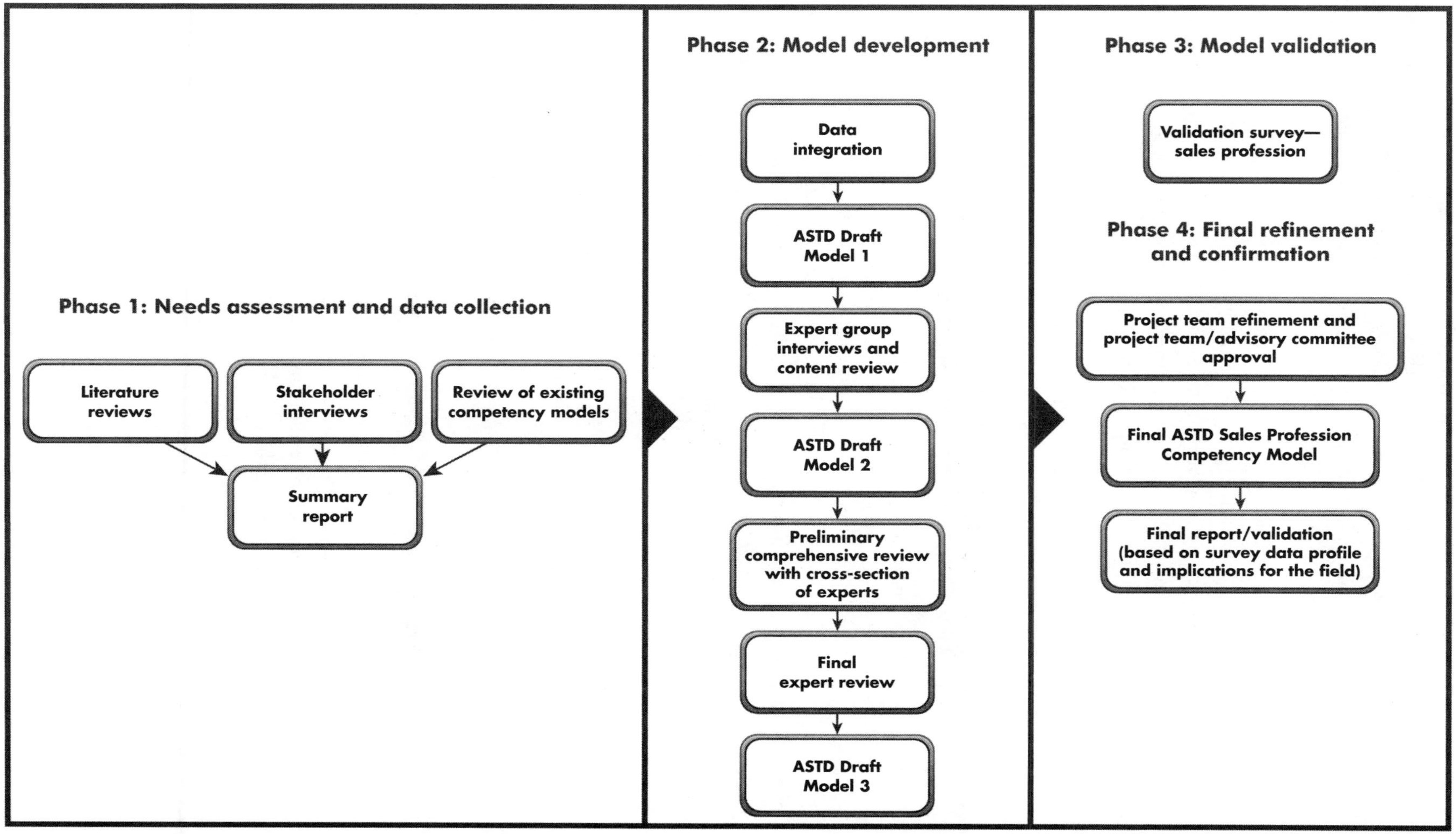

Phase 1: Needs assessment and data collection

- Literature reviews
- Stakeholder interviews
- Review of existing competency models
- Summary report

Phase 2: Model development

- Data integration
- ASTD Draft Model 1
- Expert group interviews and content review
- ASTD Draft Model 2
- Preliminary comprehensive review with cross-section of experts
- Final expert review
- ASTD Draft Model 3

Phase 3: Model validation

- Validation survey—sales profession

Phase 4: Final refinement and confirmation

- Project team refinement and project team/advisory committee approval
- Final ASTD Sales Profession Competency Model
- Final report/validation (based on survey data profile and implications for the field)

A competency-based approach applied to the sales organization can provide a firm foundation for the processes and activities needed for training and development. With such an approach, development efforts aimed at helping salespeople gain basic sales skills, technology skills, or management skills are relevant and immediately applicable.

Salespeople must continually develop new skills to contribute to the growth of their companies. The only way for companies to grow and compete in a rapidly changing global business environment is to have a skilled sales team that is innovative, understands the economic landscape and marketplace, and is driven to excel within its industry. This requires the right people, with the right skills, at the right time. The tools and systems created by a competency-based approach to sales team development can help organizations maximize the potential of their sales force.

The Purpose of This Report

This report is intended to

▲ provide clarity to the discussion and definition of "world-class selling"
▲ identify trends and drivers with the greatest impact on the current and future practices of sales training and development
▲ describe a competency model that is comprehensive, prescriptive, forward thinking, and actionable
▲ provide a foundation for a competency-based approach to selling on an organizational as well as an individual level.

By clearly defining the roles, competencies, and areas of expertise that salespeople need to succeed, ASTD is confident that the findings in this report will support those interested in increasing the performance of their sales teams and, ultimately, delivering results to the organization.

What You Will Find in This Report

The main body of this report has seven chapters. Chapter 1 discusses important trends facing the sales profession in the coming years. Chapter 2 provides a brief overview of the evolution of the selling profession and explains the importance of aligning the competency model and sales processes for maximum performance. A high-level description of the ASTD World-Class Sales Competency Model composes chapter 3. Chapters 4 through 6 examine the model components—roles, areas of expertise, and competencies—drilling down to provide a complete explanation of each. Chapter 7 includes a call to action for implementing a competency-based approach to selling and underscores the importance of assessing organizational readiness for change.

The report also includes six appendixes, including the competency model dictionary (Appendix A), a selection of assessment tools (Appendix B), a history of the ASTD competency models (Appendix C), the research methodology (Appendix D), and the research summary and statistics (Appendix E). Appendix F contains a listing of individuals and organizations—including ASTD's local chapters in the United States—that contributed to the study. The six appendixes are followed by a glossary, references, and an index.

Interested in using the results of this research in your organization?

Organizations may license the results of *World-Class Selling: New Sales Competencies*. For more information on licensing the model and results of this study, contact ASTD at 1640 King Street, Box 1443, Alexandria, VA 22313; 703.683.8100; or www .astd.org.

Chapter 1

Defining the Sales Profession

Give us clear vision that we may know where to stand and what to stand for—because unless we stand for something we shall fall for anything.

—Peter Marshall

In this chapter:

- Review five major trends shaping the sales profession.
- Discover the implications of those trends for the buyer-seller relationship.
- Learn how professional selling has evolved into a system that creates unique competency requirements for its participants.
- Learn how a competency-based approach can drive sales performance in your organization.

The ultimate goal of any reader of this book is to improve sales team performance in his or her organization. To do that, we must proceed with a shared understanding of the context in which change is to be effected. That context is created by several major elements:

- ▲ the evolution of professional selling as a system that involves multiple processes and participants
- ▲ trends and drivers in global business and in sales that have had enormous impact on professional selling
- ▲ the need for sales training and development to keep pace with change and equip sales team members to be successful in their jobs
- ▲ the fact that sales training is often occasional at best in many organizations—a responsibility shared among many people and owned by none.

In this chapter, we review these elements and set the stage for an entirely new approach to sales training and development—an approach that stems from a new competency model designed for all members of the sales profession and that clearly spells out what sales team members need to know and be able to do at work, depending on the role they are playing at the time.

A World Buffeted by Trends

Technological advances over the past two decades have shrunk our world, creating a global economy that is rich in information. This new, smaller world has

Innovative New Sales Techniques

Category management: a retailing concept in which the total range of products sold by a retailer is broken down into discrete groups of similar or related products; these groups are known as product categories. An important facet of category management is the shift in the relationship between retailer and supplier: Instead of the traditional adversarial relationship, the relationship moves to one of collaboration, exchange of information and data, and joint business building. The focus of all negotiations is centered on the effects of the turnover of the total category, not just the sales on the individual products therein (Jones, Stevens, and Chonko, 2005).

Buyer facilitation: a customer-focused selling approach that begins with identifying the buyer's needs and proceeds through providing information, educating the buyer, and then demonstrating the product's value and results; emphasizes influence over manipulation (Hall, 1999).

Team selling: using the full resources of your company to sell an account through all of their relevant decision makers (Waterhouse Group, 2007).

Consultative selling: a sales approach that depends on a relationship between buyer and seller, featuring trust, credibility, and mutual understanding; leverages the value proposition and a compelling business case for the solution (Consultative Selling, www.sales-sense.com).

changed the relationship between buyer and seller permanently; consequently, salespeople have had to adapt. Empowered, informed buyers require innovative approaches to reach them. Salespeople have invented such new techniques as category management, buyer facilitation, and team selling. In a classic snowball effect, these new techniques have created the need for new and expanded knowledge, skills, and abilities on the part of the salesperson. Therefore, global market development trends have powerful implications for salespeople, the sales profession itself, and for sales organizations.

The ASTD 2008 World-Class Sales Competency Study team identified five major trends driving change in the sales profession. These trends and their implications were identified through extensive research that included

▲ interviews and focus groups with more than 250 thought leaders and practitioners in sales training and development (see Appendix F for a partial list of interviewees and focus group attendees)

▲ a review of numerous studies, surveys, and articles related to trends affecting the sales profession

▲ survey responses from more than 2,000 salespeople, sales trainers, and sales managers.

Trends Shaping the Sales Profession

1. Globalization

Every day, more companies are developing strategies to distribute their products or services to new customers, in new industries, and in more locations. Salespeople are often the front line of a company's presence in a new country, but can face potential language, cultural, and geographic challenges that require specialized knowledge to overcome. These dynamics increase the level of teaming necessary to create the right solution to meet customer demands. These teaming requirements can strain communications and information flow across departmental boundaries and slow down the solution definition process that leads to the creation of powerful customer presentations. Understanding logistical implications as well as cultural differences within the buyer-seller relationship poses a unique challenge to sales success and is critical to sustaining long-term relationships.

2. Competition

As organizations seek to expand, intense and often brutal competition can be a fact of business life. Historically, strategy development was typically the purview of the marketing function, and execution was the responsibility of the sales team. Today, savvy sales managers have come to realize that success will not come in a strategic void. Selling is volatile and changing; a hierarchical approach to planning and execution does not meet the requirements for agility in a churning sales landscape. To meet revenue goals while penetrating customer organizations and maintaining solid customer relationships, frontline sales managers must be empowered to make decisions, maintain momentum in the sales process, and acquire the right resources in support of the sale. Sales teams must have (and sales trainers must develop) strategy-building capabilities to cultivate customer-centered relationships and create adept responses to opportunities, requirement changes, and competitive threats as they emerge.

3. Technology

To stay competitive, organizations must increase their ability to create and disseminate knowledge, yet workers' ability to process and retain enormous amounts of information has been stretched to the limit. For salespeople, these natural human limitations can strain the buyer-seller relationship. The field of professional selling has attempted to leverage technology to make up for those normal human limitations and to facilitate the buying-selling process.

Salespeople are no longer the gatekeepers of information about products and services. Buyers pursue their own early education, which forces salespeople to enter the process later. As a result, salespeople have fewer opportunities to define customer needs or answer questions about client specifications and business goals. It is more difficult for organizations to build customer loyalty by leveraging a personal approach in the sales process, requiring sales teams to be more exact and precise after the buyer does engage. This smaller margin for error demands the increased sophistication of sales-team technology, which salespeople must become skilled at using. Handheld devices, mobile computing, instant messaging, and social networking have revolutionized how salespeople navigate the sales processes.

Technological advances have created new venues and channels for selling. For example, the "click to talk live" feature of many websites blends customer service with telesales in a call-center environment. Selling is also becoming the responsibility of nontraditional sales roles, and companies are cross-training installation, service, product-development, and other staff in sales techniques.

4. Demographics

Sales managers must balance the tension of building a culture of teamwork with the need for increased levels of praise and feedback for individual achievement. Compounding the difficulty of these changes is the desire of younger employees who are seeking, and even demanding, to relate to their leaders as peers.

—Tim Ohai, president, Growth & Associates

Think About It

Buyers are increasingly sophisticated. Their knowledge of sales processes, sales tactics, and your competitors' offerings continually grows—making it harder to identify, negotiate, and close deals. Considering that these same buyers are expecting the sales professional to share the responsibility of achieving positive outcomes for the buyer's business, salespeople are often overwhelmed when their own company adds its own change initiatives to the mix. So how do the leaders of your organization manage these dynamics? How do they divide their time between revenue generation and cost management activities? With all of the shifts and pressures in the market, is it enough?

Innovative New People Development Techniques

Talent management: ASTD defines talent management as an organizational approach to leading people by building culture, engagement, capability, and capacity through integrated talent acquisition, development, and deployment processes that are aligned to business goals.

Leadership development: any activity that enhances the quality of leadership within an individual or organization and that focuses on developing the leadership abilities and attitudes of individuals.

Organizational performance: the outputs or results of an organization as measured against its goals and objectives. (Source: ASTD)

The Customer Is the Content

Al Pelham, PhD, of the College of New Jersey, has researched gaps in sales training content and delivery. In his work, he cites emerging trends toward greater salesperson responsibility for reducing buyer logistics costs, higher standards of quality control, greater mass-customization potential, and an increased demand for sellers to be problem solvers, not just pushers of standard problem solutions. Pelham says, "Salespeople need to upgrade their knowledge of the customer, the customer's industry, and the customer's customer" (Pelham, 2006).

Salespeople need to probe for problems, needs, and opportunities that are top-of-mind for the buyer.

—Tom Snyder, Huthwaite

For the first time in history, sales managers may find themselves managing members of three or four distinct generations in the workplace. In industrialized markets, these diverse workers bring differing approaches to their work, their learning, and the ways in which they respond to management and hierarchy. While many older workers prefer to work independently, younger workers place value on collaboration and enjoy working in teams. While older workers respect tenure and experience, younger workers expect a flatter organization and a say in their work and how they approach it. These differences call for adjustments on both organizational and personal levels.

Organizationally, managers must strive to build a less rigid, nonhierarchical environment within the sales organization that encourages independence and shared authority. Sales managers must balance building a team culture with the need for individual recognition.

Younger employees seek, and even demand, to relate to their leaders as peers. They are forcing changes within the sales team, causing a ripple effect in talent management, leadership development, and organizational performance strategies. On a personal level, sales managers must be willing to let go of what has made them successful in previous years and embrace what will make them successful in the years to come.

The United States and many other industrialized nations are also facing the imminent retirement of hundreds of thousands of skilled, knowledgeable workers. Despite the fact that technology has rendered many jobs obsolete, the need for skilled salespeople remains great: In its 2007 Talent Shortage Survey, Manpower discovered—for the second year in a row—that business-to-business sales positions are the hardest to fill in the United States and several other countries. A 2007 survey by CSO Insights revealed that nearly 15 percent of responding organizations planned to increase the size of their sales teams by 21 percent or more (Dickie and Trailer, 2007).

While most other professions can rely on a steady supply of potential employees from high school, college, or workforce-development programs, the sales profession lacks a comparable system to generate new talent. Over the past five years, colleges and universities have begun to offer courses in professional selling, but not nearly enough to meet the need.

Implications: Changes in Buyers' Expectations

Buyer expectations are rapidly changing. As they become more knowledgeable and informed, they expect the same from salespeople. They expect salespeople to be stakeholders in the success of both organizations and to work as partners to find advantageous business solutions. Increased competition means that buyers have many more choices and can be more discriminating and demanding. Further, the requirements of a rigid bottom line and brutal competition have driven the commoditization of many products.

The buyer-seller relationship contract has irrevocably changed. Here is how:

Increased responsibility for the salesperson. Buyers are demanding more. Higher expectations for attaining business results are being placed on sales professionals by buyers who are expected to make the correct purchase decision.

> *Buyers are now demanding an understanding of their business, objective interpretation of their needs, and a clearer translation into implementation actions.*

—Dave Stein, ES Research Group

Salespeople are under increased pressure to attain the goals of both the selling organization and the buying organization. Salespeople are learning that they must be willing to accept responsibility for ensuring the success of the buyer and the seller, as defined by each party.

Increased emphasis on consultative selling. Salespeople continue to transition from transactional selling to consultative selling, which leverages a true partnership mentality. More firms are striving to become trusted advisors to their customers. As a result, salespeople are focusing on developing deeper relationships and personal networks inside their target companies as well as within the specific industry.

Skills such as listening, analyzing, problem solving, and questioning help buyers navigate the complexity of the solution and the plethora of available information. Communication skills such as active listening can help sellers identify root problems and hidden obstacles that affect the buyer's business success. Building rapport, demonstrating patience, and exercising astute timing contribute to building the foundation for a trusting buyer-seller relationship.

Increased seller responsiveness. Historically, the role of the sales manager has been to focus on monthly or quarterly results. That environment forces many sales professionals into a commodity selling situation that is more transactional, especially when the end of the month is near. However, in today's competitive landscape, sales must focus on maintaining professionalism with buyers who may not have the same timeframe in mind or who may have strong negotiating skills. The salesperson must stay focused on delivering value to the buyer based on mutually agreed-upon goals and objectives. This requires taking the client's best interest into account while providing a relevant solution to the business issues at hand.

Generations at Work

Changing demographics have a notable effect on sales organizations across a variety of industries and geographies. In a 2006 IBM and ASTD study on the impact of changing workforce demographics on the learning function, 239 learning executives identified their primary concerns regarding this generational shift:

- Important issue, little action: Most companies are ill prepared to adapt to the changing workforce.
- Passing the torch of experience: Transferring knowledge between generations is becoming a critical capability for today's organization.
- Beyond "one size fits all": Learning executives believe there are clear differences in the learning preferences of workers from different generations.
- Avoiding roadblocks to learning: Older workers may find more barriers to participating in learning activities.
- Bypassing the learning curve: Getting new employees rapidly up to speed is taking on a new priority (Lesser and Rivera, 2006).

Key Definitions in Sales

The word *sell* is derived from the Icelandic word *selja* and the Anglo Saxon word *syllan;* both mean "to serve" or "to give." The *American Heritage Dictionary* defines a sale as "the exchange of goods or services for an amount of money or its equivalent [or] the act of selling."

A sale must therefore be a unique transaction with deliverables and an exchange of money or its equivalent. A transaction is a distinct event in the overall sales process.

A *sales process* is a series of tactical and strategic steps that leads to the sales transaction. Sales processes comprise methodologies or approaches designed to help the selling organization close more business deals.

A Sales Adaptation Checklist

How well do your sales training efforts keep pace with change? Check the items that represent strengths for you:

☐ How does your sales organization measure sales team productivity? Do you know how to use these measures to help roll out effective training solutions?

☐ What challenges are sales team members facing on a regular basis? How are key organizational linkages addressing these challenges?

☐ What is the number one complaint of your customers and your sales team members?

☐ How does your sales training content help attain your organization's key strategies, goals, and objectives?

☐ Which training content helps sales team members? Which content does not help them? Which content requires the most attention to keep customers satisfied and engaged?

☐ How are your senior leaders measured? What is the relationship between their goals and sales team goals?

☐ What is your company's position in the market? In relation to that position, how adequate is each component of the sales training mix (product knowledge, selling skills, industry knowledge, and knowledge of your company)?

☐ How does your training program help sales team members differentiate themselves as your company's top competitors?

(continued on the next page)

Increased emphasis on profitability. Traditionally, sales organizations have focused on volume of individual activity as an indicator of productivity. As such, the sales professional's compensation came when he or she met or exceeded his or her sales quotas. Now, more firms are examining the profitability and productivity of salesperson activity, rather than frequency or volume.

Organizations are working hard to ensure their sales team members use time appropriately and productively. Sales training and development professionals are uniquely positioned to work with salespeople to help them be productive, profitable, and, ultimately, world class.

Defining the Sales Profession

Profession: An occupation, such as law, medicine, or engineering, that requires considerable training and specialized study.

—*The American Heritage Dictionary of the English Language,* Fourth Edition

As we have discussed, the buyer-seller relationship has undergone many changes over time. Salespeople have attempted to rise to the challenge of meeting or exceeding buyer expectations. Often, theirs has been a *reactive* approach to market, buyer, and technological forces. The same has been true for the development of sales training approaches—reactive, rather than proactive, and they are often outdated by the time they are rolled out.

Further, sales training often takes place in a vacuum. There is no clear professional consensus on the roles salespeople play and the necessary knowledge and skills to succeed in those roles. Salespeople have been left to develop their own unique approaches and, in many cases, to pursue their own training where they can find it.

To become truly competent, salespeople must learn to customize and personalize their approaches based on inputs from buyers. It requires each salesperson to deliver value to the customer in a uniquely tailored fashion and to define *what is expected of a competent professional.* But, without a universal framework around which to build that definition, true effectiveness has been elusive.

To lay out what knowledge, skills, and abilities are necessary for the successful salesperson, we must first arrive at a useful definition for the profession itself. This involves setting some boundaries, identifying what lies within the scope of the sales profession and what should remain outside it. To establish those boundaries, the ASTD 2008 World-Class Sales Competency Study team agreed that the successful selling organization involves more people than just those individuals who carry a sales quota—but does not include the entire revenue-generation system required by companies.

No widely accepted definition of professional selling existed at the time our research commenced. The research team realized that it was difficult for academics, practitioners, consultants, and trainers to move the profession forward in its absence. Therefore, the research team attempted to answer the following questions:

▲ Who is in the sales profession?
▲ What do they know that makes them successful?
▲ What do they do that makes them successful?

To help with these research questions, the team crafted a definition of professional selling that placed the profession within the context of the promotion mix while establishing its boundaries.

To ASTD, the sales profession is

"The occupation required to effectively develop, manage, enable, and execute a mutually beneficial, interpersonal exchange of goods, services, or solutions for equitable value within the full context of the buying and selling relationship."

The ramifications of this definition should not be underestimated. This definition not only helps frame the model found within *World-Class Selling: New Sales Competencies,* but also helps the advancement of the sales profession. This definition sets forth that

▲ selling requires a *systems approach* to be effective
▲ the focus of the profession is on the *human agents involved in the exchange* between customer and seller
▲ the purpose of the profession is *a financial exchange based on value between the buyer and the seller.*

This definition has become the foundation upon which the ASTD 2008 World-Class Sales Competency Study was built. With the adoption of this definition, selling should no longer be viewed as an isolated or purely tactical function. Rather, the profession has evolved to include people who perform multiple sales-related roles. These roles include not only people who carry sales quotas, but also those who perform related tasks in the context of a larger, shared performance culture.

The sales profession includes all of the people in an organization who are directly responsible for sales performance, whether they directly sell or support those who do. All of these people are aware of the organization's business strategy and leverage technology in pursuit of its goals, but they vary in their job duties and measures of success. Together, these individuals work together to accomplish the revenue-acquisition goals of the organization

A Sales Adaptation Checklist (continued)

☐ How well does communication flow from your sales team to other important value-creating team members? How well does the communication flow help sales team members transfer relevant knowledge and co-create customized solutions?

☐ How well does your sales culture support training solutions that you believe to be important and relevant?

Is Professional Selling Really a Profession?

To define the boundaries of the sales profession, it is useful to understand the occupation of sales itself and its relationship to other occupations. The sales occupation is generally considered to be part of the marketing profession. This profession is largely concerned with what academics and practitioners call the "Four Ps" of marketing: product, price, placement, and promotion. The Four Ps work together to help an organization increase market share, build customer loyalty and trust, and bring solutions to market. For the purposes of this report, the relationship of selling to the marketing profession was analyzed.

Within the Four Ps, selling usually is found within the promotion mix and is often called "professional selling" (see figure 1-1). Understanding the promotion mix and the relationship of selling to other pursuits within the promotion mix raises the question, "How does professional selling differ from advertising, public relations, and sales promotions?"

Figure 1-1. Elements of the Promotion Mix

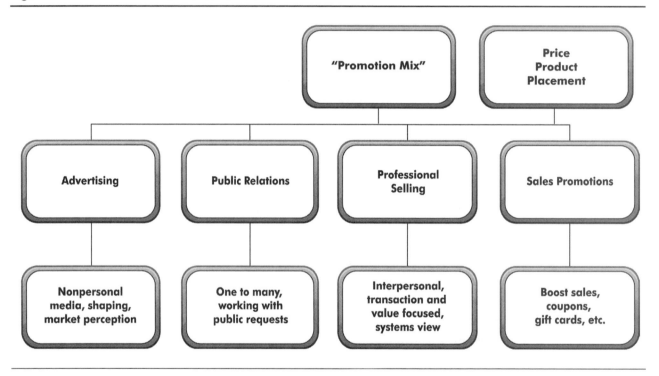

Advertising: leverages the use of nonpersonal media, such as periodicals, television, and radio, to shape market perception.

Public relations: uses "push" techniques, such as press releases and speaking engagements, to promote and polish the organization's public image.

Professional selling: defined as face-to-face and personal promotion of the marketing and sales message to current and prospective buyers.

Sales promotions: leverages specific techniques designed to boost sales, such as coupons, contests, special pricing, and so forth.

Most people are familiar with these efforts as they are used by prominent consumer brands, such as food, fuel, and pharmaceutical companies.

Within advertising, public relations, and sales promotions, the requirements and advancement paths are clearly defined. Trade organizations, educational conferences, and university degree programs have formalized requirements for success in these professions. Each of these occupations has defined its boundaries and set expectations for the professional members.

Unfortunately, professional selling has not followed suit in its definition and professional rigor. In fact, the debate still continues as to whether the sales profession is a profession at all.

alongside their counterparts in marketing, advertising, public relations, and promotion.

People who meet the definition of professional selling typically fall into one of four functional areas: personal selling, sales operations, sales training and development, and sales management:

- ▲ **Personal selling.** People within this function establish a primary personal relationship while generating customer interest; position, qualify, negotiate, and close opportunities; design, communicate, and generate customer enthusiasm for products, services, or solutions. They typically carry a sales quota.
- ▲ **Sales operations.** People within this function influence supporting sales organizations, including task substitution, order entry and fulfillment, tool/system development and implementation, sales methodology and process definition and implementation, and compensation planning.
- ▲ **Sales training and development.** People within this function design and deliver sales training and development offerings, including curriculum, course, and material development; the evaluation of learner progress; the integration of learning initiatives with sales activity; and the delivery of learning solutions.
- ▲ **Sales management.** People within this function provide strategy and direction to the sales process; manage resources to achieve business, operational, or organizational goals; and direct and manage others.

These four functional areas must work together in a world-class sales organization.

In the Next Chapter

Our new definition of professional selling makes clear who is part of the sales profession and what they do. This understanding helps to determine, then, what those sales professionals need to know and do to be successful. Chapter 2 describes the rise of the sales professional as a knowledge worker, shows how the shift to consultative selling requires new competencies, and demonstrates how the sales process must be aligned to competencies to create a world-class sales organization.

A Sales Acumen Checklist

How well do you understand the sales organization's business strategies? Here are some ways to increase the relevancy and timeliness of your approach. Check all those that represent areas of strength for you:

- ☐ understanding of how salespeople are compensated
- ☐ understanding of the sales compensation plan components that drive toward specific business objectives
- ☐ steps of the sales process
- ☐ the key value proposition of each product or service offered
- ☐ benefits that clients have in choosing your organization over another
- ☐ strategies for managing sales territory and sales team alignment
- ☐ specific "sales jargon" used by sales teams in your organization
- ☐ the top priority in your sales leader's opinion (this year and next).

Chapter 2

The Power of Alignment

Those who build great companies understand that the ultimate throttle on growth for any great company is not markets, or technology, or competition, or products. It is one thing above all others: the ability to get and keep enough of the right people.

—Jim Collins, *Good to Great*

In this chapter:

- Understand how and why salespeople have become knowledge workers.
- Discover why the shift to consultative selling requires new competencies—and what they are.
- Learn how to leverage competencies and align the sales processes to create a world-class sales organization.

Technology can be replicated. Processes can be copied. Strategies can be countered. But an organization's people can create an entirely different kind of advantage—indeed, perhaps its only true competitive advantage. People can make decisions to innovatively leverage technology, correct a broken process, and adjust a deficient strategy. The right people, with the right competencies, can enable a selling organization to successfully position itself in the market. Therefore, it is absolutely crucial to develop the unique knowledge, skills, and abilities that sales professionals need to succeed in today's business environment.

This can be challenging: There has been a dramatic shift in the sales profession over the past 15 years. Today, the people who generate revenue must be true knowledge workers. They must be able to generate data, turn it into information, and wield it as knowledge. They must then transform that knowledge into an effective solution for the buyer. Salespeople must possess both intellectual and emotional intelligence, be able to think on their feet, and be able to comprehend and solve business problems. They must incorporate their organization's vision, mission, products, and services into a sales process that builds a positive relationship with clients. Your organization can equip sales professionals for these challenges by understanding what they need to know and do to be successful. That understanding is the key to creating successful buyer-seller relationships.

Embrace the Complexity

The complexity of each unique selling environment is compounded by the complexity of each unique buying environment, creating exponentially more difficult selling scenarios. Why?

Buying organizations are savvier. The amount of information readily accessible to buyers has increased dramatically. Buyers often know the seller's full range of product offerings and pricing options and use this information in negotiating deals with the slimmest of margins.

The rate of change has become more rapid. Buying organizations, as well as selling organizations, are having a difficult time keeping up with these changes.

Buyers leverage technology much more efficiently. Technology helps buyers gain information and manage partnerships in new ways.

The global economy now demands that sales professionals deal effectively in a multicultural business environment. What is acceptable business practice in one part of the world is not acceptable in another. Buyers expect sellers to be sensitive to these differences, while taking advantage of these differences when it benefits buyers most.

Although the demands on salespeople are complex, most organizations' approach to sales training has not kept pace. Underneath all of the new technology initiatives, motivational techniques, and measurement approaches lies the same sales process created more than 100 years ago.

The first company to define a successful sales process and develop corresponding support structures was National Cash Register (NCR) Corporation in the late 1800s. The NCR philosophy was

- ▲ know your customer
- ▲ know your product
- ▲ be ready for the customer to buy
- ▲ stay engaged with the customer after the sale (Friedman, 2004).

More than a century later, that approach still surrounds even the most complicated sales systems and processes. However, what has changed dramatically are the competencies required to execute the approach.

> *In the 20-plus years since I first became a salesperson, the sales profession has lacked real clarity on the benchmarks required for world-class sales execution. This has proved a frustration to the salespeople themselves as well as to any trainer or manager tasked with developing a sales team.* World-Class Selling: New Sales Competencies *bridges that gap authoritatively for the entire sales profession. I would have loved this book in my previous life in sales management and sales training and development, and I look forward to using it now as a consultant with my clients.*

—Giles Watkins, advisor, McKinsey & Company

Breaking Down the Complexity

In the early 1900s, a major shift in selling focus occurred: a shift from *product-centric* selling to *process-centric* selling. Companies began to understand the *psychology of the transaction decision* and studied how buying behavior works.

By the 1980s and 1990s, workplace technology increased the complexity of selling as organizations experimented with online account management, virtual customer interfaces, and centralized customer support. The focus evolved to a *solution-oriented* or *consultative selling* approach, driven by the greater knowledge, speed, and flexibility demanded by buyers. Today, the entire experience—from need definition through re-purchase—focuses on providing value, as buyers look beyond return-on-investment and the overall value of their purchase decisions.

According to Brian Lambert, director of ASTD Sales Training Drivers, "The development of this model is a crucial step in the definition and advancement of professional selling standards. It can be used by a variety of people—including leaders, managers, and salespeople—to align the entire selling system behind a clear focus that balances the complexity of market demands with the need to maximize and leverage individual talent to accelerate sales performance."

To accommodate that shift and to position their salespeople for success, sales organizations must adopt a *competency-based* approach to managing the buying and selling experience. This is the approach that *World-Class Selling: New Sales Competencies* can help your organization understand and create.

Excellence Through Alignment

Professional selling is a system. It is not simply a department or a function; rather, it is composed of interrelated processes. While these processes can be selected and ordered in numerous ways, each process requires competencies—a combination of knowledge, skills, and abilities—to complete. Because the needs of the business require salespeople to play different roles, these competencies must be present throughout the organization. Further, the processes in the sales system should be selected and ordered—in other words, aligned—with the requisite competencies to drive high performance. Developing core competencies without aligning the processes simply creates competency in a vacuum; without carefully designed context, the sales system will not function as intended. This alignment can play out in multiple areas and affect important processes such as

Talent management. Studies have shown that a deliberate approach to talent management, including the recruitment, selection, orientation, engagement, and retention of top sales performers, results in annual sales force turnover of less than 10 percent (BPT Partners, 2006). Top sales organizations focus closely on the proper identification and selection of new sales team members for the best fit with sales culture, selling system, and types of solutions being sold. Aligning talent management practices and world-class sales competencies enables your organization to maximize the talent it has and develop the talent it needs.

Skills development. Sales training and development should create knowledge and develop skills and abilities, rather than just rote product knowledge. When sales leaders coach and develop their team members, an overt link with world-class sales competencies broadens the scope of the coaching activity and permits each salesperson to set career-advancement goals that are realistically tied to organizational needs.

Think About It

Marketing professionals develop new products based on extensive focus groups and market research. Customer service teams receive and process feedback from customers. Salespeople engage in sales activities that lead them to discover new competitive knowledge. Operations staff attend conferences and online webcasts to learn about new sales technologies. Recruiters interview hundreds of salespeople in a year. The vice president of sales talks to the CEO about the way the competition is reorganizing its sales team. Each of these activities involves a unique set of competencies. By understanding what those competencies are and aligning the sales process so that it values and maximizes their use, your organization can position itself for a successful future.

Salespeople Value Sales Training

In 2007, ASTD surveyed 210 sales trainers and 179 salespeople (Lambert, 2007). Overwhelmingly, respondents said that they value sales training and believe it to be very or extremely important.

When asked about the skills required to be successful in their jobs, survey respondents indicated these top five areas:

- asking effective or productive questions of customers
- becoming a better listener
- selling with the customer's best interest in mind
- making ethical decisions
- leveraging sales approaches that are adaptable from one situation to the next.

Respondents were also asked what kind of knowledge is required to be successful in their jobs. Valuable knowledge areas include

- customer requirements and potential uses of the product or service
- product knowledge
- company knowledge (of the selling company)
- knowledge about competitor companies.

Alignment Balances Competence and Capacity

An organization will often build its sales team to support revenue generation. Often, leaders will work hard to build a sustainable model that helps optimize the customer experience. Sales team member efforts support customer service actions, and sales managers interact with leadership teams in other departments. The efforts of the leadership team to create and sustain revenue-generation activities are therefore directly affected by how well everyone in the organization works together to support revenue generation,

(continued on the next page)

Sales process execution. Salespeople must be equipped with the appropriate knowledge and skills to execute the processes your organization requires. Yet, 81 percent of sales organizations say that they do not have a consultative sales process or are not following the one they have (Gist and Mosher, 2004). If organizations do not articulate specific, consistent steps for salespeople to follow, they risk overlooking core activities, falling short in execution, or alienating customers.

Even if all this makes sense to you, you might be wondering, "Who is responsible for the alignment of our sales system?" Is there a single point of accountability, or is ownership shared among groups? More important, how is that working? The people who are responsible for personal selling, sales operations, sales training, and sales management cannot build and monitor these functions separately. To align and enable world-class selling, they must work cooperatively and align all aspects of these functions as part of one system. You cannot have alignment without accountability, nor accountability without alignment.

Tackling Alignment Within the Sales System

Salespeople are the front line of any business that sells a product or service. As the faces of the company, their skills and knowledge must be of the highest quality possible. Yet, training sales team members often falls to their managers as an incidental responsibility. According to ASTD research conducted in 2008, many organizations report that sales managers receive no specific education in delivering sales training. Further, two in three self-described "sales trainers" spend less than half their time actually conducting sales training. As the ways in which salespeople communicate with and advise their clients change, their training requirements become increasingly sophisticated, resulting in instructional needs that most sales managers lack the training and the time to meet (ASTD, 2008).

While it is understandable that the development of salespeople is often casual, given the productivity pressures of the sales profession, advanced learning beyond basic product information and skills training is arguably nonexistent. A Nightingale Conant–MI/SMGuru.com survey found that 51 percent of sales managers say they do not have the time to develop and coach their sales teams, and 67 percent say they are not using or are sporadically using sales coaching (AMI, 2005). Yet, 50 percent of sales trainers say that coaching is extremely important.

A New Definition of Sales Training

To create and sustain an environment for world-class sales performance, the training and development of sales teams must be holistic, all-encompassing, and proactive. There must be a paradigm shift in thinking. Sales training must quickly and deliberately evolve from an occasional activity by sales managers to an intentional effort that is directly tied to business strategy and measured according to business outcomes. Sales professionals must be knowledgeable, dedicated, and guided by a competency-based approach to develop and hone their skills.

A quantum shift to a competency-based approach will help sales trainers align their efforts with the real needs of the business and the roles that salespeople play. Sales trainers will be more effective in helping their organizations attain business outcomes and results by focusing on sales team member knowledge, skills, and abilities that are closely linked to workplace demands. Sales training and development staff will be able to work proactively with hiring managers to select new employees who demonstrate the predetermined competencies and expertise required for success in each position. These competencies then become part of the performance management system that monitors and evaluates each employee's performance on the job. Finally, these competencies will lay out clearly what each worker needs for possible promotions and the assumption of new roles and responsibilities.

Functional Areas of Revenue Generation

Successful businesses are built on delivering value and satisfaction for customers, executing strategies effectively, managing costs, and generating revenue. Arguably, no functional area is held more accountable than professional selling for bringing in revenue and driving business growth. However, organizational leaders must recognize that there are other key functions that have a profound impact on sales success and revenue generation.

Figure 2-1 shows how organizational functions support competence and capacity. All of these functions, working together, are necessary to achieve world-class sales results—even though not all are directly responsible for revenue generation. When properly aligned and integrated, the sales system becomes more than the sum of its parts—and the use of competency-based development tools and practices in all functional areas can truly maximize its value.

A competency-based approach can help an organization identify, develop, coach, manage, and promote sales professionals with the right knowledge, skills, and abilities that are consistent with the definition of world-class sales competencies. This in turn will bring the entire operation into smooth alignment and increase productivity across the organization.

Sales Competence for Functions Directly Responsible for Revenue Generation

Sales operations. Sales operations oversees and implements the back-office processes, tools, and systems designed to support and manage sales team members. As world-class selling becomes more of a management science, more

---

Alignment Balances Competence and Capacity (continued)

no matter their role. It is every person's job to support the mission of the organization; every employee should understand his or her potential impact on the overall sales effort. Organizations can ensure that understanding by aligning sales *capacity* with sales *competence*.

Sales capacity. Sales capacity is an easy concept to understand, but a difficult one to execute. It rests on the premise that the more sales capacity an organization has, the easier it is to sell products and solutions. Conversely, the less sales capacity that exists, the harder it will be. Sales capacity can be measured by leadership position, market share, and customer loyalty. Solid performance in these areas is built upon an organization's business strategy, processes, tools, and innovation. Sales capacity can "create space" for sales professionals to occupy and allows them to produce the desired outputs. Without sales capacity, even the highest performing sales professional will have difficulty achieving results.

Sales competence. Sales competence comprises the knowledge, skills, and abilities of sales team members. By understanding what it takes to achieve sales competence, organizations can effectively address the challenge of executing higher-level strategies with tactical finesse and successful revenue generation. More important, sales competence helps organizations focus on what customers want and need despite rapid changes in the market. *World-Class Selling: New Sales Competencies* contains the validated definition of world-class sales competence and provides a solid foundation for sales excellence.

Figure 2-1. Organizational Functions Alignment and Integration

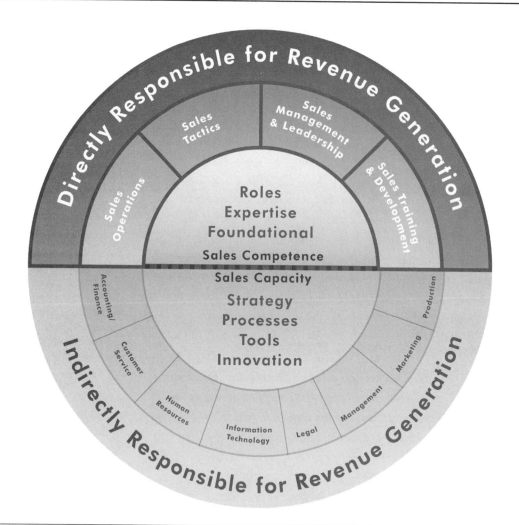

organizations are measuring their sales teams through more effective sales operations. When the efforts of sales operations staff are aligned with the process used by the sales team, an organization can increase its *sales capacity*. This, in turn, drives increased *sales competence* on the part of sales team members. The outcomes of well-designed and well-implemented sales operations initiatives can help the management team make better decisions with regard to setting quotas, determining coverage for sales territories, and achieving internal support necessary to achieve sales targets.

Sales operations managers who are responsible for defining tools, systems, and processes can benefit from *World-Class Selling: New Sales Competencies* by understanding the knowledge, skills, and abilities of sales team members in various roles and designing operational parameters and supports. For example, you might increase a salesperson's customer-facing activities or decrease his or her administrative work.

Tactical selling. World-class selling requires a dedicated sales team that is able to execute a well-defined sales process. Tactical selling is more than "overcoming objections" or "cold calling." Tactical selling aligns the sales process with the crucial buyer-seller relationship through the definition of actions, processes, and steps required for success. While most salespeople understand the importance of listening to the customer, few are able to stay tactically focused on the right tasks at the right time that lead to the biggest return-on-investment.

Sales team members who are responsible for tactical selling can benefit from *World-Class Selling: New Sales Competencies* by prioritizing tasks based on the model. They can improve the focus on the customer by identifying ways to improve the tactical selling skills identified in the model. Sales team members can also benefit from improved decision-making, problem-solving, and project management skills, which were identified as some of the most important competencies within the model.

Sales management. World-class selling requires the organization to recognize that the sales team is an important competitive advantage. Many senior-level executives are increasing their support and visibility with the sales organization. In fact, it is often said that the CEO is the most important salesperson in the organization. Obviously, executive-level sponsorship and leadership is critical to the overall alignment of the organization to support sales professionals. While many sales managers take a short-term focus, *World-Class Selling: New Sales Competencies* calls for a balance between the short term and the long term. To accomplish this, it is imperative that an organization that seeks world-class sales align its sales strategy tactics with the competency model.

Sales strategy is no longer the exclusive realm of the marketing department; rather, it is an important consideration for the long-term success and improved performance of the sales team. Identifying, sourcing, and hiring sales team members with the requisite competencies for strategic direction and execution is an important ingredient for your organization's success.

Sales training and development. World-class selling requires the sales organization to determine sales performance requirements associated with business strategies and to engineer performance improvement initiatives designed to develop the knowledge, skills, and abilities that salespeople need to meet those requirements. A continuous improvement approach, based on the ASTD World-Class Sales Competency Model, will help sales training and development professionals to identify capability gaps and recommend solutions designed to overcome those gaps.

Sales trainers can use *World-Class Selling: New Sales Competencies* to drive a competency-based approach to planning and developing capability based on a solid understanding of critical levers that will most likely increase sales results. They also can use the world-class model to design and develop learning solutions tailored to the unique sales culture found in most sales organizations, and

Think About It

Sales strategy is no longer the exclusive realm of the marketing department; rather, it is an important consideration for the long-term success and improved performance of the sales team. Identifying, sourcing, and hiring sales team members with the requisite competencies for strategic direction and execution is an important ingredient for your organization's success.

Avoiding Common Tactical Errors

The ASTD World-Class Sales Competency Model helps organizations achieve success through an understanding of individual competencies and can help rectify common tactical errors. For example:

Mistake: Selling organizations often forget about buyer decision-making processes. This sounds basic, but it is often overlooked. Sales professionals must understand and study how buyers make decisions about value. Individuals indirectly responsible for revenue generation must understand the needs of sales team members to be as successful as possible at building customer loyalty. Understanding the necessary competencies for people within the sales profession helps achieve alignment.

Mistake: Selling organizations often underestimate the complexity of the sales process. Selling is a series of interrelated processes and projects. These projects can be managed, streamlined, and more efficiently delivered by people who possess the right competencies. The integration of complex selling processes can be executed in varying ways depending on the environment; understanding and developing salesperson competencies should serve as a starting point to becoming a world-class selling organization.

Mistake: Selling organizations often underestimate what is important to the customer. While many organizations spend time and money on increasing sales capacity, they forget how their efforts affect the customer. The customer may not appreciate new steps in the sales process, newly re-organized sales territories, or the steep discount on the product or services they do not need. Changes in the sales team do have an impact on the customer. While many organizations focus on value and achieving customer loyalty, the best indication of world-class sales performance can be summed up in one word: *trust*.

they can tailor rapid design and delivery methods to better support the sales team through an integrated use of virtual, collaborative, and classroom training as appropriate.

Sales Capacity for Functional Areas Indirectly Responsible for Revenue Generation

Marketing. The profession of selling is as much of a "subset" of marketing as it is a separate profession. Both occupations are separate but equal in driving revenue for an organization. When they work together successfully, an organization will achieve greater profits and drive more revenue. Marketing professionals can benefit from this book by tailoring their marketing materials and design strategies to leverage the competencies of salespeople.

Management. Many organizations, whether they sell services or solutions, rely on managers to define requirements, hire the right people, manage communication, and create the service offering for customers. Managers can benefit from *World-Class Selling: New Sales Competencies* by understanding how to work with sales professionals to create the right service or product, define scope, manage risk, maintain quality, and manage processes that support sales success.

Human resources. Human resource functions are critical to the success of the sales organization. HR compensation, hiring, and development practices for sales professionals must encompass the entire continuum of the sales transaction. The right talent must be hired into the best sales positions that fit individual strengths and weaknesses, and then those people must be developed and retained. HR professionals who understand *World-Class Selling: New Sales Competencies* are in a better position to provide proper assessment, compensation, and training practices for sales teams that support the revenue-generation efforts of the company.

Customer service. Customer service staff work alongside sales professionals to create a positive buying atmosphere and experience for customers. Customer service is a value-added service that is often integral to the success of the sale. Customer service professionals can benefit from understanding world-class selling competencies and gaining a deeper understanding of how sales team members articulate value.

Information technology. Information technology and its deployment and support can make or break the effectiveness of a salesperson. IT professionals can enable the sales process and often will help troubleshoot sales calls from the field. By understanding *World-Class Selling: New Sales Competencies*, IT professionals can provide their sales colleagues with technology that helps maximize knowledge, skills, and abilities while navigating the steps of the sales process.

Production. A production organization is the crucial business unit that produces what the sales professional is selling. This could be the actual manufacturing facility (for products), or the service organization that codes software, programs the database, or customizes the solution, to name but a few. *World-Class Selling: New Sales Competencies* can help production teams appreciate the constraints often placed on sales team members and help them understand the context of the buyer-seller relationship.

Accounting and finance. Accounting and finance organizations play a vital role in helping sales professionals price products and build a return-on-investment strategy that resonates with buyers. Accounting and finance professionals who understand *World-Class Selling: New Sales Competencies* are in a better position to streamline billing, collection, and finance functions for sales transactions.

Legal. The legal administration of internal forms, documentation, and other paperwork is crucial to properly selling the product and/or service. Often an organization will provide some sort of legal support for the sales professional, or the sales professional might outsource this function. Obviously, the more legal requirements are placed on salespeople, the less time they have available for selling. Legal employees who understand *World-Class Selling: New Sales Competencies* can proactively identify ways to help salespeople lighten their administrative workload to allow for more value-added and customer-facing activities.

In the Next Chapter

Chapter 3 provides an overview of the ASTD World-Class Sales Competency Model, which includes the competencies and areas of expertise that sales team members must have and the roles that they will play to succeed in the future.

Chapter 3

A Model of World-Class Sales Competency

A bad system will beat a good person every time.

—W. Edwards Deming

———————▲———————

In this chapter:

- Examine the ASTD World-Class Sales Competency Model.
- Learn about the research premises that drove the development of the model.
- Understand how a competency-based approach can positively affect sales performance.

As the world of selling has become more complex, so have its demands on salespeople. Over the past 15 years, researchers have found that one of the key determinants of sales team member performance was role variability. For example, within the turbulent business environment, sales professionals fill multiple roles, both formally and informally, and are faced with making many decisions that drive the outcomes of their work. Sales team members who clearly understand their roles are those who are most successful in their work.

Conversely, a vaguely defined role can have a negative impact on a salesperson's job satisfaction and performance. It can impair his or her ability to communicate with other salespeople and understand what is necessary for success. Sales trainers and sales managers often are tasked with helping salespeople who are struggling. Unfortunately, many of the approaches available to them do not really address the problem. Those outmoded approaches do not encompass the wide variety of processes, tools, or resources that world-class sales performance requires and fail to approach it as an integrated system. Effective sales training helps salespeople and their managers

- ▲ close more business deals
- ▲ decrease new-hire ramp-up times
- ▲ accelerate the development of high performers and sales leaders
- ▲ retain high performers and sales leaders
- ▲ implement robust coaching programs
- ▲ manage important customer-facing knowledge
- ▲ enable business growth-oriented change
- ▲ design and deliver relevant training.

A clear definition of world-class sales competencies can help organizations better prepare salespeople to tackle the increasingly complex challenges of selling in a global marketplace with collapsed timeframes and sophisticated solutions. It is time to evolve the way organizations view that preparation and to change to a more systematic competency mindset from the just-in-time, on-the-job skill acquisition that many companies have used. As part of that, the current focus must shift.

Developing an Externally-Focused, Market-Driven Model

It is critical that organizations adopt a market-oriented view when designing and developing sales training. Competency models based on internal systems, processes, and tools will miss the mark. An externally focused model, however, based on market changes and incorporating customer needs and industry trends, will help organizations drive more revenue.

This focus on the external market is proven to work. According to HR Chally, a consulting firm headquartered in Cleveland, Ohio, competencies form the foundation for superior customer relationships (2008). In today's buying and selling relationships, customers expect salespeople to change along with them. They expect salespeople to be professionals who can understand changes in the customer's business and to identify and satisfy their needs.

In conducting the research for *World-Class Selling: New Sales Competencies,* the ASTD research team convened a special session of advisory panelists to discuss changing buyer expectations and how those expectations create the need for new sales competencies. They suggested that buyers most want:

Business understanding and savvy. Salespeople must deeply understand the customer's business. This means knowing the customers' systems, strategies, challenges, and organizational culture. Intimate customer knowledge is now a prerequisite to being a value-added professional.

Creativity and out-of-the-box thinking. When buyers have a business problem and pursue outside assistance, it is frequently because they perceive their problem as unique and unsuited to conventional internal solutions. They want innovation and fresh ideas for solving their problems. This type of thinking is a major source of value in today's salesperson.

Problem solving. Customers want salespeople to think beyond technical features and functions to the actual implementation of the product or service in the customer's unique business environment. Customers want to know what the offering will do for them. The new sales professional must be a business consultant who can visualize a solution and ensure that it delivers results for the customer.

The ASTD World-Class Sales Competency Model was created with the input of more than 2,000 thought leaders, experts, and practitioners in the sales profession. It was created by sales professionals for sales professionals. The model provides a common language and framework for selling competence that defines the field—for today and for years to come.

Accessibility. If anything has changed in the workplace in the past decade, it is the connectivity of today's workforce. Desk phones, desktop computers, and pagers have been replaced by cell phones, laptops, and mobile communication devices, creating a customer expectation that sellers are available 24/7.

Personal accountability. Customers are tired of pass-the-buck sellers. They do not want a salesperson to close the deal and run; they want to work with a business partner who is personally committed to a successful outcome. Business-to-business customers are usually accountable for the results inside their organizations, and they want a partner in that accountability.

Loyalty and team spirit. Customers have little or no control over what happens inside the selling company, yet the inner workings of the sales function can have a dramatic impact on the buying experience. For this reason, buyers expect salespeople to be their internal advocates, adapting the selling company's processes and practices to the customer's benefit.

A solutions mindset. The word *solution* has been overused in the sales arena, but its prevalence does point to a major shift in customer expectations. Customers no longer buy products or services; they buy solutions to their business problems. They expect a professional salesperson to diagnose, prescribe, and resolve their issues, not just sell them products.

These seven needs are real customer expectations that have evolved in the past five to 10 years. They are not secret; they are demands that salespeople encounter every day. So the question becomes, "How does your sales training equip sales team members to meet these expectations?" Sales executives must put these demands in the context of their own sales force and create an organization of people who can meet these customer needs with the right skills and abilities. Adopting a competency-based model for sales training and development is the key.

This is how world-class sales organizations set themselves apart. Their sales forces have evolved with their customers, cultivating new and complementary capabilities. They have identified the organizational approach that drives success with their customers, and they provide their salespeople with the necessary knowledge, skills, and abilities to navigate that approach. This book reveals the results of ASTD's research into the foundational competencies required to sell with success, and unveils an innovative new model that shows organizations how to leverage those competencies to move into new markets, capture market share, and excel at delivering value to customers.

> *We can never really change someone; people must change themselves. But we can help. We can be a resource. We can nurture, encourage, and support.*
>
> —Stephen R. Covey

Think About It

These seven needs are real customer expectations that have evolved in the past five to 10 years. They are not secret; they are demands that salespeople encounter every day. So the question becomes, "How does your sales training equip sales team members to meet these expectations?"

Competence versus Intelligence

The idea of understanding *competence* as opposed to *intelligence* was first framed in the early 1970s by David McClelland, a former Harvard psychologist who conducted research with the U.S. government. McClelland sought an unbiased, objective measure of people's aptitude as well as their potential to succeed within a given job. A catalyst for the use of the word *competency* in the management field was Richard Boyatzis' book *The Competent Manager* (1982). It is from this early work that many of the attempts to define competency as a research construct have emerged.

Result: A service that an employee renders to others.

Output: A tangible product that an individual delivers to others, especially colleagues, customers, or clients.

Source: McLagan and Suhadolnik (1991).

How Sales Teams Define Competence

To understand *competence,* we must first understand that its building blocks are a person's ability to process and make sense of information from the environment. This information is then turned into knowledge, skills, and abilities. *Knowledge* is what a person knows about a specific topic, such as information about market trends. *Skills* are the things that people have learned to do, such as performing a sales call. *Abilities* refer to the capacity to do something or perform a task, whether or not it is skillful. They are known in shorthand as KSAs. These three elements—knowledge, skills, and abilities—are the cornerstones of *competence.* Collectively, they form a *competency.*

Often, organizations strive to manage or change salesperson behavior to achieve a goal. Managers learn to measure important metrics of salesperson activity, such as the number of calls to make an appointment or the number of proposals to close a deal. Many managers determine whom to hire based on the past behavior of the salesperson—again, often measured by metrics. Because the sales profession is so quantifiable, it seems appropriate to use past metrics as a determinant of future success, because they seem to be reflective of a salesperson's ability to get the job done.

But because selling is really about attaining business results, competencies can better help sales managers, sales trainers, and sales leaders understand and define the knowledge, skills, and abilities salespeople need to produce results. Competencies provide a far more effective way to predict future results and outputs.

Highly competent salespeople exhibit the right behavior at the right time, with the right level of skill. For many salespeople, this ability is developed naturally. New salespeople are expected to learn the most effective way to accomplish a task, and often learn it by trial and error.

This on-the-job approach to developing sales competency begs the question: "Why are some salespeople more effective than others?" Hypothetically speaking, if people can experience the same environmental dynamics, their results should be similar. Yet the role of sales professionals is more complex than their working environment or work processes.

Effectiveness derives from a person's behavior. Goal setting, performance management, attention to detail, and teambuilding skills provide the foundation for effectiveness. Taking initiative, inspiring, setting an example, delegating, coaching, creating, learning, coordinating, and acting strategically are demonstrable results or outputs of effectiveness.

Because of the complexity of buyer-seller relationships, highly effective salespeople have their own internal frameworks for organizing knowledge and responding to needs. In other words, their hidden competencies become observable through their actions, in the form of an output. Then, based on customer response, salespeople reinforce their positive attributes and correct or remediate their negative ones. Yet this process of reinforcement and correction is often completely unconscious.

A results-based competency model highlights the competencies required to produce outputs or results. The key to improving performance lies in externally defining and organizing world-class sales competencies, which include knowledge, skills, and abilities. When those are made overt and integrated into the sales system, an organization can engage in world-class selling.

> *World-Class Selling: New Sales Competencies is more than a book; it is a tool that any organization with a sales force must have. Shave years off aligning performance improvement initiatives with sales competencies through this validated, forward-thinking work that will help you transform from traditional training function to strategic business partner.*

—Tina K. Busch, vice president, learning and performance, Pitney Bowes, Inc.

Premises of the ASTD World-Class Sales Competency Model

In conducting the research required for *World-Class Selling: New Sales Competencies,* there were several premises that influenced the model design and research methodology. They include the following:

The profession of selling is a system. The research team did not focus on any one single job title, role, or skill area. Rather, the team set out to identify and define what it takes to become a world-class selling organization, encompassing not only the people responsible and accountable for generating revenue, but also the people who develop and directly support them.

The whole is greater than the sum of the parts. The blend of competencies, skills, areas of expertise, and roles adds power and utility to the model. Any one part of the model, viewed in isolation, would narrow the definition of world-class sales competencies. Taken as a whole, however, the model can be used in a variety of ways within a variety of circumstances, industries, markets, and geographies.

The model provides a solid foundation. Because it is formed by understanding what sales professionals need to know and do to be successful, the final validated model provides a solid foundation for building talent management programs, training programs, coaching programs, and other organization-specific, competency-based deliverables through wholesale adoption of the model or licensing of the model for commercial purposes.

Know What You Do Not Know

In the early 1970s, Noel Burch, an employee of Gordon Training International, developed a four-quadrant model that defines people's varying levels of consciousness about what they do and do not know. He coined four new terms:

Unconscious incompetence. As an unconscious incompetent, you do not know what you do not know. You lack knowledge and skills in the area in question and are unaware of this gap. For example, you do not know that you cannot tie your shoes when you are two years old.

Conscious incompetence. As a conscious incompetent, you realize that you are not as expert as perhaps you thought you were or thought you could be. For example, you become aware you can tie your shoes, but you cannot tie them without help when you are four or five years old.

Conscious competence. Becoming consciously competent often takes a while, as you steadily learn about the new area, either through experience or more formal learning. This process can go in fits and starts as you learn, forget, plateau, and start anew. For example, you work at learning to tie your shoes with coaching and training. You become aware that you have to think about the steps involved when you are five or six years old.

Unconscious competence. Eventually you reach a point where you no longer have to think about what you are doing and are competent without the significant effort that characterizes the state of conscious competence. For example, after a few years of practice, you no longer think about it, and you can just tie your shoes.

Source: ChangingMinds.org (2002–2009).

Think About It

There is a global shortage of highly competent salespeople. Further, organizations often do not understand the competencies required for their salespeople to succeed. However, customers will not be lenient. They know which competencies and outputs are most important to them when it comes to interactions with salespeople. It is time to train for competency, not just hire for it—because there just are not as many salespeople to hire.

- The firm Manpower discovered for the second year in a row that vacancies in business-to-business sales positions were the hardest to fill in the United States and several other countries (Talent Shortage Survey Results, 2007).
- The authors of the 2007 Annual Sales Performance Optimization Survey of 1,300 selling organizations wrote, "For the third year in a row, [we] continue to see that most firms plan to add net-new sales representatives; and we see nearly 15 percent of all firms planning to increase the size of their sales teams by 21 percent or more" (Dickie and Trailer, 2007).

The model is applicable across all types of organizations. The model is worded in such a way that the foundational competencies, areas of expertise, and roles apply to as many different types of business-to-business selling organizations as possible, including those that sell to the public sector.

The model is relevant to multiple levels of the organization. The model can be aligned to support people at novice, intermediate, and expert levels within the sales organization as well as people with varying degrees of tenure.

The model is validated qualitatively and quantitatively. By following a standardized and well-documented approach and utilizing a third-party organization to validate results, ASTD has ensured that the World-Class Sales Competency Model is statistically valid. The qualitative information gathered through interviews and focus groups was reviewed and met face validity and content validity standards. The quantitative data collected contains enough responses to be applicable and generalizable to each population (see Appendix D for the research methodology employed).

The model is future oriented. By its design, competency modeling captures the knowledge, skills, and abilities of individuals at a specific time. By asking the advisory panel, interviewees, and focus group members to project themselves three years into the future, the research team took a forward-thinking approach and developed a model that will be relevant for years to come.

The ultimate goal is exemplary performance. The research team remained grounded in the premise that the model should not focus on adequate performance of each sales competency; rather, the focus should be on those individuals who model exemplary performance and provide many of an organization's key outputs and results.

The model is focused on improving sales performance through learning. While there are many ways to approach competency modeling, the research team focused extensively on the ability and use of the model in a learning, training, and development context. This ensured that the model is relevant and appropriate to sales professionals who are skilled at developing competency statements, conducting job analysis, and modeling best practices.

The research methodology and approach outlined in Appendix D of this book were created to define world-class selling and uncover the requisite competencies for success in the sales field. More broadly, the methodology also allowed the research team to determine the competencies required of all people in the sales profession. Although not all organizations utilize all of the competencies, it helps to be aware of them and how they may be leveraged in competitor organizations.

The ASTD approach to competency modeling combines the visible attributes of knowledge and skill with behavior and actions to produce a clearer picture for success in a specific job: the expected results and outputs. Sales managers, trainers, coaches, and consultants can all use the competency model for multiple purposes—employee recruitment, selection, or assessment; curriculum and training material development; informing coaching, counseling, and mentoring relationships; and benchmarking.

The goal of the ASTD World-Class Sales Competency Model is to bring these traditional uses together to meet the specific needs of the sales organization.

A Model of World-Class Sales Competencies

The ASTD World-Class Sales Competency Model is represented as a pyramid. It includes three layers of increasingly specific ability:

Roles are broad areas of responsibility. Roles are not the same as job titles; they are much more fluid. Playing different roles is analogous to maintaining a collection of hats—when the situation requires, the sales professional can slip out of one hat and into another one. Different hats or roles require different areas of expertise and competencies to be successful.

Areas of expertise (AOEs) represent knowledge and skill in specific sales areas or specialties. A person may possess expertise in one or more of the AOEs, and each AOE will incorporate multiple competencies.

Competencies are focused, narrower areas of knowledge, skill, and ability. They are common to the sales profession regardless of specialty—and critical to all. Competencies are grouped into four major categories: partnering, insight, solutions, and effectiveness.

Each foundational competency and AOE includes a definition, a list of key skills and knowledge statements, a list of key actions, and sample outputs.

For a full listing of the definitions, key actions, and key knowledge areas, see Appendix A; for a full listing of every component in the model and its associated importance ratings, see Appendix E.

Hypothetically Speaking...

Let us drill down through a hypothetical sales organization—starting at the executive level—and look at a few examples of how the roles, AOEs, and competencies depicted in Figure 3-1 might come into play for a few specific positions.

Example: Chief Learning Officer

Because an organization's chief learning officer (CLO) is responsible for the learning and development of sales team members, he or she needs expertise in

Competency: A cluster of related knowledge, skills, abilities, and behaviors that affects a major part of one's job. A competency should correlate with performance on the job and have the ability to be measured.

Competency model: Structures "designed to define the knowledge, skills, and attitudes required for high performance...[and that] allow for a highly targeted training needs assessment and provide a road map to more objectively manage talent for competitive advantage" (Derven, 2008).

Think About It

The boundary between visible and hidden competencies poses a dilemma for many sales team leaders. For example, what truly separates the peak performers from everyone else? Is it what they have learned or how they are wired? Can innate abilities be taught? Salesperson competency contains a complex hierarchy of interrelated and interdependent factors and abilities that must be understood in relation to the factors influencing the performance of an individual, all within his or her unique job setting.

Of course, a person's ability to perform depends upon his or her knowledge, skills, and abilities; however, focusing solely on one as the determinant of others does not approach selling as a profession. Have you ever hired a peak performer from another organization who did not perform well in the new organization? It would seem that the individual's knowledge, skill, and ability to perform within the system had more to do with success than just individual traits. The key is to define success in terms that are greater than just the past performance of the highest performers. Success should be defined as the ability to apply the right competency to the right situation to achieve high performance...now.

Figure 3-1. The ASTD Model World-Class Sales Competency Model

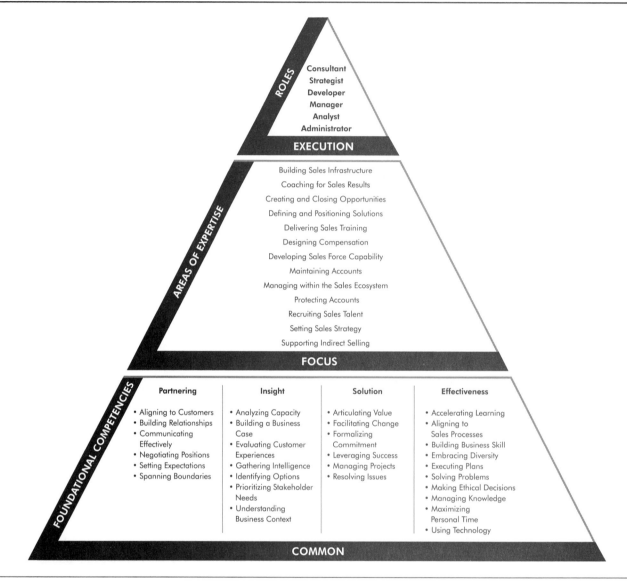

© 2009. ASTD. All rights reserved.

these sales areas of expertise—developing sales force capability, delivering sales training, and coaching for sales results—but probably manages sales professionals who perform these functions. The CLO should have strong skills and knowledge in the foundational competencies that affect the sales organization, including

▲ Analyzing organizational capacity
▲ Understanding business context
▲ Building business skill

▲ Managing knowledge
▲ Accelerating learning
▲ Executing plans
▲ Aligning to sales processes.

Example: Vice President of Sales

A vice president of sales typically manages people at all points of the sales cycle—those who are directly responsible for revenue generation and those who directly support them. Their direct reports are pre-sales specialists, salespeople, sales managers, and sales executives, as well as those who work in sales operations. The VP of sales might also oversee salesperson development or the selection of training solutions if there is no CLO in the organization.

The VP of sales may focus on the manager and strategist roles. Because he or she is responsible for managing, motivating, and rewarding sales team members, expertise in setting sales strategy, managing within the sales ecosystem, and designing compensation are required. For this job title, foundational competencies in the partnering and solutions categories should be strong.

Example: External Consultant

Obviously, external consultants will focus on a consulting role. They will likely help in defining and positioning solutions and setting sales strategy. Their strongest foundational competencies are likely to fall in the partnering and insight categories.

Example: Sales Trainer

A sales trainer might report to the CLO, the head of human resources, the VP of sales, or the sales manager. He or she mostly plays a developer role, and focuses on the delivering sales training area of expertise. Strong foundational competencies in communicating effectively, building business skills, using technology, and accelerating learning are important for success in this job.

Example: Sales Manager

In most organizations, sales managers are likely to manage revenue-generating salespeople; their staffs might include a sales trainer. Their direct reports might also include those in market research or sales operations. Sales managers focus on playing the analyst and manager roles, but certainly will weigh in on strategy as well. He or she will be skilled in creating and closing opportunities, protecting accounts, supporting indirect selling, managing within the sales ecosystem, maintaining accounts, and recruiting sales talent. Sales managers should have strong foundational competencies across the four categories.

In the Next Chapter

This chapter provided an overview of the ASTD World-Class Sales Competency Model. The next chapter is the first of the in-depth descriptions of the model's components. Chapter 4 explains the six roles—consultant, strategist, developer, manager, analyst, and administrator—and how they fit into the ASTD World-Class Sales Competency Model. It also illustrates how the roles link to competencies.

Chapter 4

Roles

Be what you are. This is the first step toward becoming better than you are.

—Julius Charles Hare

In this chapter:

- Understand the difference between roles and job titles.
- Learn how roles help sales professionals address customer needs more effectively.
- Understand how roles determine what competencies and areas of expertise salespeople should develop.

As described in chapter 3, the ASTD World-Class Sales Competency Model consists of three parts: roles, areas of expertise, and foundational competencies. This chapter explains the roles. We have likened roles to the "hats" that people wear throughout a day, a month, or a year. Roles are not job titles but rather a term that reflects the different hats we are expected to wear in response to the fluid and constantly changing demands of the buyer-seller relationship.

Choosing the right role at the right time is truly the crux of the matter—correctly interpreting those customer demands and how to respond. This is how world-class sales organizations should strive to operate—but they can only do so if salespeople have already been equipped with the requisite knowledge, skills, and abilities to meet the demands of the roles they must play as trusted business advisors.

> Roles are not job titles but rather a term that reflects the different hats we are expected to wear in response to the fluid and constantly changing demands of the buyer-seller relationship.

To become trusted business advisors to internal and external customers, sales professionals must build credibility and operate ethically, despite the multiple challenges they face in every interaction. A clear understanding of—and development path to—roles can help, because roles describe how to work effectively with different people in varying situations. They provide a clearer picture of professional selling by spelling out all those various "hats" and serve as a guideline to help sales professionals determine what skills and knowledge are best for a specific situation.

21st Century sales excellence requires a robust set of competencies for a wide range of roles. And while the management thereof can be a complex task, World-Class Selling: New Sales Competencies *provides a roadmap and checkpoints to keep us on the right road throughout the journey.*

—Jamie Barrette, vice president, North America. Mercuri International

The ASTD 2008 World-Class Sales Competency Study identified six roles that are critical to a successful buyer-seller relationship (see figure 4-1). Each of these six roles is defined as a broad area of responsibility within an organization's sales function. Each role requires a different combination of competencies and areas of expertise to perform effectively. For example, someone in the strategist role would likely develop the setting sales strategy AOE and would be skilled in several insight competencies such as prioritizing stakeholder needs and identifying options.

The ASTD World-Class Sales Competency Model defines the six roles as:

Consultant:

- ▲ leverages expertise and resources to build strong advisory relationships
- ▲ suggests best courses of action based on data and helps with rational decision making
- ▲ guides the decision making of others, including internal or external customers
- ▲ recognizes opportunities for products, services, or solutions to bring parties together to create a mutually beneficial relationship
- ▲ acts as the point person in negotiating transactions, fulfilling documented agreements, and building the relationships that are essential to long-term partnering.

Strategist:

- ▲ envisions ways of operating or achieving goals that do not currently exist

Figure 4-1. Roles

- articulates the vision in a way that facilitates its transformation to an operational reality, in response to challenges or opportunities
- applies or leads the application of innovative ideas and systems to create a competitive advantage for the organization.

Developer:

- creates business, organizational, or operational solutions or performance improvement initiatives by designing, developing, and delivering specific processes, systems, tools, events, or products intended to add value
- creates or contributes to plans, specifications, or designs that guide individual, product, or process development activities.

Manager:

- exercises direction and supervision of an organization or department
- controls and allocates resources and budgetary expenditures and enforces accountability for and compliance with work-related policies and procedures.

Analyst:

- collects, synthesizes, deconstructs, and reconfigures information (for example, ideas, facts, raw data) to provide insight to others
- works with customers to determine and document business needs
- documents requirements, processes, or methods in the most appropriate manner
- understands technology, systems, and tools for use within the sales environment.

Administrator:

- performs procedure-based activities that are often scheduled on a regular basis or require documentation
- are typically involved with activities that require compliance with established processes, practices, or operational rules.

It Is Not About Job Titles

Sales roles and job titles are not the same thing. Fundamentally, a job title represents a place on the organizational chart—a function that an employee carries out on behalf of the organization. By contrast, roles are the behavioral responses to the buyer-seller relationship and can literally change by the minute. People can play many roles, but most hold only one job title.

However, a job title often can be a collection of roles. For example, someone holding the title of sales manager may have to perform a number of roles,

Think About It

How was your sales team or sales department created? Was it built from the ground up with a singular purpose, or did it evolve over time? What impact has the customer experience had on the roles of your sales team as they approach the market? This book explains what world-class salespeople need to know and do to be successful. Understanding this approach will allow for more flexibility, adaptability, and agility in how sales teams approach the market.

such as strategist, developer, consultant, and so forth. Conversely, one role may be divided among many people. Consider how the role of developing salespeople is often spread among sales trainers, sales managers, and the salespeople themselves.

Historically, sales organizations have been built around the sales transaction, adding salespeople as needed to staff the number of accounts and manage the transactions. Given enough accounts, the organization grows to include extra layers of management to provide oversight. Then, supplementary functions are added—sales operations, sales training, and so forth—in an effort to help the "sales team sell more." Each of these functions can benefit from an understanding of roles. The roles identified in *World-Class Selling: New Sales Competencies* help to provide clarity and focus in everyday activities.

Further, it is crucial to understand how a competency-based approach to "sales work" differs. Rather than letting customer demands—as demonstrated by increasing accounts—determine the structure and staffing of their sales organizations, world-class companies take a proactive approach. They know what roles their salespeople will play and equip them with the requisite knowledge, skills, and abilities to respond effectively to customer demands.

The Roles in Action

Admittedly, operating within a selling system can be chaotic. Customer demands change constantly. The solution that addresses a customer's need in one moment may not be applicable in the next. So how does a sales manager guide members of the sales team to make sure they respond in the best way? This is where the sales roles can really come to life. Consider the following examples:

Example 1. The phone rings and the caller asks for the sales manager. The caller reports, "New sales are down in the organization." What should the sales manager do? He or she has options that draw on different roles, depending on the reason for the downturn.

▲ Are sales down because there is a lack of capability in the sales force? The manager might want to develop that capability as a developer.
▲ Are sales down because sales team members are not managing their time well? The manager might want to drive some activity discipline as a manager.
▲ Are sales down because the market is declining? The manager may want to recalibrate the sales strategy of the team to target different opportunities as a Strategist.

Example 2. A customer sends an email to his or her salesperson, indicating that the customer is not happy. What should the salesperson do? He or she should adopt the appropriate role based on the requirements of the buyer-seller relationship.

▲ Is the customer unhappy because an undiscovered need is not being met? The salesperson might want to spend some time guiding the customer through need recognition and offering possible solutions, in his or her role as a *consultant*.

▲ Is the customer unhappy because the buying organization has received an incorrect invoice and does not know how to fix it? The sales representative might inform the customer of the process to fix the problem and walk the customer through that process as an *administrator*.

Example 3. During a staff meeting, a sales trainer is informed that "the last training initiative did not work" to increase sales revenue. What should the sales trainer do? The answer depends on what the system requires in that situation.

▲ Did the training fail because it had no visible metrics defined to show results beyond overall revenue? The sales trainer might want to define other indicators of success (behavior change, increased knowledge, shorter sales cycles) to track as an *analyst*.

▲ Did the training fail because there was no on-the-job reinforcement? The sales trainer might want to help the sales leader see the need for such a solution as a *consultant*.

▲ Did the training fail because the vendor selected did not deliver as promised? The sales trainer might want to evaluate other vendors and other solutions to deliver the value required as a *developer*.

The benefit of implementing a competency-based approach is that, regardless of the situation or the role the salesperson is required to play at any given time, he or she is already prepared to play that role—with the requisite knowledge, skills, and abilities that populate the appropriate area of expertise. By taking a proactive look at what the buyer-seller relationship might require and developing those competencies in its salespeople, an organization can position itself for world-class sales.

Where Is the Profit Motive?

Some readers may wonder which roles are directly responsible for revenue generation. As explained in chapter 2, everyone in the sales organization is directly or indirectly responsible for revenue generation. Those who generate revenue and those who support and surround them must work together to achieve the definition of "world-class." Sales team members might be compensated differently or be closer to the point of sale, but everyone should focus on activities that help advance the sale, synchronize with the customer buying process, stay in tune with market conditions, and increase the profit of each individual sale. In other words, every role requires a degree of responsibility for revenue generation.

Think About It

The benefit of implementing a competency-based approach is that, regardless of the situation or the role the salesperson is required to play at any given time, he or she is already prepared to play that role—with the requisite knowledge, skills, and abilities that populate the appropriate area of expertise.

Think About It

There is a global shortage of highly competent salespeople. Further, organizations often do not understand the competencies required for their salespeople to succeed. However, customers will not be lenient. They know which competencies and outputs are most important to them when it comes to interactions with salespeople. It is time to train for competency, not just hire for it—because there just are not as many salespeople to hire.

• The firm Manpower discovered for the second year in a row that vacancies in business-to-business sales positions were the hardest to fill in the United States and several other countries (Talent Shortage Survey Results, 2007).

• The authors of the 2007 Annual Sales Performance Optimization Survey of 1,300 selling organizations wrote, "For the third year in a row, [we] continue to see that most firms plan to add net-new sales representatives; and we see nearly 15 percent of all firms planning to increase the size of their sales teams by 21 percent or more" (Dickie and Trailer, 2007).

Playing by the Roles

As mentioned previously, roles are not unique to any one person in an organization, and sales team members might play multiple roles, depending on the situation. In fact, more than 48 percent of survey respondents indicate that each role is moderately important (above a 4). Respondents were asked to rate the importance of each of the sales roles, from greatest (5) to least important (1). Table 4-1 shows the roles as ranked by the survey respondents.

Table 4-1. Role rankings.

Role	High to Low
Consultant	3.95
Strategist	3.93
Developer	3.81
Manager	3.60
Analyst	3.54
Administrator	3.38

To be effective in one's job, the importance of the roles varies depending on organizational level or function. Table 4-2 illustrates that sales team members who bear the most direct responsibility for revenue generation are the most likely to place more importance on the strategist and consultant roles; however, they also indicate that the other roles are important depending on the context or the situation. Table 4-2 shows the roles as they relate to job titles, from greatest (5) to least important (1), as ranked by the survey respondents.

Validating the Roles

In the current model, survey respondents indicate that the six roles cover most sales team job responsibilities. Only 1 percent of respondents selected "Other" as a choice when selecting the roles most relevant to them. All roles have importance ratings far above the minimum average score of 3.5 (ratings were made on a five-point scale, with 1 being "unnecessary" and 5 being "essential").

Linking Roles and Competencies

As defined previously, roles are broad areas of responsibility that require a certain combination of competencies and AOEs to perform effectively. Thus, it is important to understand which competencies and AOEs are most important for particular roles. Most competencies and AOEs have some relevance for

Table 4-2. Importance of Roles by Job Title

	Consultant	Strategist	Developer	Manager	Analyst	Administrator
Sales Executive	4.10	4.30	3.95	4.03	3.61	3.56
Sales Manager	3.97	4.20	3.91	4.32	3.75	3.47
Sales Representative	3.79	3.66	3.39	3.16	3.41	3.18
Sales Specialist	3.65	3.72	3.43	3.18	3.48	3.35
Pre-Sales Consultant	4.06	3.50	3.38	2.81	3.44	3.31
Operations Manager	3.96	4.13	3.96	4.22	3.91	3.78
Operations Executive	4.10	4.20	3.80	3.65	3.55	3.70
Sales Compensation Planner	3.83	3.67	3.50	3.67	4.00	4.00
Sales Operations Infrastructure Developer	4.00	3.67	3.83	3.83	4.17	4.00
Sales Operations Researcher/Analyst	4.00	4.00	4.00	4.00	4.00	4.00
Sales Recruiter	3.89	3.78	3.56	4.00	3.78	3.89
Sales Training Manager	4.04	4.15	4.03	3.96	3.67	3.68
Sales Training Executive	3.94	4.26	4.08	4.15	3.56	3.46
Sales Trainer	4.12	3.82	4.06	3.27	3.39	3.08
Sales Training Designer and Developer	4.02	3.55	4.43	2.84	3.61	3.16
Sales Researcher	3.65	3.48	3.48	3.17	3.17	3.17
Sales Professor/ Academic	3.98	3.71	3.90	3.56	3.44	3.40

each role. For example, it is easy to see that a foundational competency such as identifying options is important to the successful execution of any of the roles. However, some roles rely more heavily on certain competencies and AOEs than others.

Table 4-3 presents the correlations between importance ratings of roles and foundational competencies according to the survey data. Table 4-4 presents the correlations between importance ratings of roles and sales areas of expertise.

The numbers in the table are correlation coefficients with a possible range of −1.0 to +1.0. The closer the correlation coefficient is to +1.0, the stronger the positive relationship. Both tables highlight the strongest correlations. In each row, the role with the strongest relationship is highlighted in the darkest color.

Table 4-3. Correlation of Roles to Foundational Competencies

	Consultant	Strategist	Developer	Manager	Analyst	Administrator
Spanning Boundaries	0.32	0.34	0.29	0.18	0.22	0.17
Communicating Effectively	0.28	0.24	0.20	0.09	0.12	0.07
Aligning to Customers	0.19	0.16	0.13	0.04	0.09	0.07
Setting Expectations	0.34	0.29	0.27	0.15	0.21	0.11
Negotiating Positions	0.29	0.31	0.26	0.15	0.19	0.13
Building Relationships	0.25	0.21	0.18	0.04	0.04	−0.02
Analyzing Organizational Capacity	0.27	0.29	0.30	0.24	0.26	0.20
Understanding the Business Context	0.30	0.29	0.30	0.24	0.28	0.23
Evaluating Customer Experiences	0.29	0.33	0.34	0.24	0.28	0.19
Gathering Intelligence	0.31	0.29	0.31	0.22	0.30	0.24
Prioritizing Stakeholder Needs	0.26	0.30	0.30	0.20	0.21	0.18
Identifying Options	0.33	0.32	0.31	0.20	0.27	0.17
Building a Business Case	0.29	0.34	0.36	0.27	0.29	0.20
Facilitating Change	0.29	0.30	0.27	0.18	0.21	0.13
Formalizing Commitment	0.26	0.29	0.24	0.15	0.22	0.20
Resolving Issues	0.25	0.34	0.29	0.22	0.28	0.24
Managing Projects	0.24	0.30	0.26	0.25	0.27	0.25
Leveraging Success	0.27	0.34	0.33	0.23	0.24	0.24
Articulating Value	0.35	0.31	0.36	0.17	0.29	0.13
Building Business Skill	0.32	0.29	0.26	0.21	0.29	0.22
Solving Problems	0.36	0.26	0.31	0.16	0.25	0.14
Embracing Diversity	0.27	0.26	0.31	0.18	0.20	0.18
Making Ethical Decisions	0.28	0.18	0.26	0.12	0.14	0.13
Managing Knowledge	0.39	0.26	0.31	0.17	0.26	0.20
Using Technology	0.22	0.23	0.22	0.11	0.19	0.19
Accelerating Learning	0.28	0.23	0.29	0.12	0.20	0.17
Executing Plans	0.35	0.34	0.32	0.21	0.23	0.10
Maximizing Personal Time	0.34	0.29	0.29	0.20	0.25	0.15
Aligning to Sales Process	0.27	0.22	0.18	0.07	0.21	0.19

Strongest correlation   Next strongest correlation   Least correlation

Table 4-4. Correlation of Roles to Sales Areas of Expertise

	Consultant	Strategist	Developer	Manager	Analyst	Administrator
Creating and Closing Opportunities	0.09	0.19	0.03	0.15	0.11	0.15
Protecting Accounts	0.13	0.21	0.11	0.17	0.17	0.17
Defining and Positioning Solutions	0.24	0.37	0.31	0.29	0.37	0.26
Supporting Indirect Selling	0.17	0.32	0.19	0.30	0.27	0.31
Setting Sales Strategy	0.21	0.47	0.28	0.45	0.32	0.26
Managing within the Sales Ecosystem	0.22	0.38	0.32	0.50	0.39	0.37
Developing Sales Force Capability	0.23	0.39	0.44	0.38	0.29	0.22
Delivering Sales Training	0.20	0.24	0.40	0.30	0.21	0.19
Coaching for Sales Results	0.26	0.31	0.37	0.38	0.22	0.20
Building Sales Infrastructure	0.21	0.38	0.38	0.42	0.31	0.28
Designing Compensation	0.12	0.33	0.28	0.47	0.32	0.34
Maintaining Accounts	0.08	0.23	0.08	0.28	0.24	0.33
Recruiting Sales Talent	0.15	0.35	0.29	0.50	0.28	0.31

[ ] Strongest correlation   [ ] Next strongest correlation   [ ] Least correlation

The second strongest correlation is highlighted in a medium color and the lowest correlation is not shaded.

In the Next Chapter

Chapter 5 contains a detailed discussion of the areas of expertise—the specific technical and professional skills and knowledge required for success within the sales organization.

Chapter 5

Areas of Expertise

An expert is someone who knows some of the worst mistakes that can be made in his or her field, and how to avoid them.

—Werner Karl Heisenberg

In this chapter:

- Learn which specific technical and professional skills are required of sales professionals.
- Understand how areas of expertise (AOEs) go above and beyond foundational competencies.
- See how AOEs vary in importance depending on the role being played by the sales professional.

How is the sales profession different from other professions? The middle section of the ASTD World-Class Sales Competency Model (see figure 5-1) comprises areas of expertise, which are defined as the specific technical and professional knowledge and skills required for success in the sales organization.

Think of AOEs as the knowledge and skills a salesperson must have, above and beyond the foundational competencies. To be proficient in an AOE, a salesperson must demonstrate a combination of the relevant foundational

Figure 5-1. Areas of Expertise

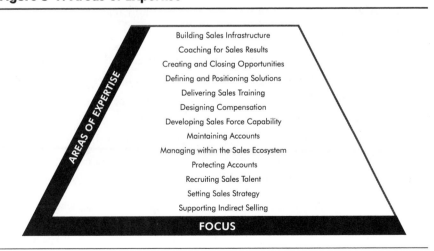

competencies and unique professional knowledge and skills. The model lists the AOEs in alphabetical order. While the validation survey asked respondents to define the knowledge and skills that all sales professionals must possess in general, your organization may wish to define levels of proficiency within each AOE, which can help you customize the ASTD World-Class Sales Competency Model to your organization's needs and selling system.

It Is About Focus

In the model, the areas of expertise reflect the current state of the sales profession—for those sales team members directly responsible for revenue generation as well as those who manage, develop, or support them—with an eye toward the future state. As organizations evolve, new technologies emerge, and needs change, sales team members are often asked to take on new responsibilities and readjust their focus. Some specialty areas remain fairly stable over time, while others change significantly. For example, over the past decade, the skills required to create and close deals have shifted from overcoming objections to consultative questioning. The AOEs presented in this report reflect how sales team members currently focus their work and also describe practices that are becoming increasingly important.

The AOEs presented in this report reflect how sales team members currently focus their work and also describe practices that are becoming increasingly important.

What Is Important?

Some AOEs might receive a lower importance rating by sales professionals as a group because they are not used as frequently. In fact, sales team members are much more likely to provide higher importance ratings for AOEs in which they spend more time. However, it is important to note that time spent and importance do not correlate directly. It is possible to spend very little time in areas that are essential to effective job performance; or a great deal of time on areas that are less essential. The key point to remember is that although perceived importance and time spent are both relative to the individual's job, all of the AOEs in this publication are important and relevant for the sales organization overall.

Although all 13 areas of expertise are important (that is, having an average importance rating of 3.0 or higher; see table 5-1), it is unlikely that all would be equally important for every job. Effective performance of one's job might not require any expertise in certain areas. Some AOEs might receive a lower importance rating by sales professionals as a group because they are not used as frequently, such as designing sales compensation. In fact, sales professionals are much more likely to provide higher importance ratings for AOEs in which they spend more time.

Table 5-1. Areas of Expertise, Ranked by Importance

Area of Expertise	Mean
Protecting Accounts	4.06
Creating and Closing Opportunities	4.05
Setting Sales Strategy	3.78
Maintaining Accounts	3.74
Coaching for Sales Results	3.70
Developing Sales Force Capability	3.67
Building Sales Infrastructure	3.65
Delivering Sales Training	3.61
Defining and Positioning Solutions	3.49
Supporting Indirect Selling	3.35
Managing within the Sales Ecosystem	3.27
Recruiting Sales Talent	3.15
Designing Compensation	3.00

It Is All Relative to the Job

Almost one-third (31 percent) of survey respondents identified creating and closing opportunities or maintaining accounts as their primary area of expertise. More than 40 percent of respondents identified the following three AOEs as their primary one: creating and closing opportunities, maintaining accounts, or protecting accounts.

While the popularity of these AOEs is evident, it is also clear that many sales professionals spend their time in more than one AOE. In fact, 63 percent of professionals define three to five AOEs as moderately to extremely important to their job. This indicates that sales team members are often providing expertise in multiple areas and must apply a broad range of skills. This is a key research finding, demonstrating that success in the profession is not defined by solid performance in a single AOE; rather, professional selling is a multi-disciplinary profession.

World-Class Selling: New Sales Competencies *brings together brilliant information, analysis, and ideas about the evolution of the sales profession to inspire new generations of salespeople, sales managers, and sales trainers.*

—Beth Rogers, chair, UK Sales Board

Sales organizations need people with a number of different job titles to carry out the required work. The research team set out to define a standard set of job titles for use during the World-Class Sales Competency research. The job titles in table 2-1 were presented to survey respondents, who were asked to select the title that most closely aligns to their current job as they perform it. Because all AOEs were scored as moderately important or higher (above 3.0), the research team aggregated the responses to define which AOEs equated to more than 50 percent of the respondents' importance rankings. The AOEs listed in table 5-2 are considered the most relevant and important for the execution of each job title.

The Role of Technology

Even though the effect of technology is not called out separately in the model, its role should not be overlooked. The technical sophistication of products in today's organizations is increasing, creating the need for higher levels of salesperson knowledge (especially product training) and technical savvy. Sales team members must educate themselves and their customers—often with the use of technology. Many organizations have stratified their sales efforts to create different levels of service that respond to customer needs.

As a result of this increased sophistication in the buyer-seller relationship, there is greater emphasis on the use of technology to manage group collaboration and as a way to stay on top of the knowledge required for sales success. A paradigm shift in the way sales professionals interact with their clients also increases the use of technology for communication. All of these factors position technology as an enabler of sales team success.

Keys to Unlocking the AOEs

Each AOE includes a list of key knowledge areas and key actions (see Appendix A). Key knowledge areas list the range of theoretical and procedural knowledge required for success in the AOE. Because there is so much depth of knowledge for each AOE, the ASTD World-Class Sales Competency Model does not list specific theories or approaches unless they are particularly important for the AOE.

Key actions list the behaviors and activities required for a person to function effectively in the AOE. Usually, key actions are readily observable and portray the day-to-day work of sales team members in each AOE. Experts in each specialty area have validated all of the key knowledge areas and actions. A review of the ratings shows that the AOEs have a high degree of validity (see Appendix E).

Table 5-2. How Areas of Expertise Relate to Job Titles in the ASTD World-Class Sales Competency Model

Sales Job Titles	Most Important Areas of Expertise by Job Title
Sales Executive	1. Creating and Closing Opportunities 2. Setting Sales Strategy 3. Maintaining Accounts
Sales Manager	1. Creating and Closing Opportunities 2. Setting Sales Strategy 3. Developing Sales Force Capability 4. Coaching for Sales Results
Sales Representative	1. Creating and Closing Opportunities 2. Protecting Accounts 3. Maintaining Accounts
Sales Specialist	1. Creating and Closing Opportunities 2. Protecting Accounts 3. Maintaining Accounts
Pre-Sales Consultant	1. Creating and Closing Opportunities 2. Protecting Accounts 3. Defining and Positioning Solutions
Operations Manager	1. Creating and Closing Opportunities 2. Protecting Accounts 3. Supporting Indirect Selling 4. Coaching for Sales Results 5. Maintaining Accounts
Operations Executive	1. Creating and Closing Opportunities 2. Protecting Accounts 3. Defining and Positioning Solutions 4. Setting Sales Strategy 5. Coaching for Sales Results 6. Building Sales Infrastructure
Sales Compensation Planner	1. Setting Sales Strategy 2. Designing Compensation 3. Maintaining Accounts
Sales Operations Infrastructure Developer	1. Creating and Closing Opportunities 2. Setting Sales Strategy 3. Developing Sales Force Capability 4. Building Sales Infrastructure
Sales Recruiter	1. Creating and Closing Opportunities 2. Defining and Positioning Solutions 3. Setting Sales Strategy 4. Building Sales Infrastructure 5. Recruiting Sales Talent
Sales Training Manager	1. Creating and Closing Opportunities 2. Developing Sales Force Capability 3. Delivering Sales Training 4. Coaching for Sales Results
Sales Training Executive	1. Creating and Closing Opportunities 2. Setting Sales Strategy 3. Developing Sales Force Capability 4. Delivering Sales Training

Notice how often creating and closing opportunities appears in table 5-2. Clearly, all sales professionals are keenly aware of its importance, no matter what their job title is.

(continued on the next page)

Table 5-2. How Areas of Expertise Relate to Job Titles in the ASTD World-Class Sales Competency Model (continued)

Sales Job Titles	Most Important Areas of Expertise by Job Title
Sales Trainer	1. Creating and Closing Opportunities 2. Developing Sales Force Capability 3. Delivering Sales Training 4. Coaching for Sales Results
Sales Training Designer and Developer	1. Developing Sales Force Capability 2. Delivering Sales Training 3. Coaching for Sales Results
Sales Researcher	1. Creating and Closing Opportunities 2. Protecting Accounts 3. Setting Sales Strategy 4. Delivering Sales Training
Sales Professor/Academic	1. Creating and Closing Opportunities 2. Protecting Accounts 3. Setting Sales Strategy 4. Delivering Sales Training

In the Next Chapter

This chapter provided an overview of the areas of expertise found within ASTD's World-Class Sales Competency Model. Chapter 6 explains the foundational competencies—grouped into the key categories of partnering, insight, solution, and effectiveness—and how they fit into the ASTD World-Class Sales Competency Model.

Chapter 6

Foundational Competencies

Avoid competency traps. Do not stay only where you are good at things, go out and be challenged.

—Andrew Creighton

———————▲———————

Competencies are the basic building blocks of a competency model. In this case, they form the foundation of the pyramid that graphically represents the model. The foundational competencies identified in the ASTD World-Class Sales Competency Model are common, core, and critical to all sales professionals regardless of job title. They are also applicable to all roles within the model (see chapter 4).

It is important to understand that competencies are the clusters of skills, knowledge, abilities, and behaviors required for job success. Competencies are required for sales professionals to achieve world-class results. They also have many applications for organizations and individuals. Organizations can use competencies to define selection criteria for new hires or placements on the sales team and to guide their training and development. Employees can use competencies as a roadmap to their own success on the job—and sales professionals can use the ASTD World-Class Sales Competency Model to guide the training and development of sales team members.

The ASTD 2008 World-Class Sales Competency Study identified 29 foundational competencies as common, core, and critical to all sales professionals, regardless of role (see figure 6-1). These 29 foundational competencies cluster into four categories, logical groupings that help sales team members define and assess their level of competence. Each competency contains a list of key actions (see Appendix A).

In this chapter:

- Understand the competency groupings used in the ASTD World-Class Sales Competency Model.
- Learn how foundational competencies apply to all sales professionals, regardless of the job title they hold.
- Discover the 10 most important foundational competencies in the ASTD World-Class Sales Competency Model.

55

Figure 6-1. Foundational Competencies

The competency clusters are:

Partnering competencies. These competencies enable the effective creation and leveraging of relationships within the sales context and facilitate sales interactions. This cluster includes

- ▲ Aligning to customers
- ▲ Building relationships
- ▲ Communicating effectively
- ▲ Negotiating positions
- ▲ Setting expectations
- ▲ Spanning boundaries.

Insight competencies. These competencies enable the development of robust analysis and synthesis skills. They permit sales team members to use information effectively and efficiently. This cluster includes

- ▲ Analyzing capacity
- ▲ Building a business case
- ▲ Evaluating customer experiences
- ▲ Gathering intelligence
- ▲ Identifying options
- ▲ Prioritizing stakeholder needs
- ▲ Understanding business context.

Solution competencies. These competencies enable the effective development of strategies and generation of support for the resulting solutions. This cluster includes

- ▲ Articulating value
- ▲ Facilitating change
- ▲ Formalizing commitment
- ▲ Leveraging success

- ▲ Managing projects
- ▲ Resolving issues.

Effectiveness competencies. These competencies enable the demonstration and development of personal effectiveness and responsibility. This cluster includes

- ▲ Accelerating learning
- ▲ Aligning to sales processes
- ▲ Building business skill
- ▲ Embracing diversity
- ▲ Executing plans
- ▲ Solving problems
- ▲ Making ethical decisions
- ▲ Managing knowledge
- ▲ Maximizing personal time
- ▲ Using technology.

Defining the Relevant Behaviors

Foundational competencies define the relevant behaviors for *all* sales professionals. To varying degrees, everyone in the sales organization must display some aspect of each competency. For example, it is difficult to imagine any salesperson being successful without the ability to articulate value or solve problems. However, the way these competencies are used can depend on the particular job held by the salesperson.

The following illustrations show how the foundational competency, prioritizing stakeholder needs, has relevance for both a sales manager and a sales trainer:

Sales manager: Sales managers often are charged with making resource decisions, deciding when to spend money and on what. They must prioritize stakeholder needs to decide which expenditures must be made to meet sales or business goals and whether expenditures can be delayed. For example, an outside sales team might request new mobile technology at the same time sales support staff is requesting new customer relationship management (CRM) software.

Sales trainer: Sales trainers are often responsible for evaluating training requests and deciding which to handle first in an environment of tight staffing and fiscal responsibility. They must prioritize stakeholder needs to decide which requests will result immediately in a new customized learning program, which might be answered with off-the-shelf materials or external courses, and which must be tabled until further resources become available.

Although the competencies in the ASTD World-Class Sales Competency Model are foundational, few sales professionals will be strong in every one.

Because all sales team members—regardless of level or experience—have unique strengths and development needs relative to the overall competency profile, it is impossible to construct a model that applies perfectly to everyone. Instead, the model is designed to cover most of the relevant skills and knowledge areas for a large majority of people in the sales organization.

The Top 10 Foundational Competencies

What does the data say about the top 10 foundational competencies, regardless of their position within each of the competency areas? Remembering that the foundational competencies apply to all roles in the sales profession, clearly partnering is the key. As shown in table 6-1, the partnering competencies of building relationships, communicating effectively, and aligning to customers were ranked as the top three in importance by survey respondents.

Selecting the right sales training partner is a monumental challenge for corporate training organizations. Millions are wasted every year because many sales training buyers do not have a complete understanding of the competencies required for sales jobs within their companies, the gaps that exist among sales personnel, and the capabilities of alternative vendors to close those gaps. World-Class Selling: New Sales Competencies will go a long way in helping buyers and sellers of outsourced sales training to close those gaps—a job that MUST be done.

—Dave Stein, president,
ES Research Group

Quick Check

How important are the top 10 competencies to you and your organization? More important, how well is each competency addressed in sales training and supported by ongoing learning and development?

Competency	Who Needs It? (salespeople, trainers, managers, sales operations)	Who Receives Training Support?
• Building Relationships • Communicating Effectively • Aligning to Customers • Facilitating Change • Negotiating Positions • Setting Expectations • Executing Plans • Aligning to Sales Processes • Making Ethical Decisions • Maximizing Personal Time		

How is each competency identified above delivered to sales professionals? Is there only one group receiving this type of support? What about the other individuals within the sales profession, such as trainers, operations staff, recruiters, sales managers, and salespeople?

Table 6-1. The Top 10 Foundational Competencies

Category	Competency	
Partnering	Building Relationships	4.43
Partnering	Communicating Effectively	4.38
Partnering	Aligning to Customers	4.36
Solution	Facilitating Change	4.26
Partnering	Negotiating Positions	4.19
Partnering	Setting Expectations	4.17
Effectiveness	Executing Plans	4.16
Effectiveness	Aligning to Sales Processes	4.16
Effectiveness	Making Ethical Decisions	4.14
Effectiveness	Maximizing Personal Time	4.13

What Is Important?

So what do the data tell us regarding importance? In a ranking of overall importance, partnering and effectiveness competencies appear at the top of the list. Survey respondents rated each competency in terms of its importance for effectiveness in their current job. Table 6-2 shows the average current importance rating for all 29 competencies, grouped by category (partnering, insight, solution, and effectiveness) and appearing in descending order of importance. All of the competencies are more than moderately important (that is, rated 3.0 or above), and no single competency is dramatically more important than the others.

Table 6-2. Foundational Competencies Ranked by Category

Category	Competency	
	Building Relationships	4.43
	Communicating Effectively	4.38
Partnering	Aligning to Customers	4.36
	Negotiating Positions	4.19
	Setting Expectations	4.17
	Spanning Boundaries	4.04
	Partnering Competencies Average	**4.26**

(continued on the next page)

Table 6-2. Foundational Competencies Ranked by Category (continued)

Category	Competency	
Insight	Prioritizing Stakeholder Needs	4.07
	Identifying Options	4.03
	Evaluating Customer Experiences	4.00
	Gathering Intelligence	3.99
	Understanding the Business Context	3.98
	Building a Business Case	3.88
	Analyzing Organizational Capacity	3.88
	Insight Competencies Average	*3.98*
Solution	Facilitating Change	4.26
	Leveraging Success	4.10
	Formalizing Commitment	4.08
	Managing Projects	4.05
	Articulating Value	4.04
	Resolving Issues	4.02
	Solution Competencies Average	*4.09*
Effectiveness	Executing Plans	4.16
	Aligning to Sales Processes	4.16
	Making Ethical Decisions	4.14
	Maximizing Personal Time	4.13
	Accelerating Learning	4.12
	Embracing Diversity	4.06
	Managing Knowledge	4.06
	Solving Problems	4.04
	Using Technology	3.97
	Building Business Skill	3.88
	Effectiveness Competencies Average	*4.07*

The ranking of the competencies is relatively stable and shows few differences in importance across organizational level (for example, executive or salesperson); area of expertise (for example, coaching or managing); or industry (for example, consulting or manufacturing). Additional analyses show that the importance of the competencies is unaffected by age, race, gender, or national origin.

In the Next Chapter

The final chapter in this book, chapter 7, is a call to action. It tells you how to assess whether your organizational culture is ready and receptive to implementing the ASTD World-Class Sales Competency Model. It shows you how to use the model as a blueprint for success and describes how a competency-based approach to selling works. You will find helpful tips for change management, as well as a personal charge to take responsibility for embracing your own learning and professional growth.

Chapter 7

A Call to Action

Nothing endures but change.

—Heraclitus

———————▲———————

In chapter 2, we introduced the concept of balancing capacity with competence. Sales capacity can look and feel different in different organizations. Some organizations may develop specific go-to-market plans based on market research or innovation, while others gather their top sales executives to identify critical opportunities with customers in strategic markets or industries. Some organizations may implement specific process improvements designed to help salespeople sell more, while others invest in new technology to manage the buyer-seller relationship.

All of those efforts can improve or increase sales *capacity* and, while they are important, this book focuses on a critical and often overlooked contributor to excellence: sales *competence*.

The ASTD World-Class Sales Competency Model defines the knowledge, skills, and abilities required for sales competence. It provides a blueprint for successfully engineering the performance of sales professionals, showing them how to adapt and change in response to the challenges of global business without losing their focus on the customer. The model defines how sales professionals should operate, what responsibilities they should carry, and how they should interact to generate revenue and support the mission of the organization.

The new economy requires fresh thinking to meet the sophisticated demands of today's customer. The "old school" method of gauging performance just by the numbers is no longer good

In this chapter:

- Learn how to use the ASTD World-Class Sales Competency Model to improve performance directly and indirectly.
- Assess your organization's readiness for change.
- Find out how you can use this book in your specific occupation.

enough. Today's environment requires a more rigorous approach of identifying and measuring the competencies necessary to truly separate those who react to demand versus those who can create it.

—Jeff Del Rossa, Global Practice Leader. Sales Talent Optimization Practice, Development Dimensions International

To be more specific, sales professionals must fully understand the complexity of the system within which they operate. They must become better at solving problems, responding to market conditions, turning data into information, and assimilating it as knowledge. This requires advanced skills, and it is those skills that will allow sales professionals to continue to provide value to customers.

Assessing Your Organization's Readiness for Change

The typical sales organization conducts activities across the spectrum of marketing, selling, and fulfillment. Sales teams are often given goals that are loosely defined and difficult to measure:

- Drive revenue for the selling organization.
- Create and maintain successful client relationships.
- Build trust and loyalty with every client interaction.
- Capture more market share for the selling organization.
- Align the functional areas of selling to the vision and strategy of the selling organization.
- Maximize sales process efficiency.
- Maintain visibility and accountability through technology.

A solid understanding of professional selling competencies and an intentional process for developing those competencies can help salespeople set, understand, and exceed these goals, thus driving revenue and improving performance in your world-class sales organization. But this is easier said than done. If your organization is like many others around the world, you have probably witnessed several shifts in how your organization approaches markets and buyers. These shifts make it more difficult to attain goals. For example, your organization's selling efforts likely have shifted

- from an *ad-hoc* selling approach to a *process-centric* selling approach
- from a focus on a *single-transaction decision* to a focus on *how buyers make specific decisions* about value
- from *product or service selling* to *solution-oriented* or *consultative selling*
- from an understanding of the *transaction experience* to an understanding of the *customer experience*
- from *hiring to fill a position* to *hiring for talent*
- from *opportunistic revenue results* to *strategic revenue generation.*

All of these shifts require a balance between capacity and competence. While many managers strive for balance, success will depend on where your organization is and where it wants to go. So where should you start? The ASTD sales effectiveness levels can help you assess your organization's critical work-related outputs and how well these outputs support your sales goals. Each of the five levels builds upon the previous ones and is critical to striking the right balance between competence and capacity. It is important to note that these levels are not completely hierarchical. In other words, you can start building the higher levels before completing the build out of the prior one.

The levels are sales science, sales process, sales relationships, sales technology, and sales competence. As your organization progresses through the five levels, your understanding of the keys to world-class sales effectiveness will become clearer and more sophisticated. Assessing your organization against the sales effectiveness levels (see figure 7-1) will help you understand how well your organization balances capacity and competence to achieve desired results.

> *This book is a tremendous resource for building an outstanding sales organization. It should be regularly referenced by everyone who works with sales organizations, particularly training and organizational development specialists. It provides an eminently comprehensive body of knowledge on all aspects of sales operations and sales force capabilities.*
>
> —Lance Cotton, Google Enterprise Sales Training

Level I: Sales Science

It all starts with sales science: *what* you are doing. Your organization has probably spent a great deal of time defining its approaches, methodologies, and

Figure 7-1. The ASTD Sales Effectiveness Levels

Level 5: Sales Competence

Level 4: Sales Technology

Level 3: Sales Relationships

Level 2: Sales Process

Level 1: Sales Science

Take action!

Identify how the ASTD World-Class Sales Competency Model can help your organization reinforce this rigorous approach to sales. How can the competencies, areas of expertise, and roles be used to support a system that is designed around the science of selling?

Take action!

Identify how the ASTD World-Class Sales Competency Model can help your organization standardize a sales process. How can the competencies, areas of expertise, and roles support a system that is designed to reinforce a consistent, repeatable sales process?

Take action!

Identify how the ASTD World-Class Sales Competency Model can help your organization provide guidance on every aspect of the transaction decision. How can the competencies, areas of expertise, and roles support a system that influences how your customers buy?

processes for selling. Your team has probably worked hard at finding out what buyers want. You have tried to teach salespeople how to sell by making a sales presentation, utilizing negotiation techniques, or leaving a compelling voice mail. To be effective, you had to stay focused on the transaction itself. By isolating the transaction as a specific moment in time, and building the "science" necessary to control as many variables as possible, you could tell new salespeople and sales managers what happened during the sale, why it happened, and how to avoid any missteps in the future. No matter how simple the product or complex the solution, your sales team needs to explain, teach, and influence.

Level II: Sales Process

Once you understand *what* you are trying to do as a sales organization, it is time to define *how*. Your organization worked hard on fully understanding what occurs between buyer and seller within an individual transaction and, as a result, has probably completed more transactions. You then defined a unique series of repeatable steps that culminate in a transaction. By analyzing how sales work is accomplished, sales managers and salespeople are able to train better; facilitate transactions better; and, most important, understand what it takes to sell effectively. As products and solutions continue to become more complicated, the sales process must be in place to cope with the higher level of complexity.

Level III: Sales Relationships

Once you have a sales process, it is time to focus on the relationship. Your organization probably has helped its salespeople shift from a transaction focus to a relationship focus. That change has had a dramatic effect on the salesperson's role, transforming it from simple order taker to strategic partner.

Once that relationship was established, buyers broadened their focus beyond limited issues and needs. They began looking for solutions to business problems, as opposed to purchasing products and services and managing their own implementation. Organizations began requiring more sophisticated back-office tracking of vendors as well as protecting shareholder value. As a result, salespeople began helping the buyer facilitate a buying decision—*consultative selling*. Salespeople were taught to become stronger problem solvers and to engage multiple stakeholders so that they were not subject to the whims of one decision maker. Other members of the sales team were brought into the transaction to guide the various steps of the decision process.

Level IV: Sales Technology

Once you have solidly defined the science, standardized the process, and cultivated relationships for maximum influence, it is time to focus on technology. Your organization may have struggled to cope with the Internet boom and the increased use of technology to manage knowledge. Once sales processes were well defined and buyer behavior became well understood, organizations turned to technology to help speed up salesperson reaction times to market trends, keep them abreast of important industry news, and develop a more solid understanding of their buyers. Your sales team may have turned to personal computers and handheld devices to help them stay on top of the rapidly changing business world. You may have even rolled out a customer relationship management system or sales force automation tool in an attempt to understand and map the entire transaction experience of the buyer. Technology can help your organization understand the initial needs of the customer, help deliver and fulfill a product or service, or handle invoicing, all to create the best possible transaction experience.

Level V: Sales Competence

With the firm foundation of science, process, relationship, and technology properly laid, it becomes time for the ongoing improvement of competence. Despite the myriad forces of change driving business today, understanding and consulting with buyers in pursuit of mutually beneficial solutions is still a relevant approach. The need continues for sales professionals to build and renew customer relationships, monitor and understand buyers' changing needs, and deliver ongoing value. This approach is difficult to implement consistently in a dynamic, constantly changing sales environment, but success comes with a holistic understanding of salesperson competence. Because buyers are increasingly demanding unique answers to their unique problems, salespeople must be able to customize and personalize their own selling approaches. This requires deep understanding and advanced knowledge, skills, and abilities.

Attaining all five levels of effectiveness for world-class selling requires buy-in and effort by multiple stakeholders. Whether you are a workplace learning and performance professional or an academic, a sales manager or a consultant, you can apply the ASTD World-Class Sales Competency Model to improve sales performance in your organization. Here is how.

Sales Trainer Applications

Training managers oversee a staff of practitioners that includes instructional designers, human resource managers, sales consultants, subcontractors, and salespeople. Trainers will find the ASTD World-Class Sales Competency Model useful in helping them to

Plan for and execute continuous performance improvement. To follow best practices, your training department will require staffing by skilled people who can

- assess the competency levels of existing training staff, line managers, and others who can play a part in sales team performance improvement
- manage outsourcing opportunities
- hire vendors to assist with any facet of the sales function

Take action!

Identify how the ASTD World-Class Sales Competency Model can help your organization monitor the whole transaction experience, from the initial identification of a need to the assessment of the purchased solution. How can the competencies, areas of expertise, and roles support a system that is designed to speed up and maximize information flow regarding the customer's experience?

Take action!

Identify how the ASTD World-Class Sales Competency Model can help your organization improve salesperson competence. How can the competencies, areas of expertise, and roles support a system that is designed to identify its own gaps and continuously improve performance throughout the buying relationship?

Think About It

Understanding how buyers buy is a fundamental skill that is often overlooked in sales organizations. Great sales professionals understand how their buyers buy; world-class sales organizations design their development and operations to support this process.

Think About It

Many organizations will attest that they have some sort of alignment. It is important to understand that all stages of alignment build on one another. For example, much of the knowledge new salespeople attain is grounded in Level I: Sales Science, and many customer relationship management programs are grounded in Level IV: Sales Technology. But how well can the customer relationship management programs work when the sales process is consistently adjusted or even ignored? How well can the organization strengthen its influence with customer relationships when the sales force has not been professionally developed? Alignment is not about new process or restructuring initiatives; it is about matching competency with capacity.

- identify or clarify work expectations for sales team members
- design jobs, work, or tasks for sales team members
- oversee sales training solutions and provide feedback to sales trainers
- offer advice and consultation about career planning to sales team members
- identify the professional development needs of sales team members
- document the accomplishments of sales team members
- train people who work with sales team members.

The ASTD World-Class Sales Competency Model clearly shows the knowledge, skills, abilities, and areas of expertise that are necessary for sales team training and development.

Prepare for the future. Training managers bear responsibility for setting a direction for their departments or functions. The trends identified in the ASTD World-Class Sales Competency Model provide valuable insight for designing sales strategies, processes, and tools to anticipate or react to those trends.

Reinvent the role of the training department. Many organizations are taking stock of what they expect from a training department and reinventing it to focus on improving sales team performance. However, transitioning from a traditional training function to a workplace learning and performance approach is a major change that requires careful planning, clear goals and expectations, involvement by key stakeholders, and continuous evaluation. The ASTD World-Class Sales Competency Model can offer an externally validated benchmark of what a reinvented training department and its staff should be doing.

Workplace Learning and Performance Applications

Workplace learning and performance (WLP) professionals manage employee learning and development, measure its impact on performance, and demonstrate business results based on the performance change. WLP professionals hold the same goals as sales leaders across the globe, which include

- improving human performance
- balancing individual and organizational needs
- building knowledge capital within the organization
- improving financial return.

By leveraging the specific skills and expertise of workplace learning and performance to prepare salespeople to meet the current challenges of their jobs, organizations adopt a solutions-based, performance-oriented approach that generates results.

WLP builds on a systematic process for analyzing and responding to individual, group, and organizational needs. WLP professionals can help organizations develop and hone competence through a variety of interventions, such as designing and delivering sales training or providing sales coaching. Figure 7-2 shows some of the techniques WLP professionals might apply.

WLP professionals should focus their efforts on developing sales team member knowledge, skills, and abilities based on the roles that the team members play. The goals must remain clear—attain business outcomes and achieve sales results. Adapting the ASTD World-Class Sales Competency Model for use in sales training, sales team member development, and organizational performance can align processes, tools, and activities. More important, the model can help sales team members learn, from basic skills to high technology and management, practices that are immediately applicable to their jobs, duties, and roles.

Figure 7-2. Workplace Learning and Performance for Sales Teams

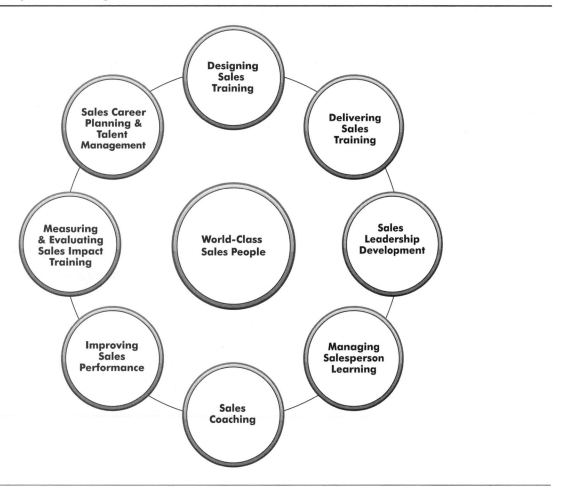

The ASTD World-Class Sales Competency Model can help you to do the following:

Achieve alignment between learning efforts and the sales process. The model clearly shows which competencies and areas of expertise are necessary for multiple roles within the sales organization. By adapting the sales process to leverage and maximize those competencies, organizations can improve their execution without sacrificing revenue generation. Further, the clear link between process and capability will make decision making about learning priorities and resources much easier.

Identify professional development needs. By using the model as a template for competency assessment, sales trainers can identify team members' professional development needs based on the roles that they play and can develop training classes or other learning programs specifically to meet those needs.

Prompt coaching on performance. Use the model to direct and improve the coaching that sales team members receive. By using the roles, competencies, and outputs described here as a reference point, sales team members can solicit concrete and timely feedback from customers and other stakeholders about their performance, which enables continuous individual improvement.

Design jobs or tasks. By understanding what sales team members know and can do and then aligning the sales process with those competencies, it becomes far easier for organizations to design jobs or tasks. Always with the desired outputs in mind, the ASTD World-Class Sales Competency Model provides a framework for maximizing salesperson capability and productivity.

Set work expectations and competency levels. By adopting the model and applying it to every role within the sales organization, you can set consistent expectations. For sales team members who want to transition from traditional selling into other roles, the model shows where to begin and what competencies they should seek to develop. They can assess, through various tools, their competence level in their desired role, then create a development plan to maximize strengths and minimize weaknesses.

Implement talent management practices. Sales team members who want to progress in their careers can clearly see and pursue the path to advancement. Further, the model is equally applicable for sales team members interested in moving to other functions such as sales training or operations.

Speak the same language. This book and the model it describes provide the basis for a common language across teams, departments, and organizations. By documenting work accomplishments in terms of the roles, competencies, and outputs described here, sales team members can show their contributions more easily and communicate across organizational boundaries more effectively.

Provide internal performance consulting. When sales trainers work to identify and address performance gaps that can drive revenue generation, they adopt a new focus for their work—that of internal performance consulting. The ASTD World-Class Sales Competency Model provides a useful and flexible framework to guide consulting engagements and assess learning and performance needs.

Prepare for the future. By questioning experts about their competency needs both now and three years into the future, ASTD has taken a future-focused approach to developing this competency model. The model takes current and future business trends into account as it describes how sales team members can prepare themselves for the future. As the sales profession heads toward an increased emphasis on results and performance, sales team members can adopt the model to anticipate and address the moving target that those results represent.

Maintain ethical standards. In the 2008 ASTD market research study referenced in chapter 2, sales team members clearly identified "making ethical decisions" as one of the top five skills necessary for success in their jobs (ASTD, 2008). Applying the ASTD World-Class Sales Competency Model consistently across the sales organization and across buyer-seller relationships provides clear conduct expectations and relieves salespeople of much of the stress that accompanies ethical dilemmas. Setting out clear performance expectations, even within the context of high revenue expectations, allows salespeople to remain focused on the buyer's best interests and balance them with individual and organizational needs.

Sales Team Member Applications

Empowered and involved sales team members are willing and able to analyze their own performance gaps, choose appropriate improvement solutions, implement the solutions, and evaluate results. The ASTD World-Class Sales Competency Model provides guidelines for this process. All salespeople, not just quota-carrying specialists, have a key stake in development. According to the trends identified in the study, sales team members must take more accountability and responsibility for sales results, no matter how long they have been with your organization. The ASTD World-Class Sales Competency Model can help support a sense of ownership for personal development through:

Synchronizing to the customer's buying process. The ASTD World-Class Sales Competency Model suggests many competencies that help sales team members maintain proper emphasis on the crucial buyer-seller relationship. This helps them assess every buyer interaction and determine the most appropriate activity to help facilitate buyer decision making.

Are You Getting in the Way of Success?

Selling organizations must provide a holistic learning and development progression rather than relying on ad-hoc sales training activities. At a minimum, the leadership of the selling organization must take a more proactive role in promoting the importance of training and development and supplying adequate resources. Right now, many company leaders are getting in the way of their sales teams' success: In a comprehensive market research study in 2008, ASTD questioned salespeople, sales trainers, and sales managers about sales training needs. Of the 271 respondents, 44 percent said that there was a lack of management buy-in to sales training in their organizations, and 42 percent said that management's short-sighted focus was an obstacle to successful sales training (ASTD, 2008).

Employing improved time management skills. The ASTD World-Class Sales Competency Model helps sales team members determine the most appropriate course of action when planning their daily, weekly, or monthly activities through more clearly defined role expectations. Armed with a more solid understanding of the roles they play, they can balance the demands placed on their time from multiple stakeholders who often have conflicting interests.

Practicing continuous personal improvement. The ASTD World-Class Sales Competency Model can help sales team members take a proactive, continuous-improvement approach to personal development and their ability to manage the sales process, leverage technology, and share knowledge internally and externally.

Increasing personal influence. The ASTD World-Class Sales Competency Model helps sales team members identify the competencies required to create and build influence with their customers. Each of the foundational competencies provides a detailed breakdown of the critical elements for building the kind of influence they need to effectively manage, direct, and advise their customers.

Sales Manager Applications

Sales managers bear primary responsibility for serving customers, achieving team goals, dealing with suppliers, and meeting distributor needs. In many organizations, sales managers are positioned to enable and measure the execution of the sales process. Likewise, sales managers are positioned around direct service delivery. Sales managers can work with their training and operations colleagues to manage organizational resources more effectively in support of the sales function. The ASTD World-Class Sales Competency Model provides a useful tool for sales managers who wish to interact effectively with the service, fulfillment, delivery, training, operations, or manufacturing functions of the organization.

The ASTD World-Class Sales Competency Model also can provide a common language by which to facilitate communication across departmental boundaries. By referring to the roles, competencies, and outputs of the sales profession, managers across departments can share a common language and work together to effect change by

Selecting the right sales organization members. The ASTD World-Class Sales Competency Model can help the sales manager assess the sales organization against a definition of *world class* during the interview process. Because many organizations focus on cultural fit and an assessment of what is required to sell in their organization, the sales manager can determine fit by clearly understanding the organization's support of the sales team (development, operations, management, and compensation) found within the model.

Analyzing and coaching performance. The ASTD World-Class Sales Competency Model offers a simple model for troubleshooting performance problems in the sales system or for planning solutions to improve performance. When sales managers become familiar with the model, they can become an internal consultant and become more adept in identifying problems, approaching salespeople, and delivering coaching.

Choosing learning solutions, managing change, and evaluating results. The ASTD World-Class Sales Competency Model suggests many possible causes for sales team performance gaps and identifies many possible solutions for change. By becoming expert at understanding the model, sales managers will learn to choose appropriate training solutions, manage change, and evaluate results.

Clearly defining expectations. The ASTD World-Class Sales Competency Model helps sales managers define what is expected of team members within the sales system. By focusing on the entire selling system and the key players within it, sales managers can ensure they provide clear guidance, make appropriate changes, and provide coaching that addresses any confusion within the system.

Coaching for improved performance. The ASTD World-Class Sales Competency Model helps sales managers better understand their team members and offers a validated dictionary of competencies that can be honed through one-on-one discussions that help motivate, change behavior, and improve focus.

Consultant Applications

Internal or external consultants working in the sales profession are often brought in to strengthen the capability and performance of the overall sales group. Sales and nonsales executives alike often rely upon the consultant's insights and past experiences when making recommendation to sales leadership. Consultants are often responsible for assessing the sales organization, recommending appropriate solutions, and guiding the implementation of those solutions. Often, the solutions center on people dynamics, like organizational structure, people processes, information flow, and behavioral alignment. The ASTD World-Class Sales Competency Model provides an externally validated benchmarking tool to use with clients to increase the capability and performance of the overall sales system, not just the sales transaction. It will help consultants to:

Assess the sales system. The ASTD World-Class Sales Competency Model helps consultants see the big picture of the sales system's roles and behavioral functions. By understanding what world class looks like, they can provide insight into how clients are delivering each of these elements. This will help client organizations to separate and accurately identify people-related gaps from nonpeople-related gaps.

Identify appropriate solutions. The ASTD World-Class Sales Competency Model helps with defining and prioritizing what solutions to propose. Organizational performance is driven by organizational competence, which is driven by individual competence. Because the model breaks desired outputs into roles and competencies, it can serve as the starting point for engineering the results the system needs to achieve through its people.

Guide implementation. The ASTD World-Class Sales Competency Model can help consultants guide and strengthen the implementation of solutions. Using the same competencies that sales team members use in delivering their services, they can leverage the model for their own performance.

Effect continuous organizational improvement. The ASTD World-Class Sales Competency Model helps consultants continuously assess clients for ongoing improvement by providing the critical anchor points for evaluating the organization. The roles, areas of expertise, and foundational competencies are universal in their application and can serve as the starting point for ensuring that the organization's sales system is functioning as it was designed.

Become a trusted advisor. The ASTD World-Class Sales Competency Model helps consultants analyze and improve their ability to become trusted advisors to their customers. Partnering competencies, insight competencies, solution competencies, and effectiveness competencies provide a roadmap for attaining this status.

Academic Applications

Administrators, faculty, and staff working in academic sales education programs can use the ASTD World-Class Sales Competency Model as a framework for assessing program needs, planning program enhancements and courses, assessing learners, formulating and implementing research, advising learners enrolled in the programs (or considering enrollment), developing faculty, and evaluating program processes and outcomes. It can be helpful in:

Assessing needs. What are the needs of sales learners and their prospective employers? The ASTD World-Class Sales Competency Model provides a framework for conducting academic program needs assessments based on the future roles those learners will play and the knowledge, skills, and abilities they will require for success.

Planning programs and courses. Professionals in academic sales education programs can use the model as a guide to establishing new courses or revising old courses in professional selling, within the context of the roles, competencies, outputs, and future trends identified, and benchmarking programs or courses against offerings at other academic institutions.

Assessing learners. The model can help in assessing differences among individual student competencies and the competencies required for success in professional selling, which can become the basis for individualized learning plans or courses of study.

Formulating and implementing a research agenda. Because the ASTD World-Class Sales Competency Model was based on an exploratory study and is intended to be an evolving process, it furnishes the basis for additional research. After all, not all important questions about professional selling have been answered here. The following questions warrant further investigation:

- How do the roles, competencies, outputs, and future trends identified by this study match the expectations of key sales-team stakeholders such as CEOs, senior executives, middle managers, and customers?
- What similarities and differences exist among the roles, competencies, and outputs identified in the United States and those in other nations or cultures?
- How does emerging technology affect the roles, competencies, and outputs of a sales professional's work?
- What roles or competencies are the most important for specific industries?
- How do roles or competencies change depending upon the size of the organization or the markets served?

Advising learners. Students enrolled in academic programs on professional selling have individualized needs for advice about what courses to take, what career goals to pursue, and how to build the competencies they need to realize their career goals. The ASTD World-Class Sales Competency Model is a useful tool for organizing such discussions. By using it, faculty and students can ensure that they are using common terminology.

Managing and developing faculty. Faculty members who teach in academic programs in marketing or selling must stay current if they are to teach effectively and provide appropriate guidance to students. Just as the ASTD World-Class Sales Competency Model is a useful tool for assessing individual student competencies and developing student plans of study, it also can be useful for assessing faculty competencies and suggesting professional development activities to build them.

Evaluating program processes and results. Just as sales team members are under increasing pressure to demonstrate that their efforts lead to payoffs for their learners and their organizations, academic programs are under pressure to demonstrate that they are delivering effective results. The ASTD World-Class Sales Competency Model is a standard against which to evaluate academic program processes and results. External review teams called in to audit instructional processes and outcomes of academic selling programs may rely on the ASTD World-Class Sales Competency Model as a benchmark against which to assess what competencies students should be building and what outputs students should be capable of producing when finished with their programs.

Conclusion

The ASTD World-Class Sales Competency Model was created with the input of more than 2,000 thought leaders, experts, and practitioners in the sales profession. It was created by sales professionals for sales professionals. The model provides a common language and framework for selling competence that defines the field—for today and for years to come.

The lasting value of the model is ensured by its broad perspective: It defines the way that people operate within the sales system, whether they are directly responsible for revenue generation or support those who are, rather than speaking from a narrow, transaction-based approach. It assumes—and celebrates— the fact that anyone who works within the sales team is a part of its success and, as such, deserves intentional, focused professional development to ensure his or her own success.

"Sales" has long been about metrics, revenue, and processes. Salesperson training and development have been conducted with little regard for the holistic effort required for sustained sales excellence. Aligning business needs and revenue goals with sales training, situated in a context that values long-term relationships and ongoing employee development, can dramatically improve the return-on-investment that your company realizes for its sales training dollars.

Although many sales organizations include workplace learning and performance professionals, not all do. The ASTD World-Class Sales Competency Model can help the people in your organization responsible for sales training— whatever their job title—speak a common language, pursue the same goals, and realize a shared vision of excellence that is world class.

Appendix A

Competency Dictionary

Contents

Appendix A

Figure A-1. The ASTD World-Class Sales Competency Model

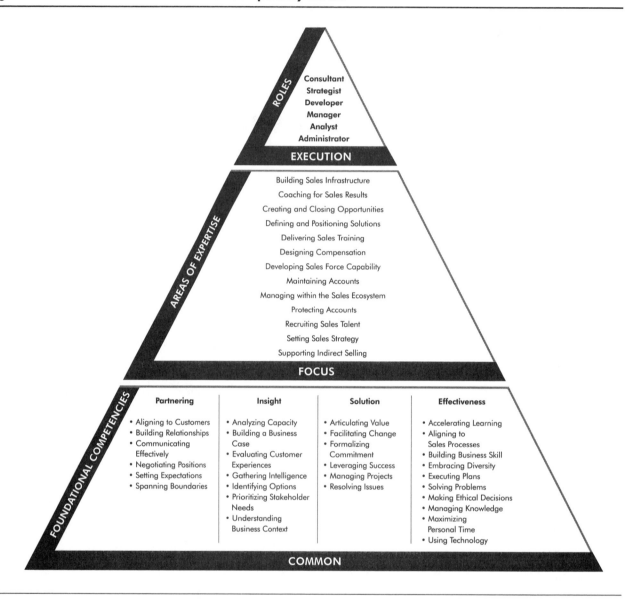

© 2009. ASTD. All rights reserved.

The ASTD World-Class Sales Competency Model

The ASTD World-Class Sales Competency Model (figure A-1) is the only widely available occupation-specific model for sales team members. It considers those who are directly responsible for revenue generation, as well as those who consult with, train, develop, and support them. Highly customizable to any kind of sales organization, the model provides structure while leaving room for unique characteristics or unusual requirements. This occupation-based model, focused intensely on the knowledge, skills, and abilities of all people within the sales organization, embraces consultants as well as inside and outside sales representatives based on the roles that they play. The model incorporates the basic tenets of workplace learning and performance, and can be used by WLP professionals and those for whom sales training is only one part of a demanding job.

The ASTD approach to competency modeling combines the visible attributes of knowledge and skill with behavior and actions to produce a clearer picture for success in a specific job: the expected results and outputs. It is represented as a pyramid and includes three layers of increasingly specific ability:

- ▲ **Roles** are broad areas of responsibility. Roles are not the same as job titles. They are much more fluid. Playing different roles is analogous to maintaining a collection of hats—when the situation requires, the sales professional can take off one hat and put on another one. Different hats or roles require different areas of expertise and competencies to be successful.
- ▲ **Areas of expertise (AOEs)** represent knowledge and skill in specific sales areas or specialties. A person may possess expertise in one or more of the AOEs, and each AOE incorporates multiple competencies.
- ▲ **Competencies** are focused, narrow areas of knowledge, skill, and ability. They are common to the sales profession regardless of specialty and critical to all. Competencies are grouped into four major categories: partnering, insight, solution, and effectiveness.

The blend of competencies, areas of expertise, and roles adds power and utility to the model. Any one part, viewed in isolation, would narrow the definition of world-class sales competencies. Taken as a whole, the model can be used in a variety of ways within a variety of circumstances, industries, markets, and geographies.

A clear definition of world-class sales competency can help organizations better prepare salespeople to tackle the increasingly complex challenges of selling in a global marketplace with collapsed timeframes and sophisticated solutions. It is time to change the way organizations view that preparation and to change from the just-in-time, on-the-job skills training that many companies use to a more systematic, competency-based approach.

Sales Roles

As we listened to our study respondents describing their current responsibilities and competency requirements, a set of sales roles emerged. Roles are not the same as job titles; they are much more fluid, depending on the application or activity. While a loose formal association may exist between roles and job titles, roles are the "hats" that people wear within the sales profession, despite specific job titles, and a single job title may involve multiple roles.

These are the sales roles:

- ▲ **Consultant.** Leverages expertise and resources to build strong advisory relationships. Suggests best courses of action and helps with rational decision making. Guides the decision making of others, including internal or external customers. Recognizes product, service, or solution opportunities for bringing parties together to actualize a mutually beneficial relationship. Acts as the point person in negotiating transactions, fulfilling documented agreements, and building the relationships that are essential to long-term partnering.

▲ **Strategist**. In response to challenges or opportunities, envisions ways of operating or achieving goals that do not currently exist. Articulates the vision in a way that facilitates its transformation to an operational reality. Applies or leads the application of innovative ideas and systems to create a business or organizational advantage.

▲ **Developer**. Creates business, organizational, or operational solutions or performance improvement initiatives by designing, developing, and delivering specific processes, systems, tools, events, or products intended to add value. Creates or contributes to plans, specifications, or designs that guide individual, product, or process development activities.

▲ **Manager**. Exercises direction and supervision of an organization or department. Controls and allocates resources and budgetary expenditures, and ensures accountabilities and compliance with work-related policies and procedures.

▲ **Analyst**. Collects, synthesizes, deconstructs, and reconfigures information (for example, ideas, facts, and raw data) to provide insight to others. Works with end users to determine and document business needs. Documents requirements, processes, or methods in the most appropriate manner. Understands technology, systems, and tools for use within the sales environment.

▲ **Administrator**. Performs procedure-based activities that are often scheduled on a regular basis or require documentation. Typically gets involved with activities that require compliance with established processes, practices, or operational rules.

These are examples of titles loosely associated with these sales roles:

Consultant titles

▲ Sales recruiter
▲ Account executive
▲ Solution architect
▲ Pre-sales technical consultant
▲ Account manager
▲ Sales specialist
▲ Client account manager

Strategist titles

▲ Sales strategy manager
▲ Operations strategy and development manager
▲ Business planning strategist
▲ Chief learning officer
▲ Vice president of sales

Developer titles

▲ Product specialist
▲ Instructional developer
▲ Knowledge engineer
▲ Compensation application engineer
▲ Sales coach

Manager titles

- ▲ Sales district manager
- ▲ Sales operations manager
- ▲ Sales training and development manager

Analyst titles

- ▲ Sales researcher
- ▲ Policy analyst
- ▲ Productivity and process analyst
- ▲ Sales analyst
- ▲ Sales incentive analyst
- ▲ Training needs analyst

Administrator titles

- ▲ Sales coordinator
- ▲ Sales configuration and quote specialist
- ▲ Operations specialist
- ▲ Order entry specialist
- ▲ Training coordinator.

Table A-1. Examples of Relationships Between Roles and AOEs

Sales Areas of Expertise	Consultant	Strategist	Developer	Manager	Analyst	Admin.
Creating and Closing Opportunities	X				X	
Managing Accounts	X					X
Defining and Positioning Solutions	X					
Supporting Indirect Selling	X			X		X
Setting Sales Strategy	X	X				
Managing within the Sales Ecosystem	X			X		
Developing Sales Force Capability	X		X		X	
Delivering Sales Training	X		X			
Coaching for Sales Results	X		X	X		
Building Sales Infrastructure	X		X			
Designing Compensation	X	X			X	
Maintaining Accounts	X				X	X
Recruiting Sales Talent	X			X	X	

Appendix A

The areas of expertise and roles identified in this model are derived from the competency model research process; however, the variations and interactions of the areas of expertise and roles will vary with each organization. Table A-1 provides an illustrative example of how areas of expertise and roles could play out. Sales professionals may customize these examples for their own company or situation. Further research is required to confirm the suggested links, but this is beyond the scope of this report.

Foundational Competencies

Four clusters comprise the foundational competencies:

- ▲ Partnering competencies
- ▲ Insight competencies
- ▲ Solution competencies
- ▲ Effectiveness competencies.

Partnering Competencies

All individuals in the sales ecosystem work interdependently with others and rely on the following competencies to facilitate these interactions:

- ▲ Spanning boundaries
- ▲ Communicating effectively
- ▲ Aligning to customers' needs
- ▲ Setting expectations
- ▲ Negotiating positions
- ▲ Building relationships.

Spanning Boundaries

Definition: Understands how interpersonal or organizational boundaries can affect success and manages them.

Key Actions:
- ▲ **Advances collaboration and positive relationships across organizational boundaries**—Sets expectations governing collaboration to minimize conflict and ensure a common focus among all internal and external stakeholders affected by the initiative.
- ▲ **Recognizes and addresses gaps among personal, team, or organizational responsibilities**—Identifies gaps between individual responsibilities and what needs to be accomplished to achieve success and takes personal accountability for positive impacts within these areas.

Communicating Effectively

Definition: Ensures that all communications are clear, focused, and based on a solid understanding of needs, using whatever medium is most appropriate

Key Actions:
- ▲ **Demonstrates active listening**—Pays close attention to what is being said and uses questioning techniques effectively to probe and clarify in pursuit of accurate understanding.
- ▲ **Achieves communication objectives**—Ensures that verbal and written communications and group presentations are well-prepared, clear, concise, accurate, and persuasive.
- ▲ **Ensures responsive communication**—Makes sure that inquiries are addressed and expedited to facilitate the needs of others.
- ▲ **Attains persuasive communication**—Successfully influences perceptions to achieve desired outcomes.

Aligning to Customers

Definition: Aligns perspective to the customer's to ensure that the concerns of the customer are understood and addressed and overall customer satisfaction is achieved.

Key Actions:

▲ **Contributes to customer satisfaction**—Understands how trust and responsiveness to customer needs builds enduring business relationships.

▲ **Advocates for the customer**—Represents the interests of the customer and ensures that a customer-oriented perspective is the touchstone for decision making.

Setting Expectations

Definition: Establishes shared expectations to minimize surprises and align stakeholders within a common understanding.

Key Actions:

▲ **Communicates expectations to all stakeholders**—Exercises personal initiative to ensure that all stakeholders understand what is required for successful implementation of a solution.

▲ **Ensures clear understanding of responsibilities**—Communicates roles and responsibilities in a way that clearly identifies who is accountable for what, when, and to what standard.

▲ **Understands and addresses potential obstacles to proposed solutions**—Identifies potential threats to a solution to avoid or manage problems in advance of their occurrence.

Negotiating Positions

Definition: Seeks to align the interests of all relevant stakeholders to create mutually beneficial agreements.

Key Actions:

▲ **Determines optimum negotiation positions**—Identifies optimum and fall-back positions prior to actual negotiations and incorporates these as strategies.

▲ **Addresses objections accordingly**—Ensures understanding of a solution and its benefits or involves the appropriate experts to help address stakeholder questions and communicates information that addresses those needs persuasively if necessary.

▲ **Builds consensus and commitment**—Leverages points of agreement and addresses points of conflict in a way that develops buy-in and commitment for moving forward.

Building Relationships

Definition: Builds and nurtures solid relationships to advance stakeholder satisfaction and professional influence in the stakeholder's organization.

Key Actions:

▲ **Actively nurtures positive relationships**—Develops and maintains positive professional relationships among stakeholders at all levels based on personal integrity and trust.

▲ **Protects and develops relationships to higher levels of trust and confidence**—Leverages professional relationships to protect partnerships and advance collaboration.

Insight Competencies

All sales professionals must develop robust information analysis and synthesis skills to use information effectively on the job. The following insight competencies are identified within the model:

- ▲ Analyzing capacity
- ▲ Understanding the customer's business
- ▲ Evaluating customer experiences
- ▲ Gathering intelligence
- ▲ Prioritizing stakeholder needs
- ▲ Identifying options
- ▲ Building a business case.

Analyzing Organizational Capacity

Definition: Assesses and weighs competing requirements against available resources to minimize risk, ensure quality deliverables, and balance capabilities with capacity.

Key Actions:

- ▲ **Assesses resources accurately**—Ensures accurate understanding of the type, quality, and quantity of resources required to achieve desired results.
- ▲ **Balances risk with goal achievement when determining next steps**—Weighs desired outcome against potential risk to prioritize options and identify an optimum path forward while protecting the interests of the company.

Understanding the Business Context

Definition: Develops a sound understanding of the business operations and priorities that serve as the context for work.

Key Actions:

- ▲ **Situates work meaningfully in terms of its relationship to other functions**—Understands an organization's divisions and the upstream, downstream, and cross-stream collaboration in which one's work is situated. Understands how the work one is engaged in contributes to the larger enterprise.
- ▲ **Contributes to the organization's success**—Understands the organization's products, services, and solutions at a level appropriate to position and sells them.

Evaluating Customer Experiences

Definition: Assesses the effectiveness and positive impact of solutions and communicates the results to the stakeholders.

Key Actions:

- ▲ **Develops and implements robust evaluations of solutions**—Uses sound methodologies to demonstrate the effectiveness of a solution at key milestones or to identify critical obstacles affecting success.
- ▲ **Communicates performance in terms of the organization's key performance drivers**—Identifies and uses key business or operational metrics that clearly express beneficial results that are understood and valued by solution stakeholders (for example, net promoter scores, total cost of ownership, return-on-investment, time to competence, and productivity ratios).

Gathering Intelligence

Definition: Systemically acquires needed information and data for effective decision making, planning, relationship building, and the well-informed execution of responsibilities.

Key Actions:

- ▲ **Determines the range, type, and scope of information needed**—Systematically assesses problems, challenges, and opportunities to ensure the right sources are utilized and critical information is collected.
- ▲ **Applies the most appropriate tools and strategies to gather needed information**—Understands which tools and strategies are best suited for fulfilling information requirements and uses these efficiently and effectively.
- ▲ **Develops sources of ongoing information**—Understands how information requirements or the quality of sources can change and creates multiple sources for collecting data and confirming its quality.

Prioritizing Stakeholder Needs

Definition: Assesses stakeholder needs in terms of their critical importance and uses this ranking to prioritize actions.

Key Actions:

- ▲ **Thoroughly diagnoses needs to identify their true nature**—Explores and identifies the root causes of needs to ensure an accurate understanding of their scope.
- ▲ **Prioritizes the most critical causes as a basis for proceeding**—Determines the most appropriate plan of action based on needs analysis and prioritizes actions, resources, and time accordingly.

Identifying Options

Definition: Determines the best course of action based on systematic assessment of what is possible in the situation.

Key Actions:

- ▲ **Explores the scope of possible solutions**—Assesses all feasible options that align with solving the challenge or need.
- ▲ **Approaches option assessment creatively**—Keeps options open ended to capture innovations perhaps not considered in conventional thinking.
- ▲ **Surveys the impact of all alternatives for selecting and prioritizing the best option**—Solicits and incorporates the input of all stakeholder experts and benefactors to ensure the best option is chosen.
- ▲ **Commits to action**—Weighs the needs, requirements, and opportunities involved before committing to the best possible option or course of action.

Building a Business Case

Definition: Builds the business case that is essential for rationalizing the investments required to advance a solution.

Key Actions:

- ▲ **Identifies critical business metrics**—Ensures valid measurements by collaborating with stakeholders to determine the most relevant business, financial, or operational metrics on which to focus.

- ▲ **Builds the value justifications required to commit resources**—Frames the input of experts in a way that ensures well-informed decision making.

- ▲ **Clearly identifies the business or financial benefits to be realized by investments**—Identifies the business and financial benefits of a solution in a way that clearly speaks to business impact.

Solution Competencies

All individuals in the sales ecosystem must develop strategies for generating support for the solutions they define, as well as strategies for making them happen. The following solution competencies are identified in the model:

- ▲ Facilitating change
- ▲ Formalizing commitment
- ▲ Resolving issues
- ▲ Managing projects
- ▲ Leveraging success
- ▲ Articulating value.

Facilitating Change

Definition: Retains an optimistic and adaptive perspective in the face of change and focuses on the positive innovations possible where change initiatives are implemented.

Key Actions:

- ▲ **Advocates change and its benefits**—Encourages others to embrace change as an opportunity rather than an obstacle to personal, operational, or business success.
- ▲ **Manages change effectively**—Ensures that work aligns with changing requirements to more accurately advance the desired change.
- ▲ **Approaches work with a proactive attitude**—Helps organizations and individuals actively engage in improving practices and attitudes by championing change, demonstrating the positive consequences of change, and exercising personal influence to encourage acceptance.

Formalizing Commitment

Definition: Ensures all commitments are formalized in sufficient detail to guide implementation of agreed-upon solutions.

Key Actions:

- ▲ **Secures appropriate commitment**—Fulfills requirements through all phases of solution design and development to build commitment and support.
- ▲ **Appropriately communicates agreements**—Ensures that verbal or written agreements are communicated in a timely fashion to stakeholders.
- ▲ **Documents agreements**—Documents and amends written agreements to accurately reflect the arrived-upon decisions in negotiation.

Resolving Issues

Definition: Works with others to quickly resolve or escalate solutions to problems.

Key Actions:

▲ **Actively monitors situations for potential problems**—Analyzes situations for potential challenges and develops associated contingency plans.

▲ **Monitors implementation or deployment to ensure success**—Takes an active interest in the success of a solution and monitors the milestones in the plan.

▲ **Acts as a focal point of escalation to expedite problem resolution**—Resolves problems directly where possible and acts as an escalation point where warranted to ensure problem resolution.

Managing Projects

Definition: Applies basic project management methods to ensure the successful progress of critical tasks.

Key Actions:

▲ **Organizes and manages work systematically**—Uses project management techniques to control scope, track and manage costs and time, determine requirements, set standards, establish communication processes, and so on.

▲ **Organizes and manages resources effectively**—Identifies and monitors people, funding, timing, and resources to ensure cost-effective and timely project or program results.

▲ **Adaptively applies methods as needed to achieve goals**—Modifies project components in the face of change or emerging requirements to better manage tasks, allocate resources, and cope with shifting work environments.

Leveraging Success

Definition: Leverages the positive impact of an action, solution, or outcome to advance or expand the level of partnership.

Key Actions:

▲ **Leverages success through active promotion**—Ensures that stakeholders appreciate both the value of the solution to the achievement of their goals and the underlying relationships as a basis for expanding a mutually beneficial collaboration.

▲ **Documents and communicates best practices**—Ensures that lessons learned are not lost, but instead captured and leveraged to realize additional opportunities.

Articulating Value

Definition: Clearly links solutions to the challenges they are meant to solve or the opportunities they are meant to actualize and confirms the validity of the solution with stakeholders.

Key Actions:

- ▲ **Ensures that criteria for decision making are shared and addressed**—Frames the benefits of a solution in a way that accurately addresses the key points and priorities of stakeholders.
- ▲ **Adapts and tailors messages as required**—Ensures that value propositions clearly speak to the needs and perspectives of all stakeholder types and levels.
- ▲ **Confirms validity of the proposed solution**—Gains stakeholder consensus on the value of the proposed solution and its efficacy in meeting the needs identified.

Effectiveness Competencies

Besides reliance on processes, methodologies, and relationships, all sales ecosystem individuals must demonstrate personal effectiveness and responsibility. These are the personal effectiveness competencies identified in the model:

- ▲ Building business skill
- ▲ Solving problems
- ▲ Embracing diversity
- ▲ Making ethical decisions
- ▲ Managing knowledge
- ▲ Using technology
- ▲ Accelerating learning
- ▲ Executing plans
- ▲ Maximizing personal time
- ▲ Aligning to sales processes.

Building Business Skill

Definition: Demonstrates business understanding to develop solutions relevant to business success.

Key Actions:

- ▲ **Incorporates business and industry acumen into work**—Understands business terminology and key processes and incorporates these accurately in conceptualizing what must be done when communicating effectively with stakeholders.
- ▲ **Exhibits business-oriented perspective in assessing needs**—Understands how businesses work to achieve profitability and uses business insight to better assess the value and priorities of work-related contributions.
- ▲ **Incorporates legal and contractual requirements into work**—Understands the purpose of standard contracts and statements of work and their role in articulating requirements and setting expectations.
- ▲ **Incorporates financial understanding into work**—Understands the role that costs and financial returns play in determining business value and incorporates this perspective into the way resources are used and solutions positioned.

Solving Problems

Definition: Creatively brings new or alternative perspectives forward to overcome difficulty or uncertainty.

Key Actions:

- ▲ **Approaches challenges creatively**—Approaches problems from a fresh perspective.
- ▲ **Crosses disciplines to frame or address challenges**—Draws from multiple disciplines or models to synthesize new approaches to problem solving.

Embracing Diversity

Definition: Values diversity (gender, ethnic, racial, cultural) and effectively leverages the insights and experiences of others to achieve goals and establish a stimulating, productive work environment.

Key Actions:

▲ **Demonstrates respect for others**—Respects the innate human dignity of every individual.

▲ **Acclimates to diverse work settings**—Demonstrates an appreciation of diverse perspectives and approaches to work and actively seeks to listen, learn, and integrate different ways of accomplishing tasks.

▲ **Harnesses diversity to create workplace synergies**—Leverages the experiences and worldviews of others to drive innovations and stimulate creativity.

Making Ethical Decisions

Definition: Adheres to ethical standards of personal conduct and business rules when making decisions or executing tasks.

Key Actions:

▲ **Demonstrates personal integrity**—Takes personal responsibility for ensuring that actions and decisions protect the integrity of the company and understands and demonstrates the values most important to the work environment.

▲ **Incorporates quality considerations into decision making**—Determines the best course of action in compliance with established quality processes, business rules, or optimum workplace practices.

Managing Knowledge

Definition: Actively captures and communicates essential information with the goal of advancing objectives or sharing best practices.

Key Actions:

▲ **Provides proactive knowledge transfer**—Understands the value of information to stakeholders and circulates it openly to improve overall performance and productivity.

▲ **Ensures that communication tools and processes advance information storage and transfer**—Recognizes and acts on obstacles to the effective storage, retrieval, or communication of information.

Using Technology

Definition: Demonstrates comfort with technology and uses technical innovations to advance the efficiency and effectiveness of work processes, procedures, and outputs.

Key Actions:

▲ **Maintains understanding of technical innovations**—Incorporates an up-to-date understanding of technical innovations and trends as well as their implications.

▲ **Uses information technology to align and expedite work**—Uses tools and systems appropriately to ensure that communications and work are delivered in a timely way and are usable by customers, colleagues, and managers.

▲ **Improves personal productivity technology**—Takes the initiative to learn new technology and incorporate its benefits into the workplace (for example, customer relationship management [CRM] systems, virtual classroom, and mobile communication devices).

Accelerating Learning

Definition: Uses conventional and innovative approaches to quickly gain and maintain the knowledge and skills necessary for effective job performance.

Key Actions:

▲ **Takes personal responsibility for development**—Monitors and addresses skill and knowledge gaps by actively soliciting performance feedback and developmental planning assistance and selects appropriate development options.

▲ **Demonstrates agility in addressing development needs**—Leverages a range of learning options and delivery media to maximize time in the acquisition of critical skills, knowledge, or values.

▲ **Leverages information to change behavior**—Accesses and incorporates essential information for the ongoing development of personal effectiveness.

Executing Plans

Definition: Organizes tasks and resources in a manner that coordinates resources efficiently, maximizes productivity, and communicates expectations and results to stakeholders.

Key Actions:

▲ **Develops plans that clearly actualize strategy**—Articulates strategies in a way that aligns activities, deliverables, and milestones.

▲ **Builds commitment to plan**—Exercises influence to ensure enthusiastic commitment and buy-in to a plan's strategy and implementation requirements.

▲ **Executes to plan, yet adapts to emergent circumstances**—Uses plans to guide activities, demonstrates responsiveness to change, and adapts plans to emerging requirements.

▲ **Delivers to plan**—Attains the goals sufficient to generate interest in continuing or expanding the organizational or business relationship into new areas of collaboration.

Maximizing Personal Time

Definition: Ensures time and effort align with priorities and provides for the most efficient use of resources.

Key Actions:

▲ **Incorporates a strategic perspective in activity planning**—Distinguishes the tactical from the strategic and the urgent from the critical as a guide to prioritizing activities.

▲ **Practices time management**—Applies appropriate time management techniques to focus, prioritize, and track tasks.

Aligning to Sales Processes

Definition: Understands the key phases of selling and how personal responsibilities affect effective execution.

Key Actions:

▲ **Aligns and relates work to sales success**—Understands how work products contribute to effective selling and ensures their solid contribution to sales success.

▲ **Incorporates selling sensibilities into work execution**—Appreciates how the term "customer" establishes an important dynamic in both internal and external business relationships, calling for consultative partnering based on mutual benefits.

▲ **Demonstrates a systemic understanding of sales**—Understands buying-selling relationships and uses this understanding to focus work in a flexible, adaptive manner that contributes to the larger network of sales relationships and facilitates the personalization and customization of sales solutions.

▲ **Ensures that work helps to advance sales**—Acts as a facilitator to sales, sales processing, or sales readiness when performing work.

Sales Areas of Expertise

Sales areas of expertise (AOEs) contain the specific technical and professional skills and knowledge required for success within professional selling. Think of sales AOEs as the knowledge and skills an individual must have and demonstrate above and beyond the foundational competencies. To function effectively in a given AOE, a person must demonstrate a blend of the appropriate foundational competencies and unique technical and professional skills and knowledge found in the AOEs. An individual may have expertise in one or more of these areas of expertise:

- ▲ Creating and closing opportunities
- ▲ Protecting accounts
- ▲ Defining and positioning solutions
- ▲ Supporting indirect selling
- ▲ Setting sales strategy
- ▲ Managing within the sales ecosystem
- ▲ Developing sales force capability
- ▲ Delivering sales training
- ▲ Coaching for sales results
- ▲ Building sales infrastructure
- ▲ Designing compensation
- ▲ Maintaining accounts
- ▲ Recruiting sales talent.

Creating and Closing Opportunities

Definition: Continuously scans for prospects to achieve new sales, expands account control, and populates account pipeline; leverages customer referrals and targets new leads; follows up on leads and assesses prospect readiness to buy; performs interest-building calls as necessary; builds and drives opportunities by generating and nurturing internal and external stakeholder interest; manages sales cycle progress; conducts or orchestrates business or technical qualifications; acquires the technical expertise required for well-targeted solution design, business case justification, and subsequent negotiations; drives or manages the resources necessary for effective negotiations, including the alignment of expert input within the negotiation strategy; and asks for the business, effectively addresses any objections or concerns, closes unique transactions, and achieves a mutually beneficial win for the buyer and seller.

Key Skills and Knowledge:

Knowledge of

- Product or service features, benefits, and value propositions
- Sales collateral resources
- Cold-calling sales techniques
- Customer-related vertical market or industry information resources
- Sales negotiation and closing methods
- Formal and ad hoc research strategies (for example, systematic exploration, personal networking, and web site scanning)
- Lead management procedures
- Cost-estimation and sizing techniques
- Personal engagement and interest-generation strategies
- Business alliance building skills (for example, client, third party, and so forth)
- Business analysis metrics and procedures (for example, health ratios and balance sheet analysis)
- Return-on-investment (ROI) and total cost of ownership (TCO) techniques
- Business workshop facilitation and management skills
- Sales cycle management skills
- Proposal development, component integration, and management practices
- Formal sales negotiation and closing methods or strategies
- Objection handling techniques
- Opportunity qualification skills
- Resource knowledge (technical, pricing, legal, and delivery and fulfillment).

Ability to

- Create compelling sales presentations
- Interpret and synthesize information from multiple sources (for example, databases, online resources, and colleagues)
- Compellingly communicate product or service benefits and features
- Determine buyer readiness from verbal and nonverbal cues
- Identify influencers, buyers, and detractors in the sales process
- Manage multiple or interrelated sales calls
- Implement environmental scanning to ensure well-targeted sales messages

- ▲ Manage leads and ensure follow-up and follow-through
- ▲ Accurately estimate costs and size solutions
- ▲ Calculate business metrics and translate product or service features meaningfully into value propositions
- ▲ Leverage vertical market and industry knowledge in product or service positioning
- ▲ Align sales activities with their respective point in the sales process
- ▲ Lead business analysis discussions.

Key Actions:

▲ **Researches and targets prospects**—Actively researches available sources to identify likely prospects based on alignment with product or service market, known business needs, typical customer profiles, business activities, competitive market position, customer challenges, product or service spend, and competitive presence in account; reviews prospects and determines where or how to allocate effort and resources; and develops approach strategy tailored to the most appropriate individuals who have decision-making authority.

▲ **Conducts interest-building calls (cold calls) when applicable**—Appropriately manages customer prospecting to connect directly with future customers while not alienating them; generates immediate, compelling customer interest in the selling organization, ensuring its product or service offers sufficient value to generate a willingness to continue the sales dialogue; and initiates exploratory discussions to schedule solid and specific follow-up sales calls in an effort to continue facilitating buying processes.

▲ **Identifies, follows up on, and manages sales leads**—Builds reciprocal lead-sharing networks to build the sales funnel with prospective clients and acts on any new lead in a timely manner to capitalize on interest and compelling needs.

▲ **Gains interest**—Leverages marketing materials to stimulate client interest; explores client curiosity from various perspectives—business, financial, and market—to capture key variables and contingencies to nurture opportunities; generates customer interest through discussion of potential benefits; and actively shapes components of each opportunity to reflect client priorities and adequately address client needs.

▲ **Qualifies opportunities**—Assesses client operations and business position for potential partnering opportunities, assesses client balance sheet and business health to determine feasibility of partnering, identifies and aligns required resources for pursuit and future solution deployment, determines scope and nature of risk as a necessary input to developing appropriate pricing and risk management strategies, and determines or orchestrates identification of opportunities and assesses requirements for third-party involvement.

▲ **Develops winning proposals**—Develops compelling value propositions aligned with customer needs, business priorities, and/or technical and operational requirements; orchestrates and aligns the technical or functional contributions of functional and technical experts; communicates key competitive advantages; works with others to ensure appropriate pricing; and manages the milestones essential for timely proposal delivery.

▲ **Builds business justification cases**—Collaborates with financial, legal, and technical experts to develop a business justification for each specific opportunity to ensure internal buy-in; enlists champions within both buyer and seller organizations; works with internal stakeholders to customize the opportunity to internal requirements while avoiding compromises that might threaten client acceptance or solution integrity; and identifies and communicates all risks associated with the opportunity and addresses these challenges with solution contingencies or fall-back positions.

▲ **Orchestrates support for negotiations**—Where warranted, coordinates the input of legal, technical, and financial experts seamlessly into the development of a negotiation strategy; ensures that stakeholders understand their role in negotiation; focuses efforts of others on achieving the business outcome; continuously checks with experts to ensure commitments are valid and can be delivered; and drives to close and asks for the business at the appropriate time.

▲ **Maintains opportunity momentum to expand sales**—Capitalizes on early wins and customer satisfaction to expand business wider and deeper into the account.

Sample Outputs:

- ▲ Prioritized prospect list
- ▲ Target prospect business or operations profile
- ▲ Sales plan or strategy
- ▲ Capture plan
- ▲ Prospect entry into sales system tracking tool
- ▲ Lead management strategies
- ▲ Follow-up activities
- ▲ Opportunity pursuit strategy
- ▲ Business health analysis
- ▲ Letters of understanding
- ▲ Sales proposals
- ▲ Responses to requests for information
- ▲ Negotiation strategy
- ▲ Business case justification
- ▲ Other outputs as appropriate.

Protecting Accounts

Definition: Gathers account intelligence and maintains current understanding of customer's business; develops and monitors sales plans; monitors and communicates sales forecasts and pipeline activities to ensure accuracy; develops expanded relationships with customers to achieve trusted advisor status and entry into business planning activities; screens account activities and protects customers from unnecessary sales or marketing activities; monitors competitive growth in accounts and builds strategies for countering competitive messages; where warranted, determines account transition readiness to sales farming and maintains customer trust during and following this transition; and ensures customer satisfaction as well as delivery or deployment alignment with contractual terms and conditions.

Key Skills and Knowledge:

Knowledge of

- ▲ Customer business and operations (for example, reporting structures and decision makers)
- ▲ Account history (prior investments and account relationships)
- ▲ Account farming procedures and practices (for example, check-ins and sponsoring marketing initiatives)
- ▲ Transition to farming practices
- ▲ Business analysis methods
- ▲ Industry research engines and resources (for example, Dun and Bradstreet and analysts reports)
- ▲ Customer organizational communication resources (websites, annual reports, press releases, and position and white papers)
- ▲ Customer business health indictors (for example, ratios)
- ▲ Account planning tools, templates, and procedures
- ▲ Account-related marketing plans
- ▲ Supply chain knowledge (lead times, response rates, and fulfillment processes)
- ▲ Funnel management practices, tools, metrics, and policies
- ▲ Deployment practices and back-office administrative or order-entry procedures
- ▲ Competitive information resources
- ▲ Contract administration and renewal processes
- ▲ Standard contractual and service level agreement (SLA) terms, conditions, and milestone metrics
- ▲ Resource management strategies.

Ability to

- ▲ Manage total customer satisfaction to optimize relationships
- ▲ Coordinate and align all account activities with overarching plan
- ▲ Determine how customers are organized and how they make purchasing decisions
- ▲ Leverage marketing programs to advance sales
- ▲ Summarize salient content from customer communication sources (for example, websites, annual reports, press releases, and position and white papers)
- ▲ Determine business health and viability using key business ratios
- ▲ Apply relevant account planning tools, templates, and procedures
- ▲ Apply funnel management practices, tools, metrics, and policies effectively to prioritize and manage selling
- ▲ Translate competitive knowledge into relevant sales practices
- ▲ Leverage contract administration and renewal into up- or cross-selling opportunities

▲ Monitor and manage contractual and service level agreement terms, conditions, and milestone metrics

▲ Set accurate customer expectations for order fulfillment (for example, lead times, response rates, and fulfillment processes).

Key Actions:

▲ **Gathers and monitors account intelligence**—Maintains account business direction in a manner consistent with client needs, establishes networks in customer business to stay abreast of current or emerging requirements, and scans relevant external publications or websites for account-related business information.

▲ **Documents account plans and sales forecasts**—Develops strategies and plans for managing account pursuit activities; assesses activities to plan; prioritizes and coordinates opportunity pursuit across multiple accounts to maintain a healthy sales funnel; and develops, communicates, and monitors sales forecasts to ensure accuracy.

▲ **Builds client executive business relationships**—Widens the breadth and depth of account penetration to achieve exposure to business planning, uses professional presence to frame selling messages in terms of client's business (rather than operational or technical) benefits, incorporates key business and financial metrics into sales positioning messages, demonstrates comfort at various business levels and possesses the social skills necessary for interacting effectively with senior level executives, and positions the company represented and the benefits of partnering as the essential components of the business relationship desired as opposed to focusing on a more purely transactional relationship.

▲ **Cultivates and develops trusted advisor status**—Ensures that product or service value propositions align and resonate with customer needs, provides on-demand consultative advice, checks the accuracy and utility of recommendations prior to their communication and avoids making inaccurate claims, conducts self professionally in all customer communications and interactions with discreteness and confidentiality when required, and credits competitive claims where warranted to maintain credibility and trust.

▲ **Protects and expands accounts**—Ensures that all contractual deployment or fulfillment obligations are met and customer satisfaction is achieved, monitors account activity to minimize rogue selling and disruptive marketing, generally maintains overall account focal point leadership, and monitors competitive activities in accounts and appropriately counters competitive messages while blocking future competitor inroads.

▲ **Manages deployment readiness and resource alignment**—Ensures accurate understanding of requirements derived from closed opportunities (for example, terms and conditions and service level agreements) and ensures knowledge is dispersed among personnel engaged in post-sale activity (for example, fulfillment and delivery); where warranted, acts as the focal point for deal education and preparation within individual geographies; and where required, facilitates the resource troubleshooting essential for successfully launching complex initiatives.

Sample Outputs:

▲ Strategic account plan

▲ Sales funnel

▲ Customer check-ups

▲ Forecast updates

▲ Sales forecasts

▲ Marketing feedback

▲ Executive-level communications

▲ Portfolio and client reviews

- ▲ Account profiles
- ▲ Service level agreements
- ▲ Legal documentation
- ▲ Management and team member updates
- ▲ Industry and competitive position papers
- ▲ Competitive analyses
- ▲ Transition plans
- ▲ Company-specific paperwork
- ▲ Solution roadmap
- ▲ Other outputs as appropriate.

Defining and Positioning Solutions

Definition: Drives the technical and technical components of opportunity qualification; translates business requirements to solution requirements; shapes solutions to capitalize on seller or partner solution advantage; coordinates the additional technical expertise required for building complex solutions; creates solutions that clearly address and align with customer business needs; conducts effective technical presentations at all appropriate levels within the client's organization; supports the sizing, scoping, and identification of delivery or deployment resources essential for accurate costing; ensures the accuracy and feasibility of all proposals and solution-oriented communications to the customer; and supports internal acceptance of proposed solutions and monitors post-sale customer satisfaction.

Key Skills and Knowledge:

Knowledge of

- ▲ Product, service, or solution technology (for example, concepts and uses)
- ▲ Solution technical foundation
- ▲ Solution configuration frameworks or templates
- ▲ Requirements analysis and management techniques
- ▲ Solution design procedures and communication conventions (written and graphical)
- ▲ Solution design methodologies, best practices, and trends
- ▲ Oral and written communication skills (sufficient for ensuring that technical concepts are meaningful to nontechnical audiences)
- ▲ Customer-facing skills
- ▲ Technical trust building and selling
- ▲ Business context of technical solution knowledge
- ▲ Solution sizing criteria
- ▲ Technical team leadership
- ▲ Vertical industry solutions
- ▲ Solution deployment or delivery practices (expectation setting and quality checking).

Ability to

- ▲ Counter competitor product or service feature and benefit messages
- ▲ Communicate features and benefits of solution-related tools or packages
- ▲ Accurately map customer's product or service operating environment
- ▲ Effectively communicate technical solutions
- ▲ Translate solution designs into meaningful customer benefits and differentiate these by stakeholder needs
- ▲ Develop trusted advisor status with customers based on technical and business acumen
- ▲ Ensure cost-effective solution deployment and delivery practices
- ▲ Manage teams and integrate their contributions.

Key Actions:

- ▲ **Performs technical qualifications**—Gathers the information required for technical solution creation based on customer's specific needs, builds technical credibility with clients to counter competitive arguments and advance the sale with the technical decision maker(s), and reviews opportunities based on technical feasibility or competitive presence within the client relationship for each individual opportunity.

▲ **Designs solutions**—Creates the technical design necessary to clearly identify solution components, their interrelationships with each other, and how they work together to solve the customer's business challenges; identifies solution components appropriate for solving a customer's unique business challenges; and validates solution ideas with customers, peers, and account teams to ensure solution integrity and feasibility.

▲ **Customizes standard products or services**—Designs solutions that are necessary to truly accommodate a customer's business needs; enlists in-house support or appropriate subject matter expertise necessary to create tailored solutions; and ensures all stakeholders (for example, sales negotiators, contract experts, and deployment or delivery personnel) understand unique solution components and/or their requirements).

▲ **Conducts technical demonstrations and benchmarks**—Demonstrates the features, benefits, value, and competitive advantage of a solution by addressing customer needs within the context of the customer's business setting; generates proof-of-concept data to create a compelling business case for selecting a specific solution; leverages benchmark data as required to technically position the beneficial results of the solution advocated; and presents performance output in a way that resonates with customers and addresses their concerns.

▲ **Contributes to solution sizing and modification**—Collaborates with functional experts (for example, colleagues in pricing, deployment, legal, and so forth) to accurately size a proposed solution and works with account teams to adapt solutions in response to new customer requirements, funding restrictions, the desire for a phased approach, and other important factors.

▲ **Articulates solution designs**—Facilitates solution positioning in a manner that effectively demonstrates understanding of the communications and positions the strategy to both technical and business stakeholders; reviews all communications and proposals for accurate solution definition and identification of benefits; and, where warranted, conducts technical presentations to ensure understanding or enlist the support of technical stakeholders within the customer's environment.

Sample Outputs:

▲ Technical demonstrations or proof-of-concept demonstrations
▲ Technical components of proposals and positioning communications
▲ Technical requirements and input to statements of work (SOWs) and delivery or deployment strategies
▲ Goals and objectives statements
▲ Technical proposals
▲ Definition of technical problems
▲ Prototypes and models
▲ Work flow or work breakdown structures
▲ Forcefield and/or root cause analyses
▲ Logical or conceptual and technical solution designs
▲ Solution presentations
▲ Other outputs as appropriate.

Supporting Indirect Selling

Definition: Conducts joint planning and marketing activities at all levels within partner organizations; conducts appropriate opportunity targeting, inventory clearance, and sales pursuit activities; builds partner business relationships essential to the maintenance of partner trust and preference; collaborates effectively with partners to present a unified position to customers; protects partner interests and ensures internal compliance with partner obligations; educates partners on products or services and motivates partner interest selling; and, where warranted, participates as a team selling member in building customer confidence in partner.

Key Skills and Knowledge:
Knowledge of

- Partner types and functions (distributors and resellers)
- Company indirect sales team focus, strategy, and direction
- Marketing promotional programs and initiatives
- Partner incentive programs
- Partner business model and financial health
- Partner market niche and product or service alignment model
- Partner loyalty and commitment-building techniques
- Partner issues escalation and resolution procedures
- Sell-with, sell-through, and sell-for techniques
- Business planning
- Business or influencing methods
- Product or service information resources
- Partner sales crediting processes and tools
- Partner scorecard metrics
- Sales forecasting and metrics management skills
- Knowledge transfer and communication skills
- Vendor requirements and certification processes.

Ability to

- Build personal relationships with partners to advance mind-share
- Leverage marketing programs and initiatives to advance partner selling
- Influence operations to ensure timely and accurate payout to partners
- Ensure timely and accurate product or service updates to partners based on the most appropriate communication method (for example, web portals and telecommunications)
- Implement partner performance assessments and evaluations impartially
- Ensure partner compliance with product or service certification requirements.

Key Actions:
- **Assesses and helps develop partner's sales force**—When appropriate, assesses the talent of the partner's sales force to leverage strengths, identify weaknesses, and address gaps.
- **Drives partner sales planning or forecasting**—Identifies likely sales prospects as well as market clusters where opportunity may exist; assesses inventory push strategies for adequacy and determines use of market-promotion funding; articulates sales goals, aligns sales metrics, and sets joint expectations with partners; tailors planning to local market requirements and conditions; gains partner commitment and establishes a

strategy for monitoring the partner's selling progress; monitors partner activities for compliance with plan; and where warranted, suggests mid-course corrections to plan.

▲ **Motivates and educates partners**—Leverages marketing promotions and discounts to advance partner selling, elevates partner preference for products or services over the competition, ensures partners are adequately prepared for accurately discussing or positioning products or services, and clearly communicates certification requirements if any exist and facilitates partner enrollment in appropriate training and testing.

▲ **Cultivates partner business relationships**—Builds understanding of partner's short- and long-term commitments; develops mutual understanding about what each stakeholder seeks to achieve in the partnership; extends partner planning and alliance-building activities to the highest levels of the partner's organization; clearly articulates the business advantages of partnering to extend the range of selling; and where warranted, helps shift partner focus from transactional to consultative selling.

▲ **Facilitates inventory balancing or clearance**—Monitors distributor warehouse flow-through for optimum efficiency, collaborates with distributors in developing strategies and making the marketing investments needed to advance or accelerate end-point selling, and troubleshoots product supply or logistics issues affecting distributor performance.

▲ **Tracks investments in partner selling to determine business impact**—Implements event-driven or quarterly tracking methods to monitor partner selling improvements; uses partner self-reports or independent data to assess return-on-investment for funds expended; and collaborates with other stakeholders to revise sales strategies or marketing events to ensure optimum yield or achievement of investment objectives (for example, sales, leads, interest generation, and market penetration).

▲ **Facilitates partner transformation**—Introduces effective selling strategies to partner organization to increase its market penetration, identifies new or expanded market opportunities, and encourages close business collaboration in business planning and investments to ensure that partners maintain their presence in the face of market trends.

▲ **Monitors and manages contract fulfillment**—Ensures that contracts serve as a frame of reference for setting expectations and guiding partner activities and ensures that contractual requirements are fulfilled.

▲ **Troubleshoots partner sales crediting**—Actively works with operations team members to correct inaccuracies and to ensure timely crediting of partner sales, collaborates with operations and other stakeholders to build or maintain optimum partner-associated processes, and helps expedite sale or order fulfillment processes.

▲ **Collaborates on team selling and positioning**—Assists partner at critical sales cycle junctions (for example, positioning, closing, and negotiation) where required; works internally to acquire optimum pricing or exemptions when appropriate; and minimizes discord with partner and presents a unified team approach to the customer.

Sample Outputs:

▲ Partner business plans
▲ Partner account plans
▲ Transformation plans
▲ Partner reviews and assessments
▲ Inventory management and turnover metrics
▲ Investment assessments and reports
▲ Market investment funding proposals
▲ Sell through or demand generation tracking results
▲ Other outputs as appropriate.

Setting Sales Strategy

Definition: Engineers world-class selling performance by helping the organization expand its understanding of a professional selling systems view; establishes long-term sales pursuit and business partnering philosophies with team and colleagues; balances short-term requirements with long-term results; recognizes and advances innovative sales practices and sales team configuration strategies; promotes integrated sales automation tools and processes; develops sales territory and organizational alignments; establishes interface processes and working relationships with key business stakeholders at the executive level to build mind-share across all functions (for example, marketing, engineering, and supply chain peers); and leads and evaluates change management programs that continuously improve sales performance.

Key Skills and Knowledge:

Knowledge of

- ▲ Emerging market and sales trend knowledge
- ▲ Company business plans, strategic direction, and goals
- ▲ Company sales and competitive policies
- ▲ Company market position and market performance information
- ▲ Cultural and market segment diversity
- ▲ Market dynamics (general and product- or service-specific trends)
- ▲ Risk management and mitigation strategies
- ▲ Competitive knowledge and best practices
- ▲ Situational leadership methods
- ▲ Sales best practice and industry sales benchmarking resources
- ▲ Companywide organizational and value-chain information
- ▲ Systemic change, diffusion, and management methods
- ▲ Program management and measurement methods
- ▲ Sales metrics and measurement methods
- ▲ Sales system, tool, or process automation information
- ▲ Workforce planning concepts
- ▲ Regulatory environment resources (global)
- ▲ Executive relationship-building strategies.

Ability to

- ▲ Synthesize industry or market knowledge toward the creation of sales force requirements
- ▲ Identify areas of risk and their probability and develop appropriate contingency plans
- ▲ Leverage and diffuse best practices in selling within the organization (industry and competitive)
- ▲ Manage complex change or transformation programs (for example, design, develop, implement, and evaluate) to preserve innovation while ensuring compliance with company policy
- ▲ Divide and allocate sales territories for maximum impact on company growth objectives
- ▲ Build executive sponsorship at the highest levels of the company.

Key Actions:

- ▲ **Identifies and articulates innovative sales practices**—Works internally to synthesize the overall business plan with market trends and data; identifies both key themes of and obstacles to sales effectiveness; solicits and validates insights from the field; develops scalable sales structure and process models that optimize current sales activities and go-to-market realities; introduces new sales practices that help deliver value; and collaborates with business management and company functions as well as sales team members to assess feasibility, costs, and benefits associated with innovative strategies.

▲ **Creates strategic plans that guide organizational, technical, process, or practice planning and implementation**—Creates development plans to set the direction and agenda for tactical sales planning, collaborates with appropriate sales management colleagues to ensure alignment with plans, works with technical personnel or vendors to provide customer-based inputs into the tools and systems support envisioned, and monitors implementation to assess success and adjusts strategy as needed.

▲ **Builds business and partner alliances to increase sales**—Forges business alliances with those who possess a shared vision of desired future state (for example, business development, product or service development, supply chain, marketing, and sales management) and enlists third-party alliances where warranted to close gaps or advance implementation toward the vision.

▲ **Provides leadership to accelerate strategy diffusion**—Develops communication and readiness strategies to generate enthusiasm for strategy and motivate the effort needed for success and leverages technology and uses events to personally champion strategy.

▲ **Configures and aligns sales territories for maximum effectiveness**—Develops or reconfigures territories to maximize sales effectiveness or technical and functional resource allocation and collaborates with regional, territory, and local sales team members to delineate responsibilities and manage territories.

Sample Outputs:

- ▲ Strategic plans
- ▲ Business models
- ▲ Territory alignment plans
- ▲ Change management strategies
- ▲ Organization-specific plans
- ▲ Annual meeting materials
- ▲ Sales team meeting agendas
- ▲ Executive summaries and briefings
- ▲ Territory planning spreadsheets
- ▲ Change management presentations
- ▲ Motivational materials
- ▲ Communication to key partners
- ▲ Best practice briefings
- ▲ Knowledge-sharing documents
- ▲ Leadership strategies
- ▲ Leadership assessments
- ▲ Other outputs as appropriate.

Managing within the Sales Ecosystem

Definition: Synthesizes team data for reporting purposes (for example, sales forecasts, team progress, delivery, and project results); monitors individual metrics achievement (for example, project completion, progress against goal, quota performance, technical coverage, and margin); monitors budgets and controls expenditures; ensures activity meets demand (for example, sales funnel activity, project management activity, technology, and margin protection); determines functional or organizational structure (for example, territory alignment, work group alignment, and team organization); conducts recruitment, hiring, promotion, termination, and career development activities; conducts performance reviews, facilitates individual development planning, and offers career development guidance; manages expectations and individual team member responsibilities; ensures optimum collaboration links among functional areas; works with peers and upper management to optimally align workload, divide labor, and allocate resources; sponsors sales force capability assessments and incorporates findings into development planning; leverages technology to improve results and operations; conducts business analysis to align business goals with team performance; and drives and manages sales-specific actions related to product or service launch and roll-out.

Key Skills and Knowledge:

Knowledge of

- Company business or sales targets and metrics
- Performance measurement and management processes and tools
- Human resources policies and procedures
- Financial concepts and spreadsheet tools
- Forecasting and aggregation methods or tools
- Funnel management and aggregation methods or tools
- Supply chain and order fulfillment processes and procedures
- Competitive sales management tactics
- Workforce planning methods
- Capability gap analysis methods
- Career counseling methods
- Behavioral interview methods
- Business organizational culture
- Organization and operations
- High-performance and team-building methods
- Risk-assessment and -management methods
- Business development methods
- Contract administration and vendor management methods
- Legal and regulatory requirements
- Profit-and-loss (P&L) management methods
- Cost-center management methods
- Business standards of conduct and ethical guidelines.

Ability to

- Convert company targets and metrics into action
- Assess individual or team strengths and weaknesses
- Ensure compliance with applicable local, national, and international laws

▲ Manage operations to ensure cost-effectiveness
▲ Manage business forecasts to ensure accuracy
▲ Build strategies for counteracting competitive tactics
▲ Identify and address workforce gaps (for example, training and hiring)
▲ Manage operations to minimize costs or maximize profits
▲ Ensure workforce compliance with standards of conduct, ethical guidelines, and specific human resources policies.

Key Actions:

▲ **Aligns tactical activities to support strategic sales plans**—Provides input to organizational planning while assessing goals in light of unique requirements and opportunities; aligns planning with organizational goals—sets priorities and expectations and identifies and addresses opportunity or resource gaps; adjusts plans to local requirements to ensure progress to established plan; and ensures alignment of all activities with upper management strategies, corporate direction, and goals.

▲ **Establishes, monitors, and controls costs that affect sales margins**—Identifies spend parameters and establishes operating budgets; tracks spending and complies with associated reporting requirements (for example, reimbursement for customer meetings and travel expenses); manages sales-related allowances and discounts to ensure appropriate margin; reallocates funding to address cost overruns; prepares and communicates quarterly and annual sales reports; manages associated sales expenditures; and drives cost-control and operational efficiencies to ensure optimum targeting of resources on most appropriate opportunities.

▲ **Aligns resources with opportunities**—Collaborates with colleagues to ensure optimum opportunity coverage using available technology and expert sales resources; balances key factors determining resource allocation to establish pursuit priorities in area of control (for example, account importance, win probability, opportunity size, and alignment to strategy); and, where necessary, troubleshoots with colleagues to ensure timely access to needed resources.

▲ **Screens administrative demands and troubleshoots back-office operations to minimize sales disruptions**—Acts as the escalation point to screen sales personnel from administrative disruptions that might otherwise dilute their focus on selling activities; screens and prioritizes incoming organizational communications for key announcements; troubleshoots operational issues around order fulfillment to ensure delivery or deployment; troubleshoots operational challenges that affect sales credit or payout to maintain positive sales morale; and collaborates with operations management to improve processes, systems, or tools for ease of use.

▲ **Ensures accurate forecasting while monitoring performance to metrics**—Ensures contributor use of planning and reporting tools or systems to establish consistency, promote accuracy, and advance real-time management assessment; conducts regularly scheduled check-ins and meetings to assess and/or troubleshoot progress to pre-determined plans; tracks account contributor performance against established metrics (for example, funnel movement, account plans, program goals, established performance objectives, and customer satisfaction); and develops and rolls up aggregate forecast as required.

▲ **Hires, promotes, and terminates to improve sales performance and address capability gaps**—Leverages management experience and knowledge of capability gaps to build well-targeted hiring criteria or conduct appropriate terminations, reviews candidate's qualification for linkage to defined competencies, supports candidate selection processes, facilitates on-boarding, clearly sets expectations for new hire performance, acts as performance resource during trial employment period, situates performance in the wider context of business goals, clearly communicates criteria for promotion and exercises this responsibility objectively, counsels contributors to address and remediate performance concerns or to resolve issues, and creates required documentation to terminate employees in a manner that minimizes challenges to this decision while protecting company assets.

▲ **Aligns reward and recognition strategies with performance goals**—Leverages company or establishes local rewards or recognition programs to advance overall sales performance, continuously assesses rewards for their motivational power and revises where necessary, administers recognition and reward selection criteria fairly to maintain morale, ensures communication of recognition or awards to leverage impact on group performance, and balances acknowledgement of individuals with the need for group solidarity to create a climate of continuous performance improvement that facilitates peer-to-peer best practices sharing.

Sample Outputs:

- ▲ Forecasts (synthesized or rolled up)
- ▲ Budgets and expenditure control plans
- ▲ Progress reports
- ▲ Responses to data requests
- ▲ Technical and functional resource plans or requests
- ▲ Workforce plans
- ▲ Hiring, termination, and promotion input and justification documents
- ▲ Hiring interview instruments and methods
- ▲ New hire training plan inputs
- ▲ New hire competency model(s) inputs
- ▲ Meetings with internal stakeholders
- ▲ Documentation for employee termination
- ▲ Talent management inputs
- ▲ Reward and recognition program plans
- ▲ Vendor selection criteria
- ▲ Flowcharts, mind maps, or other system maps
- ▲ Performance reviews
- ▲ Incentive plans
- ▲ Team-building events
- ▲ Other outputs as appropriate.

Developing Sales Force Capability

Definition: Assesses capability gaps and identifies strategies and solutions to overcome them; determines new sales performance requirements associated with business strategies; identifies learning solutions required for new product or service launch, or new sales force requirements; creates and updates sales competency profiles by meeting with relevant sales stakeholders, increasing awareness of sales context and following sound competency-based approaches to planning and development of capability; drives a competency-based approach to planning and developing capability based on a solid understanding of critical levers that will most likely increase sales results; designs and develops learning solutions essential for skill and knowledge acquisition within unique sales cultures (for example, courses, curricula, mentoring, coaching, and on-the-job resources); utilizes rapid design delivery methods where appropriate (for example, virtual, collaborative, platform, and standalone); manages program roll-outs in the most effective manner; and measures and evaluates the impact of learning solutions.

Key Skills and Knowledge:

Knowledge of

- Rapid instructional design methods
- Sales operations and fulfillment processes
- Audience learning style and preferences (individual and cultural)
- Test development (item construction and validation)
- Learning delivery systems and media
- Learning program evaluation methods (formative, summative, transfer, business impact, and ROI)
- Human performance improvement concepts
- Performance analysis methods
- Business direction and goals
- Sales cycle components and stage-specific milestones
- Blended learning techniques
- Experiential learning methods (work-based learning and on-the-job development techniques such as mentoring, job rotation, and sabbaticals)
- Learning management systems.

Ability to

- Translate business requirements or performance gaps into relevant learning improvements
- Apply approaches to learning to best meet the needs of target audiences
- Apply rapid instructional design methods to ensure responsiveness to performance challenges
- Build learning solutions sensitive to learning styles or cultural norms
- Leverage workplace opportunities to advance experiential learning (for example, mentoring, cognitive apprenticeship, and peer-to-peer tutoring)
- Construct valid and reliable tests
- Balance cost, target audience requirements, and content demands to select the most appropriate learning delivery systems and media
- Implement learning program evaluation systematically to establish a value chain that clearly connects programs to business results (for example, formative and summative).

Key Actions:

▲ **Determines competencies required to achieve sales strategy**—Understands how to align the strategic customer's needs to increased capability through the improvement of individual competencies (knowledge, skills, and attitudes); ties organization's sales strategies and business functions to competencies needed now and in the future; assesses current competencies of the team (from entry-level workers to senior executives) in relation to the requirements of the future state; and determines the priority of competencies needed.

▲ **Conducts sales-related needs assessments**—Identifies sales skill and environmental challenges, identifies required resources, analyzes and incorporates findings in a set of training solutions or support recommendations, and articulates information necessary for implementing future learning solutions while supporting organization's goals.

▲ **Designs and develops sales development programs, curricula, or learning solutions**—Partners with subject matter experts to quickly and adequately develop content; analyzes, synthesizes, and organizes content modules; develops and validates learning outcomes and/or curricula progress path; collaborates with stakeholders in determining appropriate delivery strategy and media; generates the design specifications necessary for development; implements and monitors development to plan; leverages project-based approach to learning roll-outs and solutions; selects appropriate delivery modes for learning opportunities—instructor-led classroom, online instruction, guided on-the-job experience, informal learning, or a combination of methods; proposes opportunities to drive self-directed learning (for example, job rotation, tuition reimbursement, personal development reimbursement, and professional association memberships); creates development maps for every sales team member (leaders, catalysts, developers, and enablers); and ensures development maps are meaningful to sales team leaders by tying competencies to job function within the sales team, area of expertise, or job role.

▲ **Uses learning management systems**—Provides or updates information in learning management systems to ensure accurate and timely communication of events offered; tracks participants through learning programs and, where warranted, satisfactory completion of requirements (for example, certification course and testing completion); builds usable report templates based on stakeholder needs and generates reports as needed to profile target audience progress or requirements completion; enforces data access and confidentiality norms while ensuring that participants and their management have appropriate exposure to information based on access privileges; uses data to identify program challenges as these relate to attendance or completion requirements; and uses data to inform development planning and data integration involving interfacing with other systems.

▲ **Ties learning strategy to organizational capacity**—Creates a sales-wide learning plan to address competency gaps, manage resource deployment, and measure outcomes for sales catalysts, developers, and enablers; helps the organization decide between hiring for an already developed competency, developing the competency internally, managing the skill gaps through outsourcing, or blending approaches to achieve organizational capacity; sets baseline measures by documenting every member's current competencies via assessment; identifies targets for closing the gap between current competency sets and those needed to support the future goals of the team as well as the overall organization; sets goals for internal communication and change management plans that will accompany the comprehensive action plan to address the team's skills gap; develops a separate communication and change management strategy for sales managers; and includes sales managers in the strategy.

▲ **Evaluates learning program or solution effectiveness**—Designs evaluation strategy that ties training solutions to business impact; conducts formative evaluation to ensure the integrity of learning collateral and events; ensures contribution of learning solutions to the achievement of learning objectives; aligns evaluation with appropriate indicators and measurements strategies; develops evaluation instruments; implements summative evaluation to assess learner receptivity, skill and knowledge acquisition, learning transfer to work, and business impact; mines results for lessons learned and continuous improvement of sales learning; and measures progress before and after learning takes place, including the impact on leading inputs (for example, the length of the sales cycle and closing rate), lagging outputs (for example, sales results by channel, product, and team), behavior change (for example, observable increases or decreases in targeted areas), knowledge transfer (for example, measured retention of knowledge pre-, post-, and 90 days later), and customer satisfaction.

▲ **Reports results to organizational stakeholders**—Communicates the results of learning program measurements to demonstrate accountability, ensure quality, justify investments, ensure the business impact of programs, and identify program retirement criteria; identifies implementation challenges or emerging requirements that suggest revisions; and engages in continuous improvement to ensure program effectiveness.

Sample Outputs:

▲ Learning needs assessment plans, results, and support
▲ Learning design plans and specifications
▲ Competency models
▲ Curriculum plans
▲ Lesson plans
▲ Mediated learning delivery or support content
▲ Learning measurement plans
▲ Learning evaluation reports
▲ Appropriately worded tests
▲ Company-specific certification management
▲ Sales or sales-related training content
▲ Evaluation instruments
▲ Training reports
▲ Training calendars
▲ Support materials for marketing initiatives
▲ Learning management system updates
▲ Other outputs as appropriate.

Delivering Sales Training

Definition: Understands the challenges and demands of the selling environment and is able to leverage that insight in preparation of sales training events; seeks out nontraining-related issues and creates separation between what can be targeted through training initiatives and what cannot; prepares for instruction by reviewing materials; supplements training events with real-world examples and relevant experiences; reviews training sequencing and clarifies module organization and events or activities; sets expectations and defines expected learning outcomes; delivers instruction and stimulates discussion; orchestrates interactive events that transfer knowledge or skill (for example, break-out groups and small group discussions); develops and/or manages learning attendance and performance feedback systems; manages and controls training environment within specified parameters; matches training delivery to individual sales person learning styles; and tests and scores achievement of learning outcomes.

Key Skills and Knowledge:

Knowledge of

- Platform training methods and strategies
- Sales cycle and challenges
- Rapport-building techniques
- Sales operations and fulfillment processes
- Audience learning style and preferences
- Test monitoring or proctoring methods
- Certification processes and requirements
- Learning delivery systems and media utilization strategies
- Instructor-led delivery techniques
- Learning management systems
- Online (virtual) delivery techniques
- Classroom management techniques
- Small group discussion techniques
- Questioning techniques.

Ability to

- Apply platform skills, methods, and tactics effectively to advance learning
- Adapt instructional methods to target audience requirements
- Use personal style and management techniques and media to optimize the conditions of learning
- Administer testing fairly and in a way that accurately assesses skill or knowledge acquisition
- Interpret attendance tracking and performance system data accurately
- Identify and recommend supplemental learning strategies that will reinforce and extend classroom learning
- Match experiential learning methods to appropriate content.

Key Actions:

- **Reviews and supplements learning**—Reviews and prepares for sales learning events, ensures relevance of activities and discussion to the style and interests of the target audience, supplements learning material with personal anecdotes and experiences that will bring the concepts and processes to life, links conceptual content to activities, explores varying ways that content can be applied to increase sales effectiveness, and drives toward actionable learning plans that can be implemented by participants on the job.

▲ **Motivates participants**—Generates compelling interest in course and its objectives; where relevant, bridges current with prior learning to establish continuity; relates the benefits of learning outcomes to participant interests and agendas; varies stimuli (for example, modulates voice, diversifies media, and incorporates questioning strategies) and monitors participant attention to ensure active processing of information; and ensures the relevance of activities and discussion to the style and interests of participants.

▲ **Manages instructional delivery**—Clearly explains the organization of the learning event and desired learning outcomes, organizes the facility and agenda to allow customer issues to be addressed without sacrificing the learning environment, creates a collaborative learning atmosphere through introductions or exercises, uses questioning techniques appropriately to probe and ensure understanding and broaden the utility of skills or concepts, uses set ups and summaries to maintain coherent delivery and underscore key ideas, creates interactive experiences to maximize both tacit and explicit learning, uses learning technologies effectively to support instruction and advance the achievement of objectives, and facilitates small group discussions.

▲ **Administers tests**—Reviews tests to gain familiarity with administration protocols and test construction conventions; explains and clarifies test directions; administers tests and maintains a conducive testing environment; answers participant questions appropriately, using suggested guidelines; monitors time and conducts time-checks to ensure efficient use of participant time; collects testing instruments and ensures their appropriate communication or archiving; and, where required, grades tests and reports individual and aggregate scores.

Sample Outputs:

▲ Lesson plan modifications and annotations
▲ Instructor notes or comments
▲ Participant guides and workbooks
▲ Training exercise materials
▲ Training presentation aids
▲ Participant surveys
▲ Individual and aggregate test scores
▲ Room set-up plans
▲ Management updates
▲ Training marketing materials
▲ Calendar updates
▲ Test administration and recording
▲ Company-specific certification updates
▲ Participation reports
▲ Other outputs as appropriate.

Coaching for Sales Results

Definition: Engages sales personnel in individual or group coaching; draws out the best performance of the individual or group through observation, motivation, and developmental feedback; leverages best practices and selling standards as learning tools; provides on-the-job reinforcement and corrective feedback; models appropriate and expected behaviors; develops or encourages relationships to directly grow sales talent; develops or hones sales-related subject matter expertise; identifies areas of performer excellence and maximizes development in these areas; identifies areas for improvement and addresses related obstacles; develops coaching strategies for both individuals and teams; and ensures that the sales person's best performance is linked to sales results.

Key Skills and Knowledge:
Knowledge of

- ▲ Motivation methods
- ▲ Performance observation techniques
- ▲ Listening and feedback methods
- ▲ Coaching methodology and techniques
- ▲ Organization and business strategy
- ▲ Performance review instruments and administration methods
- ▲ Counseling methods
- ▲ Business standards of conduct and ethical guidelines.

Ability to

- ▲ Assess performance objectively
- ▲ Assume various roles as needed in role-play to maximize learning (for example, sales person, customer, sales manager, and technical support)
- ▲ Employ observation to gather the most accurate depiction of performance data
- ▲ Identify "teachable moments" and uses these as program points to improve performance
- ▲ Balance performance improvement objectives with a recipient's need for a healthy self-concept.

Key Actions:
- ▲ **Observes sales person behavior to identify strengths, weaknesses, and opportunities for improvement**—Utilizes joint selling experiences to observe and evaluate; looks for trends in performance, internal relationships, and customer interactions; identifies root causes of behavior; seeks corroborating evidence of both historical and predictive performance; tests ideas through repeated experiences to avoid focusing on anomalies; schedules noncritical experiences that allow for possible failure without jeopardizing significant sales effectiveness; and documents observations and conclusions.
- ▲ **Balances corrective with positive feedback to ensure optimum guidance and performance improvement**—Identifies teaching moments to ensure individual receptiveness to feedback, provides feedback in a way that protects the dignity of recipients while identifying key components to improve and ensuring clear understanding, clearly articulates what was done correctly and where there are challenges to ensure that recipients target their improvement activities appropriately, provides salient examples to guide recipient performance, and personally supports individuals through work-related challenges.
- ▲ **Leverages motivation as a key enabler of sales performance**—Seeks to identify the motivations of both individuals and teams; engages in dialogue to uncover and reinforce effective motivational keys; analyzes the

alignment of personal motivations with organizational goals; delivers motivational communication; consistently recognizes and rewards improvements in sales behavior and selling skills; identifies and, whenever possible, removes obstacles to motivation; and matches internal and external motivational factors to create an optimum performance environment.

▲ **Links expected behaviors to strategic outcomes**—Ensures that individuals understand how their performance aligns with larger organizational or business goals, establishes consequences to show how tactical mistakes can derail strategic goals, and disabuses individuals of the idea that good performance is merely an empty ritual and shows its utility in achieving desired results in a way that can be readily understood.

▲ **Demonstrates and mentors expected sales behaviors**—Leverages sales experience to concretely demonstrate advocated sales tactics or methods; uses on-the-job opportunities or job shadowing to demonstrate best practices (for example, sales "ride-alongs," listening in on remote sales calls, and tool or system demonstrations); and personally and continuously models the positive values, attitude, and perspective expected of sales professionals.

▲ **Establishes support programs to expand and enrich new learning**—Collaborates with experienced practitioners to establish peer coaching, mentoring, or job sharing; identifies supplementary training or other resources (publications and professional associations) of potential use in performance improvement; and monitors and communicates performance innovations or new techniques that will expand or enhance performance.

Sample Outputs:

- ▲ Coaching reports
- ▲ Pre-call plan sheets
- ▲ Employee communications (pre- and postcoaching experiences)
- ▲ Sales performance reviews
- ▲ Developmental objectives for customer calls
- ▲ Individual sales performance development plans
- ▲ Customized targets and goals
- ▲ Performance contracts
- ▲ Sales contests
- ▲ Sales mentoring program agreements
- ▲ Reward and recognition programs
- ▲ Maximum potential assessments
- ▲ Employee redeployment or exit strategies
- ▲ Other outputs as appropriate.

Building Sales Infrastructure

Definition: Defines requirements essential for creating an efficient and unified sales environment, including necessary processes, procedures, tools, and systems; works with experts and stakeholders to design and implement appropriate solutions (for example, tool or system experts and organization development experts); tests systems against desired outcomes and resolves issues; maintains process, tool, or system usability and integrity; identifies and proposes innovations to advance sales force productivity; manages reporting and administrative support as required; creates and leads sales capacity planning efforts; and implements solutions with a minimal disruption to sales team productivity.

Key Skills and Knowledge:

Knowledge of

- Sales operations-related tools and technologies
- Requirements definition techniques
- Technical prototyping testing strategies
- Strategic planning methods
- Data analysis methods
- Process analysis and planning methods
- Sales stakeholder requirements (for example, business planners, sales management, sales force, and partners)
- Sales operations functions and processes
- Sales operations best practices (order entry or fulfillment and value chain maintenance)
- ROI calculation methods
- Change management methodologies.

Ability to

- Establish valid requirement feeds from all key stakeholders
- Depict key value chain process inputs, milestones, and outputs
- Build comprehensive models depicting all stakeholder interfaces
- Assess current processes and tools for gaps or inefficiencies.

Key Actions:

- **Monitors current business processes and sales productivity tools for adequacy**—Assesses current processes, systems, and tools for obstacles to productivity or agile access to sales intelligence (interface issues, usability issues, system or tool responsiveness, and data validity, reliability, and utility); identifies gaps in information flow and understands how improvements to the infrastructure can help; monitors marketplace and vendor offerings for infrastructure innovations and appropriateness to company needs; and determines ROI or break-even points to trigger investment discussions or decision making.

- **Develops and drives strategic infrastructure planning**—Collaborates with business planners, functions, and sales management to identify goals, challenges, and opportunities for improving infrastructure support; harnesses the technical resources essential for determining accurate technical and functional tool or system requirements; creates plans to guide infrastructure design and investment decisions; circulates plans among stakeholders to ensure buy-in and alignment with business, operations, and sales productivity objectives; and ensures that impact assessment has been completed and results understood by all stakeholders.

- **Manages infrastructure upkeep or revision**—Manages pilot testing and/or revisions of infrastructure solutions prior to roll-out, implements roll-out in accordance with plan and adapts those plans as necessary to meet quarterly or regional performance measures, and ensures that hardware improvements and software patches or revisions are monitored and incorporated in a way that minimizes impact on the sales function.

▲ **Drives or supports infrastructure change and alignment**—Collaborates with sales and operational management to develop change management strategies and programs; develops and coordinates change programs, communications, and training essential for program readiness and roll-out; and personally champions and advocates adoption of new systems.

▲ **Pilots and evaluates infrastructure programs**—Uses sound strategies and methods to evaluate the impact of new programs or program improvements and pilots innovations and ensures optimum usability to end users.

Sample Outputs:

▲ Process improvement flow charts

▲ Internal communications

▲ Sales team diagnostic tools

▲ Tool or system investment plans

▲ Tool or system productivity reports

▲ Infrastructure needs assessments

▲ Change management plans

▲ Other outputs as appropriate.

Designing Compensation

Definition: Researches industry sales compensation metrics and best practices; collaborates with others to ensure that the end-to-end compensation environment motivates and rewards the right sales behaviors and contributes to overall sales growth; ensures that the sales behaviors targeted for reward link to the overall sales and marketing strategy; ensures the company has required information and metrics necessary for accurate and on-time revenue credit and compensation pay-out; determines and proposes sales group or aggregate competitive compensation models; ensures compensation models balance the business interests of the company with the needs of a well-motivated sales force and the realities it faces; identifies areas of conflict between sales behaviors and compensation; introduces and explains new compensation processes or calculations to the sales force; and serves as the functional representative to the sales team for resolving compensation-related issues and processing exception requests.

Key Skills and Knowledge:

Knowledge of

- Research methods
- Industry benchmarking sources
- Payout processes, key milestones, ratios, and formulas
- Sales force motivators
- Financial compensation vehicles and metrics
- Financial modeling methods
- Business analysis methods
- Program planning and management skills
- Change management requirements
- Sales culture
- Local, regional, and/or country-level regulatory requirements
- Business performance resources.

Ability to

- Synthesize data from a variety of sources and make valid inferences
- Determine competitive yet feasible compensation metrics
- Supplement base payout with innovative reward strategies
- Identify and incorporate market competitive practices in compensation
- Generate stakeholder buy-in
- Identify the impact of current and proposed compensation policies on company health and sales force retention or recruiting.

Key Actions:

- **Assesses current compensation against best practices and innovative sales compensation options—** Identifies compensation challenges unique to sales that could be contributing to the challenges the company currently faces (for example, poor performance, misaligned or unintended reinforcement of nonpreferred sales behaviors, and loss of sales personnel); orchestrates or researches industry compensation packages; identifies trends or innovations and assesses them for applicability; and makes sound business recommendations.

▲ **Aligns compensation with business requirements and appropriate sales behaviors and metrics**—Ensures that proposed compensation models balance the business strategies with business realities and are achievable by sales team members; ensures that compensation aligns with human resource policies, regulatory requirements, and any contractual obligations; ensures that compensation promotes and reinforces productive, high-yield sales behaviors; and identifies and addresses negative or unintended consequences of current compensation strategies.

▲ **Develops and enlists support for sales compensation models and plans**—Develops sales compensation models that optimize the overall salary, commission, and bonus structure to create a well-motivated sales force and enlists the review of compensation strategies by business and sales executives and accommodates segment or regional differences where warranted.

▲ **Drives sales compensation acceptance**—Collaborates with sales and operational management team members in developing change management strategies and programs; develops and coordinates programs, communications, and awareness training essential for compensation strategy acceptance and roll-out; and champions and advocates adoption of new compensation strategies.

Sample Outputs:

▲ Sales compensation research reports
▲ Sales compensation models
▲ Strategic compensation plans
▲ Compensation training programs
▲ Compensation plan updates
▲ Executive team briefings
▲ Coding specifications for human resource or payroll systems
▲ Other outputs as appropriate.

Maintaining Accounts

Definition: Actively manages account and/or customer portfolio; conducts account performance data analysis; generates reports essential for determining account status (for example, credit analysis, account performance assessment, and contract renewal scheduling); focuses individual activities on selling priorities while determining best strategies for handling accounts (for example, renew, drop, and expand selling); fulfills and troubleshoots orders, including formalizing contracts, resolving fulfillment bottlenecks, troubleshooting off-shore fulfillment challenges, and ensuring compliance with service-level agreement terms; and provides contract administration and tracking centered on contract renewals, contract expansion opportunities, and contract terms requiring renegotiation.

Key Skills and Knowledge:
Knowledge of

- Sales system or tools
- Sales-related databases (for example, what they contain and how to access)
- Sales process
- Sales culture
- Pricing or costing formulas
- Account management processes
- Order entry and fulfillment processes
- Funnel management administration
- Contractual terms and conditions (standard)
- Report templates
- Supply chain (for example, components, strategy, processes, and key contacts)
- Customer satisfaction requirements
- Process improvement methods.

Ability to

- Collaborate effectively with account managers to meet customer needs
- Apply standard contractual terms and pricing appropriately and escalate for nonstandard conditions, where needed
- Identify account performance trends and key milestones
- Prioritize and fulfill customer requests with an appropriate sense of urgency.

Key Actions:
- **Prepares standard and ad hoc reports on account status**—Analyzes account performance and contractual status data; researches customer or account business health, credit worthiness, and other qualification variables that quantify risk; and generates reports profiling account or customer current state as scheduled or on demand.
- **Provides agile task substitution assistance to facilitate sales**—Accesses pricing information required for solution costing, including special or discount options; identifies part or component numbers required for costing solutions or providing replacements; acts in parallel with customer-facing sales in executing any back-office or operational tasks involved with aggregating data that will advance or formalize new deals; and enters order data using appropriate systems and order entry processes and tracks processing to completion.

▲ **Crafts contracts and statements of work**—Assembles standard contracts for use by others as boilerplates for noncomplex opportunities, works with legal experts to modify terms and conditions that reflect decisions reached during negotiation, communicates contracts or statements of work to stakeholders to ensure understanding of the opportunity and attendant responsibilities in execution, and ensures that contracts and statements of work move through sanctioned approval process and are archived appropriately upon signing.

▲ **Troubleshoots customer operational issues**—Acts as an important interface for resolving customer issues around order or service fulfillment; works with back-office, partner, or supply chain stakeholders to eliminate bottlenecks; revises inaccurate data entry, solicits and gains required approval, expedites customer involvement, or identifies supply chain issues for escalation; and ensures that issues are resolved to the customer's satisfaction.

▲ **Tracks and administers contracts**—Uses systems and tools to monitor contract expiration or service plan milestones, alerts sales to pending events requiring customer contact and renewal negotiations, prepares the necessary documentation required for renewal, and acts on behalf of the company when interacting with difficult customers to ensure they fulfill payment or other contractual obligations.

Sample Outputs:

▲ Standard or nonstandard contracts
▲ Statements of work
▲ Trouble reports
▲ Scheduled or ad hoc reports
▲ Project plans
▲ Meeting agendas
▲ Metrics documents
▲ Contract administration updates
▲ Data-entry modifications or updates to company-specific database
▲ Standard or customized pricing quotes
▲ Legal review documentation
▲ Customer surveys
▲ Back-office actions
▲ Other outputs as appropriate.

Recruiting Sales Talent

Definition: Ensures job descriptions are accurate and include the information essential for recruiting the sales people with the right level of knowledge, skills, abilities, and other attributes for the position; sets and aligns performance and financial expectations with sales management as well as potential candidates to establish clear recruitment parameters; orchestrates individual and professional networks, agencies, and other resources and tools required for sourcing, identifying, and selecting the most appropriate matches; conducts interviews with sales candidates; knows sales compensation plan elements and relays appropriate levels of information regarding compensation to candidates at appropriate time; maintains sensitivity to individual personalities, negotiation styles, and worldviews unique to the sales or sales support environment; contributes to effective candidate interviewing through participation in sales simulation exercises and structured behavioral interviews or other methods; provides process oversight; negotiates effectively to bring key stakeholders together and achieve a win-win deal for both the sales organization and the candidate; and facilitates sales on-boarding to ensure the mutual benefit of all recruitment stakeholders (sales organization, new hire, and recruiter).

Key Skills and Knowledge:
Knowledge of

- Psychometric tests (uses and output)
- Industry recruitment practices
- Industry networking methods
- Sales organization or company compensation structure and practices
- Sales or organization culture and personality variables
- Sales interviewing methods
- Job or position analysis methods
- Human resources recruitment policies, compliance requirements, and procedures
- Human resources operational policies (including diversity and harassment policies)
- Product, services, and solutions (target markets and customers)
- Industry vertical selling requirements
- Candidate pipeline management tools
- Local, regional, and country-level labor laws
- Interviewing methods and strategies (behavioral based and probing techniques)
- Company mission, vision, and goals
- Negotiation methods.

Ability to

- Build and maintain professional industry and professional contacts
- Influence the definition of job and salary requirements to ensure logical alignment
- Accurately interpret psychometric test output
- Validate tacit impressions of a candidate through questioning techniques
- Establish candidate relationships based on trust
- Assess emerging information against prior information for consistency
- Protect the interests of company stakeholders during negotiations.

Key Actions:

▲ **Aligns and modifies sales job profiles**—Collaborates with end-point sales management and appropriate team members to enhance standard sales position descriptions with better business needs and performance expectations; highlights key performance indicators (KPIs) and their supporting skills, knowledge, and experience; identifies unique or specific company practices or norms that may affect candidate success; and revises job profiles, validates with end-point management, and sets overall expectations based on clear recruitment objectives and parameters.

▲ **Ensures valid compensation package**—Assesses compensation package offered for the sales position and job level against industry practices and metrics, negotiates with end-point management to bring packages into alignment with market value, and finalizes compensation range as a basis for later candidate negotiations.

▲ **Monitors and maintains sales candidate pipeline**—Establishes and monitors industry-specific conferences and professional associations where prospects congregate, develops reciprocal network of contacts with colleagues to share prospect leads and references, builds candidate lists categorized by descriptors such as industry verticals or market segments, continuously updates pipeline as a basis for sale candidate prospecting, and scans industry segments for volatility.

▲ **Sources sales candidates**—Engages all available strategies (personal networking and peer recruiter information sharing), technology (job boards, social networks, and web mining), and resources (industry and professional associations) to conduct candidate searches; identifies prospects' contact information and incorporates these into solicitation strategy; and uses exploratory interviews with potential candidates to expand candidate pool with additional references.

▲ **Solicits, screens, and profiles candidates and determines person-job fit**—Conducts iterative interviews with potential candidates (for example, dialogues around KPIs), gauges interest, and assesses skill set and level of experience; evaluates prospect's information with job profile requirements to determine active candidacy; develops profile of candidate to ensure consistency of information and identify issues requiring further investigation; and narrows candidates and communicates final list to end-point management.

▲ **Facilitates sales peer team interviews and candidate testing**—Prepares candidates for end-point management and sales team interviews; facilitates behavioral or sales simulation interview scenarios that emulate real-world requirements; co-interviews candidates to ensure all critical position requirements are addressed (for example, compensation package, base and commission payout formulas, and relocation expenses); where warranted, facilitates candidate testing; debriefs candidates and end-point sales interviewees to assess match, determine fit, and make recommendations; and advises interviewers on human resources, legal, and compliance requirements.

▲ **Generates offers and conducts negotiations with sales stakeholders to closure**—Develops and communicates offer letters to candidates; conducts negotiations with candidates and end-point management to close outstanding gaps (for example, raise benefits and modify requirements); identifies area of mutual hiring acceptance and brokers key compromises; monitors candidates' bargaining behavior and claims to ensure veracity, integrity and overall fit; and resolves outstanding issues.

▲ **Supports on-boarding**—Develops appropriate on-boarding plan; briefs new hire on next steps and works with human resources to implement seamless hand-off to orientation; maintains contact with new hire to troubleshoot problems and ensure on-boarding success; and, where warranted by new hires that do not assimilate successfully, works with end-point management to refill position.

Sample Outputs:

- ▲ Job or position descriptions
- ▲ Network of industry resources and contacts
- ▲ Sales candidate pipeline of future prospects
- ▲ Psychometric test results
- ▲ Sales compensation data (amended) management meetings
- ▲ Candidate interview data
- ▲ Résumé filing and retrieval
- ▲ Coordinated candidate interviews
- ▲ Sales interview protocols (questions and strategies)
- ▲ Offer letters and cover letters
- ▲ On-boarding plan input
- ▲ Other outputs as appropriate.

Appendix B

Competency-Based Assessment and Planning Tools

We hope that the preceding pages have given you a better understanding of the competencies for sales professionals and their applications. To help you apply this new knowledge to your own circumstances, we have developed several illustrative tools:

- ▲ Worksheet B1. Self-Assessment Inventory
- ▲ Worksheet B2. Peer and Leader Assessment Inventory
- ▲ Worksheet B3. Summary of Results
- ▲ Worksheet B4. Development Planning Tool
- ▲ Worksheet B5. Learning Contract
- ▲ Worksheet B6. Sales Team Analysis Tool
- ▲ Worksheet B7. Sales Training Diagnostic.

You can use worksheets B1, B2, and B3 to create a 180- or 360-degree assessment of your strengths and development needs for use within the sales profession. They also help you understand which competencies are important to develop for your current work responsibilities and which competencies will become increasingly important in the future. Once you have that information, worksheet B4, the development planning tool, will help you brainstorm ways of filling any knowledge gaps, and worksheet B5, the learning contract, will help you formalize your development objectives with your manager. Worksheet B6, the sales team analysis tool, is designed to help identify, prioritize, and implement sales training solutions. Worksheet B7, the sales training diagnostic, outlines a seven-step process that follows the chronological steps that occur as a seller interacts with a buyer and is purposely focused on the selling side of that interaction. The diagnostic tool can serve as the foundation for your training program strategy. By following the directions at the top of each worksheet, you can complete this process in a few hours.

Worksheet B1. Self-Assessment Inventory

Step 1: Know Your Purpose

Which of the following best describes your reasons for completing a review of your professional selling competencies?

Answering this question is important because your reason(s) will affect what you need from the competency assessment process and how you should interpret the results. Place a check in all of the appropriate boxes below. You may want to rank your answers, starting with "1" as your primary reason, "2" as your secondary reason, and so on.

Q. I am reviewing my professional selling competencies

☐ to benchmark myself against the competencies described in this book

☐ to move into a new sales role that involves responsibility for leveraging new competencies, selecting individuals with specific competencies, or managing others within the selling function

☐ to document my current competency level

☐ to determine how the sales profession will evolve in the foreseeable future

☐ to benchmark my current skills against other sales professionals

☐ to use as a supplement to my performance review

☐ Other: _____

Step 2: Identify Reviewers

Given your reason(s) for entering this review process, consider which people would be best at assessing your current competency level objectively. You may wish to select people who are not within your organization, but are familiar with your work. It is important that you select several (two or three) of your peers and, if you manage people, several of your direct reports. If you do not have any direct reports, consider people in other departments with whom you interact frequently. Also, to gain a well-rounded perspective, involve your direct supervisor (leader) in this process. Please list all of your potential candidates in the spaces provided on the following pages.

Peers:

1. Name: _____

Job Title and Work Function: _____

Why will this person provide helpful information? _____

2. Name: _____

Job Title and Work Function: _____

Why will this person provide helpful information? _____

3. Name: _____

Job Title and Work Function: _____

Why will this person provide helpful information? _____

Direct Reports:

1. Name: _____

Job Title and Work Function: _____

Why will this person provide helpful information? _____

2. Name: _____

Job Title and Work Function: _____

Why will this person provide helpful information? _____

3. Name: _____

Job Title and Work Function: _____

Why will this person provide helpful information? _____

Leaders:

1. Name: _____

Job Title and Work Function: _____

Why will this person provide helpful information? _____

2. Name: _____

Job Title and Work Function: _____

Why will this person provide helpful information? _____

3. Name: _____

Job Title and Work Function: _____

Why will this person provide helpful information? _____

Step 3: Rate Yourself

In tables B1-1 through B1-14, rate your expertise in each competency area by circling the appropriate number under "Current Level of Proficiency" (expanded descriptions of each competency area are available in Appendix A). Use the following definitions to help you identify your level of proficiency:

- ▲ **None (0):** I have no knowledge of, or experience in, applying this competency.
- ▲ **Very little proficiency (1):** I possess general understanding of key principles, and I am capable of discussing this competency with others.
- ▲ **Limited proficiency (2):** I possess a solid understanding of key principles, and I am able to perform this competency with help (from reference materials or other people) as required.
- ▲ **Consistent proficiency (3):** I possess a comprehensive understanding of key principles, and I am capable of working without assistance regarding the application of this competency.

▲ **Advanced proficiency (4):** I possess substantial knowledge and expertise and can both troubleshoot complex situations and teach others the application of this competency.

▲ **Exceptional proficiency (5):** I possess extraordinary knowledge and expertise and can both troubleshoot at a national or regional level and devise innovative applications of this competency.

Use the higher number in the range if you feel strongly that you have reached this level of proficiency. Use the lower number if you are less confident that you have reached this level.

Next, cover up your "Current Level of Proficiency" answers. Go to the last column on the right and rate, on a scale from 1 to 3, how important you think each competency is for your future success in the field of professional selling. This assessment should be completely independent of which competencies you think you already have or don't have.

Use this rating scale when assessing how important each competency will be in the future:

▲ **Mildly important to future success (1)**
▲ **Important to future success (2)**
▲ **Critically important to future success (3).**

Figure B1-1 illustrates a partial example of a completed worksheet.

Figure B1-1. Example of a Completed Self-Assessment Inventory

Foundational Competencies	Current Level of Proficiency						Future Importance		
	None	Very Little	Limited	Consistent	Advanced	Exceptional	How important is this competency for future success?		
Advances collaboration and positive relationships across organizational boundaries.	0	1	2	(3)	4	5	1	(2)	3
Recognizes and addresses gaps among personal, team, or organizational responsibilities.	0	1	(2)	3	4	5	1	2	(3)
Demonstrates active listening.	0	1	2	3	(4)	5	1	(2)	3

Table B1-1. Foundational Competencies

Foundational Competencies	Current Level of Proficiency						Future Importance: How important is this competency for future success?		
	None	Very Little	Limited	Consistent	Advanced	Exceptional			
Advances collaboration and positive relationships across organizational boundaries	0	1	2	3	4	5	1	2	3
Recognizes and addresses gaps among personal, team, or organizational responsibilities	0	1	2	3	4	5	1	2	3
Demonstrates active listening	0	1	2	3	4	5	1	2	3
Achieves communication objectives	0	1	2	3	4	5	1	2	3
Ensures responsive communication	0	1	2	3	4	5	1	2	3
Attains persuasive communication	0	1	2	3	4	5	1	2	3
Contributes to customer satisfaction	0	1	2	3	4	5	1	2	3
Advocates for the customer	0	1	2	3	4	5	1	2	3
Communicates expectations to all stakeholders	0	1	2	3	4	5	1	2	3
Ensures clear understanding of responsibilities	0	1	2	3	4	5	1	2	3
Understands and addresses potential obstacles to proposed solutions	0	1	2	3	4	5	1	2	3
Determines optimum negotiation positions	0	1	2	3	4	5	1	2	3
Addresses objections accordingly	0	1	2	3	4	5	1	2	3
Builds consensus and commitment	0	1	2	3	4	5	1	2	3
Actively nurtures positive relationships	0	1	2	3	4	5	1	2	3
Protects and develops relationships to higher levels of trust and confidence	0	1	2	3	4	5	1	2	3
Assesses resources accurately	0	1	2	3	4	5	1	2	3

Competency	0	1	2	3	4	5	1	2	3
Balances risk with goal achievement when determining next steps	0	1	2	3	4	5	1	2	3
Situates work meaningfully in terms of its relationship to other functions	0	1	2	3	4	5	1	2	3
Contributes to the organization's success	0	1	2	3	4	5	1	2	3
Develops and implements robust evaluations of solutions	0	1	2	3	4	5	1	2	3
Communicates performance in terms of the organization's key performance drivers	0	1	2	3	4	5	1	2	3
Determines the range, type, and scope of information needed	0	1	2	3	4	5	1	2	3
Applies the most appropriate tools and strategies to gather needed information	0	1	2	3	4	5	1	2	3
Develops sources of ongoing information	0	1	2	3	4	5	1	2	3
Thoroughly diagnoses needs to identify their true nature	0	1	2	3	4	5	1	2	3
Prioritizes the most critical causes as a basis for proceeding	0	1	2	3	4	5	1	2	3
Explores the scope of possible solutions	0	1	2	3	4	5	1	2	3
Approaches option assessment creatively	0	1	2	3	4	5	1	2	3
Surveys the impact of all alternatives for selecting and prioritizing the best option	0	1	2	3	4	5	1	2	3
Commits to action	0	1	2	3	4	5	1	2	3
Identifies critical business metrics	0	1	2	3	4	5	1	2	3
Builds the value justifications required to commit resources	0	1	2	3	4	5	1	2	3
Clearly identifies the business or financial benefits to be realized by investments	0	1	2	3	4	5	1	2	3
Advocates change and its benefits	0	1	2	3	4	5	1	2	3
Manages change effectively	0	1	2	3	4	5	1	2	3

(continued on the next page)

Table B1-1. Foundational Competencies (continued)

Foundational Competencies	Current Level of Proficiency						Future Importance		
	None	Very Little	Limited	Consistent	Advanced	Exceptional	How important is this competency for future success?		
Approaches work with a proactive attitude	0	1	2	3	4	5	1	2	3
Secures appropriate commitment	0	1	2	3	4	5	1	2	3
Appropriately communicates agreements	0	1	2	3	4	5	1	2	3
Documents agreements	0	1	2	3	4	5	1	2	3
Actively monitors situations for potential problems	0	1	2	3	4	5	1	2	3
Monitors implementation or deployment to ensure success	0	1	2	3	4	5	1	2	3
Acts as a focal point of escalation to expedite problem resolution	0	1	2	3	4	5	1	2	3
Organizes and manages work systematically	0	1	2	3	4	5	1	2	3
Organizes and manages resources effectively	0	1	2	3	4	5	1	2	3
Adaptively applies methods as needed to achieve goals	0	1	2	3	4	5	1	2	3
Leverages success through active promotion	0	1	2	3	4	5	1	2	3
Documents and communicates best practices	0	1	2	3	4	5	1	2	3
Ensures that criteria for decision making are shared and addressed	0	1	2	3	4	5	1	2	3
Adapts and tailors messages as required	0	1	2	3	4	5	1	2	3
Confirms validity of the proposed solution	0	1	2	3	4	5	1	2	3

Competency									
Incorporates business and industry acumen into work	0	1	2	3	4	5	1	2	3
Exhibits business-oriented perspective in assessing needs	0	1	2	3	4	5	1	2	3
Incorporates legal and contractual requirements into work	0	1	2	3	4	5	1	2	3
Incorporates financial understanding into work	0	1	2	3	4	5	1	2	3
Approaches challenges creatively	0	1	2	3	4	5	1	2	3
Crosses disciplines to frame or address challenges	0	1	2	3	4	5	1	2	3
Demonstrates respect for others	0	1	2	3	4	5	1	2	3
Acclimates to diverse work settings	0	1	2	3	4	5	1	2	3
Harnesses diversity to create workplace synergies	0	1	2	3	4	5	1	2	3
Demonstrates personal integrity	0	1	2	3	4	5	1	2	3
Incorporates quality considerations into decision making	0	1	2	3	4	5	1	2	3
Provides proactive knowledge transfer	0	1	2	3	4	5	1	2	3
Ensures that communication tools and processes advance information storage and transfer	0	1	2	3	4	5	1	2	3
Maintains understanding of technical innovations	0	1	2	3	4	5	1	2	3
Uses information technology to align and expedite work	0	1	2	3	4	5	1	2	3
Improves personal productivity technology	0	1	2	3	4	5	1	2	3
Takes personal responsibility for development	0	1	2	3	4	5	1	2	3
Demonstrates agility in addressing development needs	0	1	2	3	4	5	1	2	3

(continued on the next page)

135

Table B1-1. Foundational Competencies (continued)

Foundational Competencies	Current Level of Proficiency						Future Importance		
	None	Very Little	Limited	Consistent	Advanced	Exceptional	How important is this competency for future success?		
Leverages information to change behavior	0	1	2	3	4	5	1	2	3
Develops plans that clearly actualize strategy	0	1	2	3	4	5	1	2	3
Builds commitment to plan	0	1	2	3	4	5	1	2	3
Executes to plan, yet adapts to emergent circumstances	0	1	2	3	4	5	1	2	3
Delivers to plan	0	1	2	3	4	5	1	2	3
Incorporates a strategic perspective in activity planning	0	1	2	3	4	5	1	2	3
Practices time management	0	1	2	3	4	5	1	2	3
Aligns and relates work to sales success	0	1	2	3	4	5	1	2	3
Incorporates selling sensibilities into work execution	0	1	2	3	4	5	1	2	3
Demonstrates a systemic understanding of sales	0	1	2	3	4	5	1	2	3
Ensures that work helps to advance sales	0	1	2	3	4	5	1	2	3

Table B1-2. Area of Expertise: Creating and Closing Opportunities

Creating and Closing Opportunities	Current Level of Proficiency					Future Importance
	None	Very Little	Limited	Consistent	Advanced	Exceptional	How important is this competency for future success?		
Researches and targets prospects	0	1	2	3	4	5	1	2	3
Conducts interest-building calls (cold calls) when applicable	0	1	2	3	4	5	1	2	3
Identifies, follows up on, and manages sales leads	0	1	2	3	4	5	1	2	3
Gains interest	0	1	2	3	4	5	1	2	3
Qualifies opportunities	0	1	2	3	4	5	1	2	3
Develops winning proposals	0	1	2	3	4	5	1	2	3
Builds business justification cases	0	1	2	3	4	5	1	2	3
Orchestrates support for negotiations	0	1	2	3	4	5	1	2	3
Maintains opportunity momentum to expand sales	0	1	2	3	4	5	1	2	3

Table B1-3. Area of Expertise: Protecting Accounts

Protecting Accounts	Current Level of Proficiency						Future Importance		
	None	Very Little	Limited	Consistent	Advanced	Exceptional	How important is this competency for future success?		
Gathers and monitors account intelligence	0	1	2	3	4	5	1	2	3
Documents account plans and sales forecasts	0	1	2	3	4	5	1	2	3
Builds client executive business relationships	0	1	2	3	4	5	1	2	3
Cultivates and develops trusted advisor status	0	1	2	3	4	5	1	2	3
Protects and expands accounts	0	1	2	3	4	5	1	2	3
Manages deployment readiness and resource alignment	0	1	2	3	4	5	1	2	3

Table B1-4. Area of Expertise: Defining and Positioning Solutions

Defining and Positioning Solutions	Current Level of Proficiency						Future Importance		
	None	Very Little	Limited	Consistent	Advanced	Exceptional	How important is this competency for future success?		
Performs technical qualifications	0	1	2	3	4	5	1	2	3
Designs solutions	0	1	2	3	4	5	1	2	3
Customizes standard products or services	0	1	2	3	4	5	1	2	3
Conducts technical demonstrations and benchmarks	0	1	2	3	4	5	1	2	3
Contributes to solution sizing and modification	0	1	2	3	4	5	1	2	3
Articulates solution designs	0	1	2	3	4	5	1	2	3

Table B1-5. Area of Expertise: Supporting Indirect Selling

Supporting Indirect Selling	Current Level of Proficiency						Future Importance		
	None	Very Little	Limited	Consistent	Advanced	Exceptional	How important is this competency for future success?		
Assesses and helps develop partner's sales force	0	1	2	3	4	5	1	2	3
Drives partner sales planning or forecasting	0	1	2	3	4	5	1	2	3
Motivates and educates partners	0	1	2	3	4	5	1	2	3
Cultivates partner business relationships	0	1	2	3	4	5	1	2	3
Facilitates inventory balancing or clearance	0	1	2	3	4	5	1	2	3
Tracks investments in partner selling to determine business impact	0	1	2	3	4	5	1	2	3
Facilitates partner transformation	0	1	2	3	4	5	1	2	3
Monitors and manages contract fulfillment	0	1	2	3	4	5	1	2	3
Troubleshoots partner sales crediting	0	1	2	3	4	5	1	2	3
Collaborates on team selling and positioning	0	1	2	3	4	5	1	2	3

Table B1-6. Area of Expertise: Setting Sales Strategy

Setting Sales Strategy	Current Level of Proficiency						Future Importance		
	None	Very Little	Limited	Consistent	Advanced	Exceptional	How important is this competency for future success?		
Identifies and articulates innovative sales practices	0	1	2	3	4	5	1	2	3
Creates strategic plans that guide organizational, technical, process, or practice planning and implementation	0	1	2	3	4	5	1	2	3
Builds business and partner alliances to increase sales	0	1	2	3	4	5	1	2	3
Provides leadership to accelerate strategy diffusion	0	1	2	3	4	5	1	2	3
Configures and aligns sales territories for maximum effectiveness	0	1	2	3	4	5	1	2	3

Table B1-7. Area of Expertise: Managing within the Sales Ecosystem

Managing within the Sales Ecosystem	Current Level of Proficiency						Future Importance		
	None	Very Little	Limited	Consistent	Advanced	Exceptional	How important is this competency for future success?		
Aligns tactical activities to support strategic sales plans	0	1	2	3	4	5	1	2	3
Establishes, monitors, and controls costs that affect sales margins	0	1	2	3	4	5	1	2	3
Aligns resources with opportunities	0	1	2	3	4	5	1	2	3
Screens administrative demands and troubleshoots back-office operations to minimize sales disruptions	0	1	2	3	4	5	1	2	3
Ensures accurate forecasting while monitoring performance to metrics	0	1	2	3	4	5	1	2	3
Hires, promotes, and terminates to improve sales performance and address capability gaps	0	1	2	3	4	5	1	2	3
Aligns reward and recognition strategies to performance goals	0	1	2	3	4	5	1	2	3

Table B1-8. Area of Expertise: Developing Sales Force Capability

Developing Sales Force Capability	Current Level of Proficiency						Future Importance		
	None	Very Little	Limited	Consistent	Advanced	Exceptional	How important is this competency for future success?		
	0	1	2	3	4	5	1	2	3
Determines competencies required to achieve sales strategy	0	1	2	3	4	5	1	2	3
Conducts sales-related needs assessments	0	1	2	3	4	5	1	2	3
Designs and develops sales development programs, curricula, or learning solutions	0	1	2	3	4	5	1	2	3
Uses learning management systems	0	1	2	3	4	5	1	2	3
Ties learning strategy to organizational capacity	0	1	2	3	4	5	1	2	3
Evaluates learning program or solution effectiveness	0	1	2	3	4	5	1	2	3
Reports results to organizational stakeholders	0	1	2	3	4	5	1	2	3

Table B1-9. Area of Expertise: Delivering Sales Training

Delivering Sales Training	Current Level of Proficiency						Future Importance		
	None	Very Little	Limited	Consistent	Advanced	Exceptional	How important is this competency for future success?		
	0	1	2	3	4	5	1	2	3
Reviews and supplements learning	0	1	2	3	4	5	1	2	3
Motivates participants	0	1	2	3	4	5	1	2	3
Manages instructional delivery	0	1	2	3	4	5	1	2	3
Administers tests	0	1	2	3	4	5	1	2	3

Table B1-10. Area of Expertise: Coaching for Sales Results

Coaching for Sales Results	Current Level of Proficiency						Future Importance		
	None	Very Little	Limited	Consistent	Advanced	Exceptional	How important is this competency for future success?		
Observes sales person behavior to identify strengths, weaknesses, and opportunities for improvement	0	1	2	3	4	5	1	2	3
Balances corrective with positive feedback to ensure optimum guidance and performance improvement	0	1	2	3	4	5	1	2	3
Leverages motivation as a key enabler of sales performance	0	1	2	3	4	5	1	2	3
Links expected behaviors to strategic outcomes	0	1	2	3	4	5	1	2	3
Demonstrates and mentors expected sales behaviors	0	1	2	3	4	5	1	2	3
Establishes support programs to expand and enrich new learning	0	1	2	3	4	5	1	2	3

Table B1-11. Area of Expertise: Building Sales Infrastructure

Building Sales Infrastructure	Current Level of Proficiency						Future Importance
	None	Very Little	Limited	Consistent	Advanced	Exceptional	How important is this competency for future success?
Monitors current business processes and sales productivity tools for adequacy	0	1	2	3	4	5	1 2 3
Develops and drives strategic infrastructure planning	0	1	2	3	4	5	1 2 3
Manages infrastructure upkeep or revision	0	1	2	3	4	5	1 2 3
Drives or supports infrastructure change and alignment	0	1	2	3	4	5	1 2 3
Pilots and evaluates infrastructure programs	0	1	2	3	4	5	1 2 3

Table B1-12. Area of Expertise: Designing Compensation

Designing Compensation	Current Level of Proficiency						Future Importance
	None	Very Little	Limited	Consistent	Advanced	Exceptional	How important is this competency for future success?
Assesses current compensation against best practices and innovative sales compensation options	0	1	2	3	4	5	1 2 3
Aligns compensation with business requirements and appropriate sales behaviors and metrics	0	1	2	3	4	5	1 2 3
Develops and enlists support for sales compensation models and plans	0	1	2	3	4	5	1 2 3
Drives sales compensation acceptance	0	1	2	3	4	5	1 2 3

Table B1-13. Area of Expertise: Maintaining Accounts

Maintaining Accounts	Current Level of Proficiency						Future Importance		
	None	Very Little	Limited	Consistent	Advanced	Exceptional	How important is this competency for future success?		
	0	1	2	3	4	5	1	2	3
Prepares standard and ad hoc reports on account status	0	1	2	3	4	5	1	2	3
Provides agile task substitution assistance to facilitate sales	0	1	2	3	4	5	1	2	3
Crafts contracts and statements of work	0	1	2	3	4	5	1	2	3
Troubleshoots customer operational issues	0	1	2	3	4	5	1	2	3
Tracks and administers contracts	0	1	2	3	4	5	1	2	3

Table B1-14. Area of Expertise: Recruiting Sales Talent

Maintaining Accounts	Current Level of Proficiency						Future Importance		
	None	Very Little	Limited	Consistent	Advanced	Exceptional	How important is this competency for future success?		
	0	1	2	3	4	5	1	2	3
Aligns and modifies sales job profiles	0	1	2	3	4	5	1	2	3
Ensures valid compensation package	0	1	2	3	4	5	1	2	3
Monitors and maintains sales candidate pipeline	0	1	2	3	4	5	1	2	3
Sources sales candidates	0	1	2	3	4	5	1	2	3
Solicits, screens, and profiles candidates and determines person-job fit	0	1	2	3	4	5	1	2	3
Facilitates sales peer team interviews and candidate testing	0	1	2	3	4	5	1	2	3
Generates offers and conducts negotiations with sales stakeholders to closure	0	1	2	3	4	5	1	2	3
Supports on-boarding	0	1	2	3	4	5	1	2	3

Worksheet B2. Peer and Leader Assessment Inventory

On the following pages, you will find the assessment inventory that your peers, direct reports, and leaders will use (tables B2-1 to B2-14). At the top of the worksheet, respondents are given an opportunity to identify themselves and to state their relationship to you. Although this information is helpful, the respondents should be allowed to complete the inventory anonymously. Only your supervisor must reveal his or her identity. We have also supplied you with a cover sheet that you can use when distributing the inventory.

Here are some steps and important guidelines to remember:

Guidelines:

- ▲ Ask people if they are interested in participating in this activity before you send them the inventory.
- ▲ Tell them clearly what this inventory is being used for, how long it will take, and when it is due.
- ▲ Advise respondents, other than your supervisor, that they may complete the inventory anonymously if they prefer.
- ▲ Tell respondents that you want candid, future-focused feedback, but not a personality or performance appraisal. Make them comfortable with the idea of providing honest answers. Tell them that after you've reviewed the completed assessment, you may come back to clarify, but not to challenge, their responses (if they choose to put their name on the inventory).

Steps:

1. Make photocopies of the assessment inventory. You will need one copy for each respondent.
2. Make photocopies of the cover sheet, which is on the next four pages. Be sure to address a copy to each respondent, fill out the necessary information, and staple it to the front of the assessment inventory.
3. Distribute the assessment inventory to the respondents. Note: You may wish to distribute copies of the *World-Class Selling: New Sales Competencies* book instead.
4. Send out a reminder notice a few days before the inventory is due.
5. Collect the inventories on the due date and complete the summary of results in worksheet B3.

Note: For additional copies of *World-Class Selling: New Sales Competencies,* contact ASTD at 703.683.8100 or visit www.astd.org.

Cover Sheet: Peer and Leader Assessment Inventory

From: _____

To: _____

Date: _____

Thank you for agreeing to participate in this competency assessment activity. I am trying to determine which competencies are strengths for me and which competencies I need to develop.

Please give me candid, future-focused, and honest feedback of my competencies. Below is a full set of instructions. If you need further clarification, feel free to call me at [_____].

The competencies that you are assessing derive from the ASTD World-Class Sales Competency Model, which describes the major competencies necessary for success within the sales profession. Thank you for participating in this activity.

The due date is: _____

Directions:

Please think about the person who asked you to complete this assessment. You can help him or her by providing feedback based on your personal observations of his or her work. Although this questionnaire is not a performance appraisal, answering the following questions will provide helpful guidance for the requester to develop into expanded roles within the organization. Please follow these easy steps:

1. In tables B2-1 through B2-14, indicate in the first column if you have observed the requester demonstrating the competency described. If you have not observed the person demonstrating this competency, skip to the next competency. If you have observed the person demonstrating this competency, go to step 2.

2. On a scale from 0 to 5, indicate the requester's level of proficiency in this competency. Use the following definitions to help you identify the level of expertise:

   ▲ **None (0):** The person has no knowledge of, or experience in, applying this competency.
   ▲ **Very little proficiency (1):** The person possesses general understanding of key principles, and he or she is capable of discussing this competency with others.
   ▲ **Limited proficiency (2):** The person possesses a solid understanding of key principles, and he or she is able to perform this competency with help (from reference materials or other people) as required.
   ▲ **Consistent proficiency (3):** The person possesses a comprehensive understanding of key principles, and he or she is capable of working without assistance regarding the application of this competency.
   ▲ **Advanced proficiency (4):** The person possesses substantial knowledge and expertise and can both troubleshoot complex situations and teach others the application of this competency.
   ▲ **Exceptional Proficiency (5):** The person possesses extraordinary knowledge and expertise and can both troubleshoot at a national or regional level and devise innovative applications of this competency.

3. Use the higher number if you feel strongly that the person has reached this level of expertise. Use the lower number if you are less confident that he or she has reached this level.

Competencies are grouped into four categories: partnering, insight, solution, and effectiveness. You will need the following definitions to help you with this assessment:

Partnering. Everyone who works in the sales profession works interdependently with others, relying on these competencies to facilitate interactions:

- ▲ spanning boundaries
- ▲ communicating effectively
- ▲ aligning to customers
- ▲ setting expectations
- ▲ negotiating positions
- ▲ building relationships.

Insight. Everyone in the sales profession must develop robust information analysis and synthesis skills to use information effectively on the job. These competencies demonstrate insight:

- ▲ analyzing organizational capacity
- ▲ understanding the business context
- ▲ evaluating customer experiences
- ▲ gathering intelligence
- ▲ prioritizing stakeholder needs
- ▲ identifying options
- ▲ building a business case.

Solution. Sales professionals must develop strategies for generating support for the solutions they define, as well as strategies for implementation. This involves

- ▲ facilitating change
- ▲ formalizing agreements
- ▲ resolving issues
- ▲ managing projects
- ▲ leveraging success
- ▲ articulating value.

Effectiveness. Personal effectiveness and responsibility are key to a sales professional's ability to navigate processes and cultivate relationships. These competencies demonstrate effectiveness:

- ▲ building business skills
- ▲ solving problems
- ▲ embracing diversity
- ▲ making ethical decisions
- ▲ managing knowledge
- ▲ using technology
- ▲ accelerating learning

▲ executing plans

▲ maximizing personal time

▲ aligning to the sales process.

4. Finally, cover up the "Current Level of Proficiency" answers. Go to the last column on the right and rate, on a scale from 1 to 3, how important you think this competency is for the requester's future success in the sales profession—not how competent the requester already is. Use this rating scale:

▲ **Mildly important to future success (1)**

▲ **Important to future success (2)**

▲ **Critically important to future success (3).**

See figure B2-1 for an example of a completed worksheet.

Figure B2-1. Example of a Completed Competency Assessment Inventory

Name of person being assessed: John Smith

Assessor's name (optional): _____

Relationship to the person being assessed: (Direct Report)   Peer   Supervisor   Date: 2/14/09

Foundational Competencies	Has requester demonstrated this competency? □ Yes □ No	Current Level of Proficiency						Future Importance — How important is this competency for future success?		
		None	Very Little	Limited	Consistent	Advanced	Exceptional			
		0	1	2	3	4	5	1	2	3
Advances collaboration and positive relationships across organizational boundaries—Sets expectations governing collaboration to minimize conflict and ensure a common focus among all internal and external stakeholders affected by the initiative.	□ YES ☒ NO	(0)	1	2	3	4	5	1	(2)	3
Recognizes and addresses gaps among personal, team, or organizational responsibilities—Identifies gaps among individual responsibilities and what needs to accomplished to achieve success and takes personal accountability for positive impacts within these areas.	☒ YES □ NO	0	1	2	(3)	4	5	1	(2)	3

Table B2-1. Competency Assessment Inventory

Name of person being assessed: _____ Date: _____

Assessor's name (optional): _____

Relationship to the person being assessed: _____ Direct Report   Peer   Supervisor

Foundational Competencies	Has requester demonstrated this competency? □ Yes □ No	Current Level of Proficiency						Future Importance — How important is this competency for future success?		
		None	Very Little	Limited	Consistent	Advanced	Exceptional			
Advances collaboration and positive relationships across organizational boundaries—Sets expectations governing collaboration to minimize conflict and ensure a common focus among all internal and external stakeholders affected by the initiative.	□ YES □ NO	0	1	2	3	4	5	1	2	3
Recognizes and addresses gaps among personal, team, or organizational responsibilities—Identifies gaps among individual responsibilities and what needs to be accomplished to achieve success and takes personal accountability for positive impacts within these areas.	□ YES □ NO	0	1	2	3	4	5	1	2	3
Demonstrates active listening—Pays close attention to what is being said and uses questioning techniques effectively to probe and clarify in pursuit of accurate understanding.	□ YES □ NO	0	1	2	3	4	5	1	2	3
Achieves communication objectives—Ensures that verbal and written communications and group presentations are well prepared, clear, concise, accurate, and persuasive.	□ YES □ NO	0	1	2	3	4	5	1	2	3

(continued on the next page)

Table B2-1. Competency Assessment Inventory (continued)

Foundational Competencies	Has requester demonstrated this competency? Yes / No	Current Level of Proficiency						Future Importance — How important is this competency for future success?		
		None	Very Little	Limited	Consistent	Advanced	Exceptional			
		0	1	2	3	4	5	1	2	3
Ensures responsive communication—Makes sure that inquiries are addressed and expedited to facilitate the needs of others.	☐ YES ☐ NO	0	1	2	3	4	5	1	2	3
Attains persuasive communication—Successfully influences perceptions to achieve desired outcomes.	☐ YES ☐ NO	0	1	2	3	4	5	1	2	3
Contributes to customer satisfaction—Understands how trust and responsiveness to customer needs builds enduring business relationships.	☐ YES ☐ NO	0	1	2	3	4	5	1	2	3
Advocates for the customer—Represents the interests of the customer and ensures that a customer-oriented perspective is the touchstone for decision making.	☐ YES ☐ NO	0	1	2	3	4	5	1	2	3
Communicates expectations to all stakeholders—Exercises personal initiative to ensure that all stakeholders understand what is required for successful implementation of a solution.	☐ YES ☐ NO	0	1	2	3	4	5	1	2	3
Ensures clear understanding of responsibilities—Communicates roles and responsibilities in a way that clearly identifies who is accountable for what, when, and to what standard.	☐ YES ☐ NO	0	1	2	3	4	5	1	2	3
Understands and addresses potential obstacles to proposed solutions—Identifies potential threats to a solution to avoid or manage problems in advance of their occurrence.	☐ YES ☐ NO	0	1	2	3	4	5	1	2	3

Competency		0	1	2	3	4	5	1	2	3
Determines optimum negotiation positions—Identifies optimum and fallback positions prior to actual negotiations and incorporates these as strategies.	☐ YES ☐ NO	0	1	2	3	4	5	1	2	3
Addresses objections accordingly—Ensures understanding of a solution and its benefits or involves the appropriate experts to help address stakeholder questions and communicates information that addresses those needs persuasively if necessary.	☐ YES ☐ NO	0	1	2	3	4	5	1	2	3
Builds consensus and commitment—Leverages points of agreement and addresses points of conflict in a way that develops buy-in and commitment for moving forward.	☐ YES ☐ NO	0	1	2	3	4	5	1	2	3
Actively nurtures positive relationships—Develops and maintains positive professional relationships among stakeholders at all levels based on personal integrity and trust.	☐ YES ☐ NO	0	1	2	3	4	5	1	2	3
Protects and develops relationships to higher levels of trust and confidence—Leverages professional relationships to protect partnerships and advance collaboration.	☐ YES ☐ NO	0	1	2	3	4	5	1	2	3
Assesses resources accurately—Ensures accurate understanding of the type, quality, and quantity of resources required to achieve desired results.	☐ YES ☐ NO	0	1	2	3	4	5	1	2	3
Balances risk with goal achievement when determining next steps—Weighs desired outcome against potential risk to prioritize options and identify an optimum path forward while protecting the interests of the company.	☐ YES ☐ NO	0	1	2	3	4	5	1	2	3

(continued on the next page)

Table B2-1. Competency Assessment Inventory (continued)

Foundational Competencies	Has requester demonstrated this competency? ☐ Yes ☐ No	Current Level of Proficiency						Future Importance		
		None	Very Little	Limited	Consistent	Advanced	Exceptional	How important is this competency for future success?		
Situates work meaningfully in terms of its relationship to other functions—Understands an organization's divisions and the upstream, downstream, and cross-stream collaboration in which one's work is situated. Understands how the work one is engaged in contributes to the larger enterprise.	☐ YES ☐ NO	0	1	2	3	4	5	1	2	3
Contributes to the organization's success—Understands the organization's products, services, and solutions at a level appropriate to position and sells them.	☐ YES ☐ NO	0	1	2	3	4	5	1	2	3
Develops and implements robust evaluations of solutions—Uses sound methodologies to demonstrate the effectiveness of a solution at key milestones or to identify critical obstacles affecting success.	☐ YES ☐ NO	0	1	2	3	4	5	1	2	3
Communicates performance in terms of the organization's key performance drivers—Identifies and uses key business or operational metrics that clearly express beneficial results that are understood and valued by solution stakeholders (for example, net promoter scores, total cost of ownership, return-on-investment, time to competence, and productivity ratios).	☐ YES ☐ NO	0	1	2	3	4	5	1	2	3

Competency										
Determines the range, type, and scope of information needed— Systematically assesses problems, challenges, and opportunities to ensure the right sources are utilized and critical information is collected.	☐ YES ☐ NO	0	1	2	3	4	5	1	2	3
Applies the most appropriate tools and strategies to gather needed information—Understands which tools and strategies are best suited for fulfilling information requirements and uses these efficiently and effectively.	☐ YES ☐ NO	0	1	2	3	4	5	1	2	3
Develops sources of ongoing information—Understands how information requirements or the quality of sources can change and creates multiple sources for collecting data and confirming its quality.	☐ YES ☐ NO	0	1	2	3	4	5	1	2	3
Thoroughly diagnoses needs to identify their true nature— Explores and identifies the root causes of needs to ensure an accurate understanding of their scope.	☐ YES ☐ NO	0	1	2	3	4	5	1	2	3
Prioritizes the most critical causes as a basis for proceeding—Determines the most appropriate plan of action based on needs analysis and prioritizes actions, resources, and time accordingly.	☐ YES ☐ NO	0	1	2	3	4	5	1	2	3
Explores the scope of possible solutions—Assesses all feasible options that align to solving the challenge or need.	☐ YES ☐ NO	0	1	2	3	4	5	1	2	3
Approaches option assessment creatively—Keeps options open ended to capture innovations perhaps not considered in conventional thinking.	☐ YES ☐ NO	0	1	2	3	4	5	1	2	3

(continued on the next page)

Table B2-1. Competency Assessment Inventory (continued)

Foundational Competencies	Has requester demonstrated this competency? ☐ Yes ☐ No	Current Level of Proficiency						Future Importance How important is this competency for future success?		
		None	Very Little	Limited	Consistent	Advanced	Exceptional			
Surveys the impact of all alternatives for selecting and prioritizing the best option—Solicits and incorporates the input of all stakeholder experts and benefactors to ensure the best option is chosen.	☐ YES ☐ NO	0	1	2	3	4	5	1	2	3
Commits to action—Weighs the needs, requirements, and opportunities involved before committing to the best possible option or course of action.	☐ YES ☐ NO	0	1	2	3	4	5	1	2	3
Identifies critical business metrics—Ensures valid measurements by collaborating with stakeholders to determine the most relevant business, financial, or operational metrics on which to focus.	☐ YES ☐ NO	0	1	2	3	4	5	1	2	3
Builds the value justifications required to commit resources—Frames the input of experts in a way that ensures well-informed decision making.	☐ YES ☐ NO	0	1	2	3	4	5	1	2	3
Clearly identifies the business or financial benefits to be realized by investments—Identifies the business and financial benefits of a solution in a way that clearly speaks to business impact.	☐ YES ☐ NO	0	1	2	3	4	5	1	2	3
Advocates change and its benefits—Encourages others to embrace change as an opportunity rather than an obstacle to personal, operational, or business success.	☐ YES ☐ NO	0	1	2	3	4	5	1	2	3

Competency		0	1	2	3	4	5	1	2	3
Manages change effectively—Ensures that work aligns with changing requirements to more accurately advance the desired change.	☐ YES ☐ NO	0	1	2	3	4	5	1	2	3
Approaches work with a proactive attitude—Helps organizations and individuals actively engage in improving practices and attitudes by championing change, demonstrating the positive consequences of change, and exercising personal influence to encourage acceptance.	☐ YES ☐ NO	0	1	2	3	4	5	1	2	3
Secures appropriate commitment—Fulfills requirements through all phases of solution design and development to build commitment and support.	☐ YES ☐ NO	0	1	2	3	4	5	1	2	3
Appropriately communicates agreements—Ensures that verbal or written agreements are communicated in a timely fashion to stakeholders.	☐ YES ☐ NO	0	1	2	3	4	5	1	2	3
Documents agreements—Documents and amends written agreements to accurately reflect the arrived-upon decisions in negotiation.	☐ YES ☐ NO	0	1	2	3	4	5	1	2	3
Actively monitors situations for potential problems—Analyzes situations for potential challenges and develops associated contingency plans.	☐ YES ☐ NO	0	1	2	3	4	5	1	2	3
Monitors implementation or deployment to ensure success—Takes an active interest in the success of a solution and monitors the milestones in the plan.	☐ YES ☐ NO	0	1	2	3	4	5	1	2	3

(continued on the next page)

Table B2-1. Competency Assessment Inventory (continued)

Foundational Competencies	Has requester demonstrated this competency? ☐ Yes ☐ No	Current Level of Proficiency						Future Importance — How important is this competency for future success?		
		None	Very Little	Limited	Consistent	Advanced	Exceptional			
Acts as a focal point of escalation to expedite problem resolution—Resolves problems directly where possible and acts as an escalation point where warranted to ensure problem resolution.	☐ YES ☐ NO	0	1	2	3	4	5	1	2	3
Organizes and manages work systematically—Uses project management techniques to control scope, track and manage costs and time, determine requirements, set standards, establish communication processes, and so on.	☐ YES ☐ NO	0	1	2	3	4	5	1	2	3
Organizes and manages resources effectively—Identifies and monitors people, funding, timing, and resources to ensure cost-effective and timely project or program results.	☐ YES ☐ NO	0	1	2	3	4	5	1	2	3
Adaptively applies methods as needed to achieve goals—Modifies project components in the face of change or emerging requirements to better manage tasks, allocate resources, and cope with shifting work environments.	☐ YES ☐ NO	0	1	2	3	4	5	1	2	3
Leverages success through active promotion—Ensures that stakeholders appreciate both the value of the solution to the achievement of their goals and the underlying relationships as a basis for expanding a mutually beneficial collaboration.	☐ YES ☐ NO	0	1	2	3	4	5	1	2	3

		0	1	2	3	4	5	1	2	3
Documents and communicates best practices—Ensures that lessons learned are not lost, but instead captured and leveraged to realize additional opportunities.	☐ YES ☐ NO	0	1	2	3	4	5	1	2	3
Ensures that criteria for decision making are shared and addressed—Frames the benefits of a solution in a way that accurately addresses the key points and priorities of stakeholders.	☐ YES ☐ NO	0	1	2	3	4	5	1	2	3
Adapts and tailors messages as required—Ensures that value propositions clearly speak to the needs and perspectives of all stakeholder types and levels.	☐ YES ☐ NO	0	1	2	3	4	5	1	2	3
Confirms validity of the proposed solution—Gains stakeholder consensus on the value of the proposed solution and its efficacy in meeting the needs identified.	☐ YES ☐ NO	0	1	2	3	4	5	1	2	3
Incorporates business and industry acumen into work—Understands business terminology and key processes and incorporates these accurately in conceptualizing what must be done when communicating effectively with stakeholders.	☐ YES ☐ NO	0	1	2	3	4	5	1	2	3
Exhibits business-oriented perspective in assessing needs—Understands how businesses work to achieve profitability; uses business insight to better assess the value and priorities of work-related contributions.	☐ YES ☐ NO	0	1	2	3	4	5	1	2	3

(continued on the next page)

159

Table B2-1. Competency Assessment Inventory (continued)

Foundational Competencies	Has requester demonstrated this competency? ☐ Yes ☐ No	Current Level of Proficiency						Future Importance: How important is this competency for future success?		
		None	Very Little	Limited	Consistent	Advanced	Exceptional			
Incorporates legal and contractual requirements into work—Understands the purpose of standard contracts and statements of work and their role in articulating requirements and setting expectations.	☐ YES ☐ NO	0	1	2	3	4	5	1	2	3
Incorporates financial understanding into work—Understands the role that costs and financial returns play in determining business value and incorporates this perspective into the way resources are used and solutions positioned.	☐ YES ☐ NO	0	1	2	3	4	5	1	2	3
Approaches challenges creatively—Approaches problems from a fresh perspective.	☐ YES ☐ NO	0	1	2	3	4	5	1	2	3
Crosses disciplines to frame or address challenges—Draws from multiple disciplines or models to synthesize new approaches to problem solving.	☐ YES ☐ NO	0	1	2	3	4	5	1	2	3
Demonstrates respect for others—Respects the innate human dignity of every individual.	☐ YES ☐ NO	0	1	2	3	4	5	1	2	3
Acclimates to diverse work settings—Demonstrates an appreciation of diverse perspectives and approaches to work and actively seeks to listen, learn, and integrate different ways of accomplishing tasks.	☐ YES ☐ NO	0	1	2	3	4	5	1	2	3

Competency	YES/NO	0	1	2	3	4	5	1	2	3
Harnesses diversity to create workplace synergies—Leverages the experiences and worldviews of others to drive innovations and stimulate creativity.	☐ YES ☐ NO	0	1	2	3	4	5	1	2	3
Demonstrates personal integrity—Takes personal responsibility for ensuring that actions and decisions protect the integrity of the company; understands and demonstrates the values most important to the work environment.	☐ YES ☐ NO	0	1	2	3	4	5	1	2	3
Incorporates quality considerations into decision making—Determines the best course of action in compliance with established quality processes, business rules, or optimum workplace practices.	☐ YES ☐ NO	0	1	2	3	4	5	1	2	3
Provides proactive knowledge transfer—Understands the value of information to stakeholders and circulates it openly to improve overall performance and productivity.	☐ YES ☐ NO	0	1	2	3	4	5	1	2	3
Ensures that communication tools and processes advance information storage and transfer—Recognizes and acts on obstacles to the effective storage, retrieval, or communication of information.	☐ YES ☐ NO	0	1	2	3	4	5	1	2	3
Maintains understanding of technical innovations—Incorporates an up-to-date understanding of technical innovations and trends as well as their implications.	☐ YES ☐ NO	0	1	2	3	4	5	1	2	3

(continued on the next page)

Table B2-1. Competency Assessment Inventory (continued)

Foundational Competencies	Has requester demonstrated this competency? □ Yes □ No	Current Level of Proficiency						Future Importance — How important is this competency for future success?		
		None	Very Little	Limited	Consistent	Advanced	Exceptional			
Uses information technology to align and expedite work—Uses tools and systems appropriately to ensure that communications and work are delivered in a timely way and are usable by customers, colleagues, and managers.	□ YES □ NO	0	1	2	3	4	5	1	2	3
Improves personal productivity technology—Takes the initiative to learn new technology and incorporate its benefits into the workplace (for example, customer relationship management [CRM] systems, virtual classroom, and mobile communication devices).	□ YES □ NO	0	1	2	3	4	5	1	2	3
Takes personal responsibility for development—Monitors and addresses skill and knowledge gaps by actively soliciting performance feedback and developmental planning assistance and selects appropriate development options.	□ YES □ NO	0	1	2	3	4	5	1	2	3
Demonstrates agility in addressing development needs—Leverages a range of learning options and delivery media to maximize time in the acquisition of critical skills, knowledge, or values.	□ YES □ NO	0	1	2	3	4	5	1	2	3
Leverages information to change behavior—Accesses and incorporates essential information for the ongoing development of personal effectiveness.	□ YES □ NO	0	1	2	3	4	5	1	2	3

Competency		0	1	2	3	4	5	1	2	3
Develops plans that clearly actualize strategy—Articulates strategies in a way that aligns activities, deliverables, and milestones.	☐ YES ☐ NO	0	1	2	3	4	5	1	2	3
Builds commitment to plan—Exercises influence to ensure enthusiastic commitment and buy-in to a plan's strategy and implementation requirements.	☐ YES ☐ NO	0	1	2	3	4	5	1	2	3
Executes to plan, yet adapts to emergent circumstances—Uses plans to guide activities, demonstrates responsiveness to change, and adapts plans to emerging requirements.	☐ YES ☐ NO	0	1	2	3	4	5	1	2	3
Delivers to plan—Attains the goals sufficient to generate interest in continuing or expanding the organizational or business relationship into new areas of collaboration.	☐ YES ☐ NO	0	1	2	3	4	5	1	2	3
Incorporates a strategic perspective in activity planning—Distinguishes the tactical from the strategic and the urgent from the critical as a guide to prioritizing activities.	☐ YES ☐ NO	0	1	2	3	4	5	1	2	3
Practices time management—Applies appropriate time management techniques to focus, prioritize, and track tasks.	☐ YES ☐ NO	0	1	2	3	4	5	1	2	3
Aligns and relates work to sales success—Understands how work products contribute to effective selling and ensures their solid contribution to sales success.	☐ YES ☐ NO	0	1	2	3	4	5	1	2	3
Incorporates selling sensibilities into work execution—Appreciates how the term "customer" establishes an important dynamic in both internal and external business relationships, calling for consultative partnering based on mutual benefits.	☐ YES ☐ NO	0	1	2	3	4	5	1	2	3

(continued on the next page)

Table B2-1. Competency Assessment Inventory (continued)

Foundational Competencies	Has requester demonstrated this competency? ☐ Yes ☐ No	Current Level of Proficiency					Future Importance		
		None	Very Little	Limited	Consistent	Advanced	Exceptional	How important is this competency for future success?		
Demonstrates a systemic understanding of sales—Understands buying-selling relationships and uses this understanding to focus work in a flexible, adaptive manner that contributes to the larger network of sales relationships and facilitates the personalization and customization of sales solutions.	☐ YES ☐ NO	0	1	2	3	4	5	1	2	3
Ensures that work helps to advance sales—Acts as a facilitator to sales, sales processing, or sales readiness when performing work.	☐ YES ☐ NO	0	1	2	3	4	5	1	2	3

Table B2-2. Area of Expertise: Creating and Closing Opportunities

Name of person being assessed: _____

Assessor's name (optional): _____

Relationship to the person being assessed: _____ Date: _____

Direct Report   Peer   Supervisor

Creating and Closing Opportunities	Has requester demonstrated this competency? ☐ Yes ☐ No	Current Level of Proficiency						Future Importance — How important is this competency for future success?		
		None	Very Little	Limited	Consistent	Advanced	Exceptional			
Researches and targets prospects—Actively researches available sources to identify likely prospects based on alignment to product or service market, known business needs, typical customer profiles, business activities, competitive market position, customer challenges, product or service spend, and competitive presence in account; reviews prospects and determines where or how to allocate effort and resources; and develops approach strategy tailored to the most appropriate individuals who have decision-making authority.	☐ YES ☐ NO	0	1	2	3	4	5	1	2	3
Conducts interest-building calls (cold calls) when applicable—Appropriately manages customer prospecting to connect directly with future customers while not alienating them; generates immediate, compelling customer interest in the selling organization, ensuring its product or service offers sufficient value to generate a willingness to continue the sales dialogue; and initiates exploratory discussions to schedule solid and specific follow-up sales calls in an effort to continue facilitating buying processes.	☐ YES ☐ NO	0	1	2	3	4	5	1	2	3

(continued on the next page)

Table B2-2. Area of Expertiser: Creating and Closing Opportunities (continued)

Creating and Closing Opportunities	Has requester demonstrated this competency? ☐ Yes ☐ No	Current Level of Proficiency						Future Importance — How important is this competency for future success?		
		None	Very Little	Limited	Consistent	Advanced	Exceptional			
Identifies, follows up on, and manages sales leads—Builds reciprocal lead-sharing networks to build the sales funnel with prospective clients and acts on any new lead in a timely manner to capitalize on interest and compelling needs.	☐ YES ☐ NO	0	1	2	3	4	5	1	2	3
Gains interest—Leverages marketing materials to stimulate client interest; explores client curiosity from various perspectives—business, financial, and market—to capture key variables and contingencies to nurture opportunities; generates customer interest through discussion of potential benefits; and actively shapes components of each opportunity to reflect client priorities and adequately address client needs.	☐ YES ☐ NO	0	1	2	3	4	5	1	2	3
Qualifies opportunities—Assesses client operations and business position for potential partnering opportunities, assesses client balance sheet and business health to determine feasibility of partnering, identifies and aligns required resources for pursuit and future solution deployment, determines scope and nature of risk as a necessary input to developing appropriate pricing and risk management strategies, and determines or orchestrates identification of opportunities and assesses requirements for third party involvement.	☐ YES ☐ NO	0	1	2	3	4	5	1	2	3

Competency										
Develops winning proposals—Develops compelling value propositions aligned with customer needs, business priorities, and/or technical and operational requirements; orchestrates and aligns the technical or functional contributions of functional and technical experts; communicates key competitive advantages; works with others to ensure appropriate pricing; and manages the milestones essential for timely proposal delivery.	☐ YES ☐ NO	0	1	2	3	4	5	1	2	3
Builds business justification cases—Collaborates with financial, legal, and technical experts to develop a business justification for each specific opportunity to ensure internal buy-in; enlists champions within both buyer and seller organizations; works with internal stakeholders to customize the opportunity to internal requirements while avoiding compromises that might threaten client acceptance or solution integrity; and identifies and communicates all risks associated with the opportunity and addresses these challenges with solution contingencies or fall-back positions.	☐ YES ☐ NO	0	1	2	3	4	5	1	2	3
Orchestrates support for negotiations—Where warranted, coordinates the input of legal, technical, and financial experts seamlessly into the development of a negotiation strategy; ensures that stakeholders understand their role in negotiation; focuses efforts of others on achieving the business outcome; continuously checks with experts to ensure commitments are valid and can be delivered; and drives to close and asks for the business at appropriate time.	☐ YES ☐ NO	0	1	2	3	4	5	1	2	3

(continued on the next page)

Table B2-2. Area of Expertiser: Creating and Closing Opportunities (continued)

Creating and Closing Opportunities	Has requester demonstrated this competency? ☐ Yes ☐ No	Current Level of Proficiency					Future Importance		
		None	Very Little	Limited	Consistent	Advanced	Exceptional	How important is this competency for future success?		
Maintains opportunity momentum to expand sales—Capitalizes on early wins and customer satisfaction to expand business wider and deeper into the account.	☐ YES ☐ NO	0	1	2	3	4	5	1	2	3

Table B2-3. Area of Expertise: Protecting Accounts

Name of person being assessed: _____

Assessor's name (optional): _____

Relationship to the person being assessed: Direct Report   Peer   Supervisor

Date: _____

Protecting Accounts	Has requester demonstrated this competency? ☐ Yes ☐ No	Current Level of Proficiency						Future Importance
		None	Very Little	Limited	Consistent	Advanced	Exceptional	How important is this competency for future success?
Gathers and monitors account intelligence—Maintains account business direction in a manner consistent with client needs, establishes networks in customer business to stay abreast of current or emerging requirements, and scans relevant external publications or websites for account-related business information.	☐ YES ☐ NO	0	1	2	3	4	5	1 2 3
Documents account plans and sales forecasts—Develops strategies and plans for managing account pursuit activities; assesses activities to plan; prioritizes and coordinates opportunity pursuit across multiple accounts to maintain a healthy sales funnel; and develops, communicates, and monitors sales forecasts to ensure accuracy.	☐ YES ☐ NO	0	1	2	3	4	5	1 2 3

(continued on the next page)

Table B2-3. Area of Expertise: Protecting Accounts (continued)

Protecting Accounts	Has requester demonstrated this competency? ☐ Yes ☐ No	Current Level of Proficiency						Future Importance How important is this competency for future success?		
		None	Very Little	Limited	Consistent	Advanced	Exceptional			
Builds client executive business relationships—Widens the breadth and depth of account penetration to achieve exposure to business planning, uses professional presence to frame selling messages in terms of client's business (rather than operational or technical) benefits, incorporates key business and financial metrics into sales positioning messages, demonstrates comfort at various business levels and possesses the social skills necessary for interacting effectively with senior level executives, and positions the company represented and the benefits of partnering as the essential components of the business relationship desired as opposed to focusing on a more purely transactional relationship.	☐ YES ☐ NO	0	1	2	3	4	5	1	2	3
Cultivates and develops trusted advisor status—Ensures that product or service value propositions align and resonate with customer needs, provides on-demand consultative advice, checks the accuracy and utility of recommendations prior to their communication and avoids making inaccurate claims, conducts self professionally in all customer communications and interactions with discreteness and confidentiality when required, and credits competitive claims where warranted to maintain credibility and trust.	☐ YES ☐ NO	0	1	2	3	4	5	1	2	3

		0	1	2	3	4	5	1	2	3
Protects and expands accounts—Ensures that all contractual deployment or fulfillment obligations are met and customer satisfaction is achieved, monitors account activity to minimize rogue selling and disruptive marketing, generally maintains overall account focal point leadership, and monitors competitive activities in accounts and appropriately counters competitive messages while blocking future competitor inroads.	☐ YES ☐ NO									
Manages deployment readiness and resource alignment—Ensures accurate understanding of requirements derived from closed opportunities (for example, terms and conditions and service level agreements) and ensures knowledge is dispersed among personnel engaged in post-sale activity (for example, fulfillment and delivery); where warranted, acts as the focal point for deal education and preparation within individual geographies; and, where required, facilitates the resource troubleshooting essential for successfully launching complex initiatives.	☐ YES ☐ NO									

Table B2-4. Area of Expertise: Defining and Positioning Solutions

Name of person being assessed: _____ Date: _____

Assessor's name (optional): _____

Relationship to the person being assessed: Direct Report Peer Supervisor _____

Defining and Positioning Solutions	Has requester demonstrated this competency? ☐ Yes ☐ No	Current Level of Proficiency						Future Importance — How important is this competency for future success?		
		None	Very Little	Limited	Consistent	Advanced	Exceptional			
Performs technical qualifications—Gathers the information required for technical solution creation based on customer's specific needs, builds technical credibility with clients to counter competitive arguments and advance the sale with the technical decision maker(s), and reviews opportunities based on technical feasibility or competitive presence within the client relationship for each individual opportunity.	☐ YES ☐ NO	0	1	2	3	4	5	1	2	3
Designs solutions—Creates the technical design necessary to clearly identify solution components, their interrelationships with each other, and how they work together to solve the customer's business challenges; identifies solution components appropriate for solving a customer's unique business challenges; and validates solution ideas with customers, peers, and account teams to ensure solution integrity and feasibility.	☐ YES ☐ NO	0	1	2	3	4	5	1	2	3

		0	1	2	3	4	5	1	2	3
Customizes standard products or services—Designs solutions that are necessary to truly accommodate a customer's business needs; enlists in-house support or appropriate subject matter expertise necessary to create tailored solutions; and ensures all stakeholders (for example, sales negotiators, contract experts, and deployment or delivery personnel) understand unique solution components and/or their requirements).	☐ YES ☐ NO	0	1	2	3	4	5	1	2	3
Conducts technical demonstrations and benchmarks—Demonstrates the features, benefits, value, and competitive advantage of a solution by addressing customer needs within the context of the customer's business setting; generates proof-of-concept data to create a compelling business case for selecting a specific solution; leverages benchmark data as required to technically position the beneficial results of the solution advocated; and presents performance output in a way that resonates with customers and addresses their concerns.	☐ YES ☐ NO	0	1	2	3	4	5	1	2	3
Contributes to solution sizing and modification—Collaborates with functional experts (for example, colleagues in pricing, deployment, legal, and so forth) to accurately size a proposed solution and works with account teams to adapt solutions in response to new customer requirements, funding restrictions, the desire for a phased approach, and other important factors.	☐ YES ☐ NO	0	1	2	3	4	5	1	2	3

(continued on the next page)

173

Table B2-4. Area of Expertise: Defining and Positioning Solutions (continued)

Defining and Positioning Solutions	Has requester demonstrated this competency? ☐ Yes ☐ No	Current Level of Proficiency						Future Importance — How important is this competency for future success?		
		None	Very Little	Limited	Consistent	Advanced	Exceptional			
Articulates solution designs— Facilitates solution positioning in a manner that effectively demonstrates understanding of the communications and positions the strategy to both technical and business stakeholders; reviews all communications and proposals for accurate solution definition and identification of benefits; and where warranted, conducts technical presentations to ensure understanding or enlist the support of technical stakeholders within the customer's environment.	☐ YES ☐ NO	0	1	2	3	4	5	1	2	3

Table B2-5. Area of Expertise: Supporting Indirect Selling

Name of person being assessed: _____

Assessor's name (optional): _____

Relationship to the person being assessed: Direct Report   Peer   Supervisor

Date: _____

Supporting Indirect Selling	Has requester demonstrated this competency? ☐ Yes ☐ No	Current Level of Proficiency						Future Importance — How important is this competency for future success?		
		None	Very Little	Limited	Consistent	Advanced	Exceptional			
Assesses and helps develop partner's sales force—When appropriate, assesses the talent of the partner's sales force to leverage strengths, identify weaknesses, and address gaps.	☐ YES ☐ NO	0	1	2	3	4	5	1	2	3
Drives partner sales planning or forecasting—Identifies likely sales prospects as well as market clusters where opportunity may exist; assesses inventory push strategies for adequacy and determines use of market-promotion funding; articulates sales goals, aligns sales metrics, and sets joint expectations with partners; tailors planning to local market requirements and conditions; gains partner commitment and establishes a strategy for monitoring the partner's selling progress; monitors partner activities for compliance with plan; and where warranted, suggests mid-course corrections to plan.	☐ YES ☐ NO	0	1	2	3	4	5	1	2	3

(continued on the next page)

175

Table B2-5. Area of Expertise: Supporting Indirect Selling (continued)

Supporting Indirect Selling	Has requester demonstrated this competency? ☐ Yes ☐ No	Current Level of Proficiency						Future Importance — How important is this competency for future success?		
		None	Very Little	Limited	Consistent	Advanced	Exceptional			
Motivates and educates partners—Leverages marketing promotions and discounts to advance partner selling, elevates partner preference for products or services over the competition, ensures partners are adequately prepared for accurately discussing or positioning products or services, and clearly communicates certification requirements if any exist and facilitates partner enrollment in appropriate training and testing.	☐ YES ☐ NO	0	1	2	3	4	5	1	2	3
Cultivates partner business relationships—Builds understanding of partner's short- and long-term commitments; develops mutual understanding about what each stakeholder seeks to achieve in the partnership; extends partner planning and alliance-building activities to the highest levels of the partner's organization; clearly articulates the business advantages of partnering to extend the range of selling; and where warranted, helps shift partner focus from transactional to consultative selling.	☐ YES ☐ NO	0	1	2	3	4	5	1	2	3
Facilitates inventory balancing or clearance—Monitors distributor warehouse flow-through for optimum efficiency, collaborates with distributors in developing strategies and making the marketing investments needed to advance or accelerate end-point selling, and troubleshoots product supply or logistics issues affecting distributor performance.	☐ YES ☐ NO	0	1	2	3	4	5	1	2	3

Competency		0	1	2	3	4	5	1	2	3
Tracks investments in partner selling to determine business impact—Implements event-driven or quarterly tracking methods to monitor partner selling improvements; uses partner self-reports or independent data to assess return-on-investment for funds expended; and collaborates with other stakeholders to revise sales strategies or marketing events to ensure optimum yield or achievement of investment objectives (for example, sales, leads, interest generation, and market penetration).	☐ YES ☐ NO	0	1	2	3	4	5	1	2	3
Facilitates partner transformation—Introduces effective selling strategies to partner organization to increase its market penetration, identifies new or expanded market opportunities, and encourages close business collaboration in business planning and investments to ensure that partners maintain their presence in the face of market trends.	☐ YES ☐ NO	0	1	2	3	4	5	1	2	3
Monitors and manages contract fulfillment—Ensures that contracts serve as a frame of reference for setting expectations and guiding partner activities and ensures that contractual requirements are fulfilled.	☐ YES ☐ NO	0	1	2	3	4	5	1	2	3
Troubleshoots partner sales crediting—Actively works with operations team members to correct inaccuracies and to ensure timely crediting of partner sales, collaborates with operations and other stakeholders to build or maintain optimum partner-associated processes, and helps expedite sale or order fulfillment processes.	☐ YES ☐ NO	0	1	2	3	4	5	1	2	3

(continued on the next page)

Table B2-5. Area of Expertise: Supporting Indirect Selling (continued)

Supporting Indirect Selling	Has requester demonstrated this competency? □ Yes □ No	Current Level of Proficiency					Future Importance How important is this competency for future success?		
		None	Very Little	Limited	Consistent	Advanced	Exceptional		
Collaborates on team selling and positioning—Assists partner at critical sales cycle junctions (for example, positioning, closing, and negotiation) where required; works internally to acquire optimum pricing or exemptions when appropriate; and minimizes discord with partner and presents a unified team approach to the customer.	□ YES □ NO	0	1	2	3	4	5	1	2	3

Table B2-6. Area of Expertise: Setting Sales Strategy

Name of person being assessed: _____

Date: _____

Assessor's name (optional): _____

Relationship to the person being assessed: _____ Direct Report _____ Peer _____ Supervisor

Setting Sales Strategy	Has requester demonstrated this competency? ☐ Yes ☐ No	Current Level of Proficiency						Future Importance — How important is this competency for future success?		
		None	Very Little	Limited	Consistent	Advanced	Exceptional			
Identifies and articulates innovative sales practices—Works internally to synthesize the overall business plan with market trends and data; identifies both key themes of and obstacles to sales effectiveness; solicits and validates insights from the field; develops scalable sales structure and process models that optimize current sales activities and go-to-market realities; introduces new sales practices that help deliver value; and collaborates with business management and company functions as well as sales team members to assess feasibility, costs, and benefits associated with innovative strategies.	☐ YES ☐ NO	0	1	2	3	4	5	1	2	3
Creates strategic plans that guide organizational, technical, process, or practice planning and implementation—Creates development plans to set the direction and agenda for tactical sales planning, collaborates with appropriate sales management colleagues to ensure alignment to plans, works with technical personnel or vendors to provide customer-based inputs into the tools and systems support envisioned, and monitors implementation to assess success and adjusts strategy as needed.	☐ YES ☐ NO	0	1	2	3	4	5	1	2	3

(continued on the next page)

Table B2-6. Area of Expertise: Setting Sales Strategy (continued)

Setting Sales Strategy	Has requester demonstrated this competency? ☐ Yes ☐ No	Current Level of Proficiency						Future Importance — How important is this competency for future success?		
		None	Very Little	Limited	Consistent	Advanced	Exceptional			
Builds business and partner alliances to increase sales—Forges business alliances with those who possess a shared vision of desired future state (for example, business development, product or service development, supply chain, marketing, and sales management) and enlists third party alliances where warranted to close gaps or advance implementation toward the vision.	☐ YES ☐ NO	0	1	2	3	4	5	1	2	3
Provides leadership to accelerate strategy diffusion—Develops communication and readiness strategies to generate enthusiasm for strategy and motivate the effort needed for success and leverages technology and uses events to personally champion strategy.	☐ YES ☐ NO	0	1	2	3	4	5	1	2	3
Configures and aligns sales territories for maximum effectiveness—Develops or reconfigures territories to maximize sales effectiveness or technical and functional resource allocation and collaborates with regional, territory, and local sales team members to delineate responsibilities and manage territories.	☐ YES ☐ NO	0	1	2	3	4	5	1	2	3

Table B2-7. Area of Expertise: Managing within the Sales Ecosystem

Name of person being assessed: _____

Assessor's name (optional): _____

Relationship to the person being assessed: Direct Report   Peer   Supervisor   Date: _____

Managing within the Sales Ecosystem	Has requester demonstrated this competency? ☐ Yes ☐ No	Current Level of Proficiency						Future Importance — How important is this competency for future success?		
		None	Very Little	Limited	Consistent	Advanced	Exceptional			
Aligns tactical activities to support strategic sales plans— Provides input to organizational planning while assessing goals in light of unique requirements and opportunities; aligns planning with organizational goals—sets priorities and expectations and identifies and addresses opportunity or resource gaps; adjust plans to local requirements to ensure progress to established plan; and ensures alignment of all activities with upper management strategies, corporate direction, and goals.	☐ YES ☐ NO	0	1	2	3	4	5	1	2	3
Establishes, monitors, and controls costs that affect sales margins— Identifies spend parameters and establishes operating budgets; tracks spending and complies with associated reporting requirements (for example, reimbursement for customer meetings and travel expenses); manages sales-related allowances and discounts to ensure appropriate margin; reallocates funding to address cost overruns; prepares and communicates quarterly and annual sales reports; manages associated sales expenditures; and drives cost control and operational efficiencies to ensure optimum targeting of resources on most appropriate opportunities.	☐ YES ☐ NO	0	1	2	3	4	5	1	2	3

(continued on the next page)

181

Table B2-7. Area of Expertise: Managing within the Sales Ecosystem (continued)

Managing within the Sales Ecosystem	Has requester demonstrated this competency? Yes No	Current Level of Proficiency						Future Importance — How important is this competency for future success?		
		None	Very Little	Limited	Consistent	Advanced	Exceptional			
Aligns resources with opportunities—Collaborates with colleagues to ensure optimum opportunity coverage using available technology and expert sales resources; balances key factors determining resource allocation to establish pursuit priorities in area of control (for example, account importance, win probability, opportunity size, and alignment to strategy); and, where necessary, troubleshoots with colleagues to ensure timely access to needed resources.	☐ YES ☐ NO	0	1	2	3	4	5	1	2	3
Screens administrative demands and troubleshoots back-office operations to minimize sales disruptions—Acts as the escalation point to screen sales personnel from administrative disruptions that might otherwise dilute their focus on selling activities; screens and prioritizes incoming organizational communications for key announcements; troubleshoots operational issues around order fulfillment to ensure delivery or deployment; troubleshoots operational challenges that affect sales credit or payout to maintain positive sales morale; and collaborates with operations management to improve processes, systems, or tools for ease of use.	☐ YES ☐ NO	0	1	2	3	4	5	1	2	3

Competency		0	1	2	3	4	5	1	2	3
Ensures accurate forecasting while monitoring performance to metrics—Ensures contributor use of planning and reporting tools or systems to establish consistency, promote accuracy, and advance real-time management assessment; conducts regularly scheduled check-ins and meetings to assess and/or troubleshoot progress to pre-determined plans; tracks account contributor performance against established metrics (for example, funnel movement, account plans, program goals, established performance objectives, and customer satisfaction); and develops and rolls up aggregate forecast as required.	☐ YES ☐ NO	0	1	2	3	4	5	1	2	3
Hires, promotes, and terminates to improve sales performance and address capability gaps—Leverages management experience and knowledge of capability gaps to build well-targeted hiring criteria or conduct appropriate terminations, reviews candidate's qualification for linkage to defined competencies, supports candidate selection processes, facilitates on-boarding, clearly sets expectations for new hire performance, acts as performance resource during trial employment period, situates performance in the wider context of business goals, clearly communicates criteria for promotion and exercises this responsibility objectively, counsels contributors to address and remediate performance concerns or to resolve issues, and creates required documentation to terminate employees in a manner that minimizes challenges to this decision while protecting company assets.	☐ YES ☐ NO	0	1	2	3	4	5	1	2	3

(continued on the next page)

183

Table B2-7. Area of Expertise: Managing within the Sales Ecosystem (continued)

Managing within the Sales Ecosystem	Has requester demonstrated this competency? ☐ Yes ☐ No	Current Level of Proficiency						Future Importance		
		None	Very Little	Limited	Consistent	Advanced	Exceptional	How important is this competency for future success?		
Aligns reward and recognition strategies to performance goals—leverages company or establishes local rewards or recognition programs to advance overall sales performance, continuously assesses rewards for their motivational power and revises where necessary, administers recognition and reward selection criteria fairly to maintain morale, ensures communication of recognition or awards to leverage impact on group performance, and balances acknowledgement of individuals with the need for group solidarity to create a climate of continuous performance improvement that facilitates peer-to-peer best practices sharing.	☐ YES ☐ NO	0	1	2	3	4	5	1	2	3

Table B2-8. Area of Expertise: Developing Sales Force Capability

Name of person being assessed: _____ Date: _____

Assessor's name (optional): _____

Relationship to the person being assessed: Direct Report Peer Supervisor

Developing Sales Force Capability	Has requester demonstrated this competency? ☐ Yes ☐ No	Current Level of Proficiency						Future Importance How important is this competency for future success?		
		None	Very Little	Limited	Consistent	Advanced	Exceptional			
Determines competencies required to achieve sales strategy—Understands how to align the strategic customer's needs to increased capability through the improvement of individual competencies (knowledge, skills, and attitudes); ties organization's sales strategies and business functions to competencies needed now and in the future; assesses current competencies of the team (from entry-level workers to senior executives) in relation to the requirements of the future state; and determines the priority of competencies needed.	☐ YES ☐ NO	0	1	2	3	4	5	1	2	3
Conducts sales-related needs assessments—Identifies sales skill and environmental challenges, identifies required resources, analyzes and incorporates findings in a set of training solutions or support recommendations, and articulates information necessary for implementing future learning solutions while supporting organization's goals.	☐ YES ☐ NO	0	1	2	3	4	5	1	2	3

(continued on the next page)

Table B2-8. Area of Expertise: Developing Sales Force Capability (continued)

Developing Sales Force Capability	Has requester demonstrated this competency? ☐ Yes ☐ No	Current Level of Proficiency						Future Importance		
		None	Very Little	Limited	Consistent	Advanced	Exceptional	How important is this competency for future success?		
Designs and develops sales development programs, curricula, or learning solutions— Partners with subject matter experts to quickly and adequately develop content; analyzes, synthesizes, and organizes content modules; develops and validates learning outcomes and/or curricula progress path; collaborates with stakeholders in determining appropriate delivery strategy and media; generates the design specifications necessary for development; implements and monitors development to plan; leverages project-based approach to learning rollouts and solutions; selects appropriate delivery modes for learning opportunities—instructor-led classroom, online instruction, guided on-the-job experience, informal learning, or a combination of methods; proposes opportunities to drive self-directed learning (for example, job rotation, tuition reimbursement, personal development reimbursement, and professional association memberships); creates development maps for every sales team member (leaders, catalysts, developers, and enablers); and ensures development maps are meaningful to sales team leaders by tying competencies to job function within the sales team, area of expertise, or job role.	☐ YES ☐ NO	0	1	2	3	4	5	1	2	3

		0	1	2	3	4	5	1	2	3
Uses learning management systems—Provides or updates information in learning management systems to ensure accurate and timely communication of events offered; tracks participants through learning programs and, where warranted, satisfactory completion of requirements (for example, certification course and testing completion); builds usable report templates based on stakeholder needs and generates reports as needed to profile target audience progress or requirements completion; enforces data access and confidentiality norms while ensuring that participants and their management have appropriate exposure to information based on access privileges; uses data to identify program challenges as these relate to attendance or completion requirements; and uses data to inform development planning and data integration involving interfacing with other systems.	☐ YES ☐ NO									
Ties learning strategy to organizational capacity—Creates a sales-wide learning plan to address competency gaps, manage resource deployment, and measure outcomes for sales catalysts, developers, and enablers; helps the organization decide between hiring for an already developed competency, developing the competency internally, managing the skill gaps through outsourcing, or blending approaches to achieve organizational capacity; sets baseline measures by documenting every member's current competencies via assessment; identifies targets for closing the gap between current competency sets and those needed to support the future goals of the team as well as the overall organization; sets	☐ YES ☐ NO									

(continued on the next page)

187

Table B2-8. Area of Expertise: Developing Sales Force Capability (continued)

Developing Sales Force Capability	Has requester demonstrated this competency? ☐ Yes ☐ No	Current Level of Proficiency						Future Importance — How important is this competency for future success?		
		None	Very Little	Limited	Consistent	Advanced	Exceptional	1	2	3
goals for internal communication and change management plans that will accompany the comprehensive action plan to address the team's skills gap; develops a separate communication and change management strategy for sales managers; and includes sales managers in the strategy.										
Evaluates learning program or solution effectiveness—Designs evaluation strategy that ties training solutions to business impact; conducts formative evaluation to ensure the integrity of learning collateral and events; ensures contribution of learning solutions to the achievement of learning objectives; aligns evaluation with appropriate indicators and measurements strategies; develops evaluation instruments; implements summative evaluation to assess learner receptivity, skill and knowledge acquisition, learning transfer to work, and business impact; mines results for lessons learned and continuous improvement of sales learning; and measures progress before and after learning takes place, including the impact on leading inputs (for example, the length of the sales cycle and closing rate), lagging outputs (for example, sales results by channel, product, and team), behavior change (for example, observable increases or decreases in targeted areas), knowledge transfer (for example, measured retention of knowledge pre-, post-, and 90 days later), and customer satisfaction.	☐ YES ☐ NO	0	1	2	3	4	5	1	2	3

		0	1	2	3	4	5	1	2	3
Reports results to organizational stakeholders—Communicates the results of learning program measurements to demonstrate accountability, ensure quality, justify investments, ensure the business impact of programs, and identify program retirement criteria; identifies implementation challenges or emerging requirements that suggest revisions; and engages in continuous improvement to ensure program effectiveness.	□ YES □ NO									

Table B2-9. Area of Expertise: Delivering Sales Training

Name of person being assessed: _____

Date: _____

Assessor's name (optional): _____

Relationship to the person being assessed: Direct Report   Peer   Supervisor

Delivering Sales Training	Has requester demonstrated this competency? ☐ Yes ☐ No	Current Level of Proficiency						Future Importance		
		None	Very Little	Limited	Consistent	Advanced	Exceptional	How important is this competency for future success?		
Reviews and supplements learning—Reviews and prepares for sales learning events, ensures relevance of activities and discussion to the style and interests of the target audience, supplements learning material with personal anecdotes and experiences that will bring the concepts and processes to life, links conceptual content to activities, explores varying ways that content can be applied to increase sales effectiveness, and drives toward actionable learning plans that can be implemented by participants on the job.	☐ YES ☐ NO	0	1	2	3	4	5	1	2	3
Motivates participants—Generates compelling interest in course and its objectives; where relevant, bridges current with prior learning to establish continuity; relates the benefits of learning outcomes to participant interests and agendas; varies stimuli (for example, modulates voice, diversifies media, and incorporates questioning strategies) and monitors participant attention to ensure active processing of information; and ensures the relevance of activities and discussion to the style and interests of participants.	☐ YES ☐ NO	0	1	2	3	4	5	1	2	3

	YES / NO	0	1	2	3	4	5	1	2	3
Manages instructional delivery— Clearly explains the organization of the learning event and desired learning outcomes, organizes the facility and agenda to allow customer issues to be addressed without sacrificing the learning environment, creates a collaborative learning atmosphere through introductions or exercises, uses questioning techniques appropriately to probe and ensure understanding and broaden the utility of skills or concepts, uses set ups and summaries to maintain coherent delivery and underscore key ideas, creates interactive experiences to maximize both tacit and explicit learning, uses learning technologies effectively to support instruction and advance the achievement of objectives, and facilitates small group discussions.	☐ YES ☐ NO									
Administers tests— Reviews tests to gain familiarity with administration protocols and test construction conventions; explains and clarifies test directions; administers tests and maintains a conducive testing environment; answers participant questions appropriately, using suggested guidelines; monitors time and conducts time-checks to ensure efficient use of participant time; collects testing instruments and ensures their appropriate communication or archiving; and, where required, grades tests and reports individual and aggregate scores.	☐ YES ☐ NO									

Table B2-10. Area of Expertise: Coaching for Sales Results

Name of person being assessed: _____   Date: _____

Assessor's name (optional): _____

Relationship to the person being assessed: Direct Report   Peer   Supervisor

Coaching for Sales Results	Has requester demonstrated this competency? ☐ Yes ☐ No	Current Level of Proficiency						Future Importance — How important is this competency for future success?				
		None	Very Little	Limited	Consistent	Advanced	Exceptional	1	2	3		
Observes sales person behavior to identify strengths, weaknesses, and opportunities for improvement—Utilizes joint selling experiences to observe and evaluate; looks for trends in performance, internal relationships, and customer interactions; identifies root causes of behavior; seeks corroborating evidence of both historical and predictive performance; tests ideas through repeated experiences to avoid focusing on anomalies; schedules noncritical experiences that allow for possible failure without jeopardizing significant sales effectiveness; and documents observations and conclusions.	☐ YES ☐ NO	0	1	2	3	4	5	1	2	3		
Balances corrective with positive feedback to ensure optimum guidance and performance improvement—Identifies teaching moments to ensure individual receptiveness to feedback, provides feedback in a way that protects the dignity of recipients while identifying key components to improve and ensuring clear understanding, clearly articulates what was done correctly and where there are challenges to ensure that recipients target their improvement activities appropriately, provides salient examples to guide recipient performance, and personally supports individuals through work-related challenges.	☐ YES ☐ NO	0	1	2	3	4	5	1	2	3		

	0	1	2	3	4	5	1	2	3
Leverages motivation as a key enabler of sales performance— Seeks to identify the motivations of both individuals and teams; engages in dialogue to uncover and reinforce effective motivational keys; analyzes the alignment of personal motivations with organizational goals; delivers motivational communication; consistently recognizes and rewards improvements in sales behavior and selling skills; identifies and, whenever possible, removes obstacles to motivation; and matches internal and external motivational factors to create an optimum performance environment.	☐ YES ☐ NO	1	2	3	4	5	1	2	3
Links expected behaviors to strategic outcomes— Ensures that individuals understand how their performance aligns to larger organizational or business goals, establishes consequences to show how tactical mistakes can derail strategic goals, and disabuses individuals of the idea that good performance is merely an empty ritual and shows its utility in achieving desired results in a way that can be readily understood.	☐ YES ☐ NO	1	2	3	4	5	1	2	3
Demonstrates and mentors expected sales behaviors— Leverages sales experience to concretely demonstrate advocated sales tactics or methods; uses on-the-job opportunities or job shadowing to demonstrate best practices (for example, sales "ride-alongs," listening in on remote sales calls, and tool or system demonstrations); and personally and continuously models the positive values, attitude, and perspective expected of sales professionals.	☐ YES ☐ NO	1	2	3	4	5	1	2	3

(continued on the next page)

Table B2-10. Area of Expertise: Coaching for Sales Results (continued)

Coaching for Sales Results	Has requester demonstrated this competency? ☐ Yes ☐ No	Current Level of Proficiency						Future Importance
		None	Very Little	Limited	Consistent	Advanced	Exceptional	How important is this competency for future success?
Establishes support programs to expand and enrich new learning—Collaborates with experienced practitioners to establish peer coaching, mentoring, or job sharing; identifies supplementary training or other resources (publications and professional associations) of potential use in performance improvement; and monitors and communicates performance innovations or new techniques that will expand or enhance performance.	☐ YES ☐ NO	0	1	2	3	4	5	1 2 3

Table B2-11. Area of Expertise: Building Sales Infrastructure

Name of person being assessed: _____   Date: _____

Assessor's name (optional): _____

Relationship to the person being assessed: Direct Report   Peer   Supervisor

Building Sales Infrastructure	Has requester demonstrated this competency? ☐ Yes ☐ No	Current Level of Proficiency						Future Importance — How important is this competency for future success?		
		None	Very Little	Limited	Consistent	Advanced	Exceptional			
Monitors current business processes and sales productivity tools for adequacy—Assesses current processes, systems, and tools for obstacles to productivity or agile access to sales intelligence (interface issues, usability issues, system or tool responsiveness, and data validity, reliability, and utility); identifies gaps in information flow and understands how improvements to the infrastructure can help; monitors marketplace and vendor offerings for infrastructure innovations and appropriateness to company needs; and determines ROI or breakeven points to trigger investment discussions or decision making.	☐ YES ☐ NO	0	1	2	3	4	5	1	2	3
Develops and drives strategic infrastructure planning—Collaborates with business planners, functions, and sales management to identify goals, challenges, and opportunities for improving infrastructure support; harnesses the technical resources essential for determining accurate technical and functional tool or system requirements; creates plans to guide infrastructure design and investment decisions; circulates plans among stakeholders to ensure buy-in and alignment with business, operations, and sales productivity objectives; and ensures that impact assessment has been completed and results understood by all stakeholders.	☐ YES ☐ NO	0	1	2	3	4	5	1	2	3

(continued on the next page)

195

Table B2-11. Area of Expertise: Building Sales Infrastructure (continued)

Building Sales Infrastructure	Has requester demonstrated this competency? ☐ Yes ☐ No	Current Level of Proficiency						Future Importance — How important is this competency for future success?		
		None	Very Little	Limited	Consistent	Advanced	Exceptional			
Manages infrastructure upkeep or revision—Manages pilot testing and/or revisions of infrastructure solutions prior to rollout; implements roll-out in accordance with plan and adapts those plans as necessary meet quarterly or regional performance measures, and ensures that hardware improvements and software patches or revisions are monitored and incorporated in a way that minimizes impact on the sales function.	☐ YES ☐ NO	0	1	2	3	4	5	1	2	3
Drives or supports infrastructure change and alignment—Collaborates with sales and operational management to develop change management strategies and programs; develops and coordinates change programs, communications, and training essential for program readiness and roll-out; and personally champions and advocates adoption of new systems.	☐ YES ☐ NO	0	1	2	3	4	5	1	2	3
Pilots and evaluates infrastructure programs—Uses sound strategies and methods to evaluate the impact of new programs or program improvements and pilots innovations and ensures optimum usability to end users.	☐ YES ☐ NO	0	1	2	3	4	5	1	2	3

196

Table B2-12. Area of Expertise: Designing Compensation

Name of person being assessed: _____

Assessor's name (optional): _____

Date: _____

Relationship to the person being assessed: Direct Report Peer Supervisor

Designing Compensation	Has requester demonstrated this competency? Yes No	Current Level of Proficiency					Future Importance		
		None	Very Little	Limited	Consistent	Advanced	Exceptional	How important is this competency for future success?		
Assesses current compensation against best practices and innovative sales compensation options—Identifies compensation challenges unique to sales that could be contributing to the challenges the company currently faces (for example, poor performance, misaligned or unintended reinforcement of nonpreferred sales behaviors, and loss of sales personnel); orchestrates or researches industry compensation packages; identifies trends or innovations and assesses them for applicability; and makes sound business recommendations.	YES NO	0	1	2	3	4	5	1	2	3
Aligns compensation with business requirements and appropriate sales behaviors and metrics—Ensures that proposed compensation models balance the business strategies with business realities and are achievable by sales team members; ensures that compensation aligns with human resource policies, regulatory requirements, and any contractual obligations; ensures that compensation promotes and reinforces productive, high-yield sales behaviors; and identifies and addresses negative or unintended consequences of current compensation strategies.	YES NO	0	1	2	3	4	5	1	2	3

(continued on the next page)

Table B2-12. Area of Expertise: Designing Compensation (continued)

Designing Compensation	Has requester demonstrated this competency? ☐ Yes ☐ No	Current Level of Proficiency						Future Importance — How important is this competency for future success?		
		None	Very Little	Limited	Consistent	Advanced	Exceptional			
Develops and enlists support for sales compensation models and plans—Develops sales compensation models that optimize the overall salary, commission, and bonus structure to create a well-motivated sales force and enlists the review of compensation strategies by business and sales executives and accommodates segment or regional differences where warranted.	☐ YES ☐ NO	0	1	2	3	4	5	1	2	3
Drives sales compensation acceptance—Collaborates with sales and operational management team members in developing change management strategies and programs; develops and coordinates programs, communications, and awareness training essential for compensation strategy acceptance and rollout; and champions and advocates adoption of new compensation strategies.	☐ YES ☐ NO	0	1	2	3	4	5	1	2	3

Table B2-13. Area of Expertise: Maintaining Accounts

Name of person being assessed: _____

Assessor's name (optional): _____

Relationship to the person being assessed: Direct Report   Peer   Supervisor   Date: _____

Maintaining Accounts	Has requester demonstrated this competency? ☐ Yes ☐ No	Current Level of Proficiency						Future Importance — How important is this competency for future success?		
		None	Very Little	Limited	Consistent	Advanced	Exceptional			
Prepares standard and ad hoc reports on account status—Analyzes account performance and contractual status data; researches customer or account business health, credit worthiness, and other qualification variables that quantify risk; and generates reports profiling account or customer current state as scheduled or on demand.	☐ YES ☐ NO	0	1	2	3	4	5	1	2	3
Provides agile task substitution assistance to facilitate sales—Accesses pricing information required for solution costing, including special or discount options; identifies part or component numbers required for costing solutions or providing replacements; acts in parallel with customer-facing sales in executing any back-office or operational tasks involved with aggregating data that will advance or formalize new deals; and enters order data using appropriate systems and order entry processes and tracks processing to completion.	☐ YES ☐ NO	0	1	2	3	4	5	1	2	3

(continued on the next page)

199

Table B2-13. Area of Expertise: Maintaining Accounts (continued)

Maintaining Accounts	Has requester demonstrated this competency? ☐ Yes ☐ No	Current Level of Proficiency						Future Importance How important is this competency for future success?		
		None	Very Little	Limited	Consistent	Advanced	Exceptional			
Crafts contracts and statements of work—Assembles standard contracts for use by others as boilerplates for noncomplex opportunities, works with legal experts to modify terms and conditions that reflect decisions reached during negotiation, communicates contracts or statements of work to stakeholders to ensure understanding of the opportunity and attendant responsibilities in execution, and ensures that contracts and statements of work move through sanctioned approval process and are archived appropriately upon signing.	☐ YES ☐ NO	0	1	2	3	4	5	1	2	3
Troubleshoots customer operational issues—Acts as an important interface for resolving customer issues around order or service fulfillment; works with back-office, partner, or supply chain stakeholders to eliminate bottlenecks; revises inaccurate data entry, solicits and gains required approval, expedites customer involvement, or identifies supply chain issues for escalation; and ensures that issues are resolved to the customer's satisfaction.	☐ YES ☐ NO	0	1	2	3	4	5	1	2	3

Tracks and administers contracts—Uses systems and tools to monitor contract expiration or service plan milestones, alerts sales to pending events requiring customer contact and renewal negotiations, prepares the necessary documentation required for renewal, and acts on behalf of the company when interacting with difficult customers to ensure they fulfill payment or other contractual obligations.	☐ YES ☐ NO	0	1	2	3	4	5	1	2	3

Table B2-14. Area of Expertise: Recruiting Sales Talent

Name of person being assessed: _____   Date: _____

Assessor's name (optional): _____

Relationship to the person being assessed: _____   Direct Report _____   Peer _____   Supervisor _____

Recruiting Sales Talent	Has requester demonstrated this competency? ☐ Yes ☐ No	Current Level of Proficiency						Future Importance — How important is this competency for future success?		
		None	Very Little	Limited	Consistent	Advanced	Exceptional			
Aligns and modifies sales job profiles—Collaborates with end-point sales management and appropriate team members to enhance standard sales position descriptions with better business needs and performance expectations; highlights key performance indicators (KPIs) and their supporting skills, knowledge, and experience; identifies unique or specific company practices or norms that may affect candidate success; and revises job profiles, validates with end-point management, and sets overall expectations based on clear recruitment objectives and parameters.	☐ YES ☐ NO	0	1	2	3	4	5	1	2	3
Ensures valid compensation package—Assesses compensation package offered for the sales position and job level against industry practices and metrics, negotiates with endpoint management to bring packages into alignment with market value, and finalizes compensation range as a basis for later candidate negotiations.	☐ YES ☐ NO	0	1	2	3	4	5	1	2	3

(continued on the next page)

Competency										
Monitors and maintains sales candidate pipeline—Establishes and monitors industry-specific conferences and professional associations where prospects congregate, develops reciprocal network of contacts with colleagues to share prospect leads and references, builds candidate lists categorized by descriptors such as industry verticals or market segments, continuously updates pipeline as a basis for sale candidate prospecting, and scans industry segments for volatility.	☐ YES ☐ NO	0	1	2	3	1	2	3	4	5
Sources sales candidates—Engages all available strategies (personal networking and peer recruiter information sharing), technology (job boards, social networks, and web mining), and resources (industry and professional associations) to conduct candidate searches; identifies prospects' contact information and incorporates these into solicitation strategy; and uses exploratory interviews with potential candidates to expand candidate pool with additional references.	☐ YES ☐ NO	0	1	2	3	1	2	3	4	5
Solicits, screens, and profiles candidates and determines person-job fit—Conducts iterative interviews with potential candidates (for example, dialogues around key performance indicators [KPIs]), gauges interest, and assesses skill set and level of experience; evaluates prospect's information with job profile requirements to determine active candidacy; develops profile of candidate to ensure consistency of information and identify issues requiring further investigation; and narrows candidates and communicates final list to end-point management.	☐ YES ☐ NO	0	1	2	3	1	2	3	4	5

Table B2-14. Area of Expertise: Recruiting Sales Talent (continued)

Recruiting Sales Talent	Has requester demonstrated this competency? □ Yes □ No	Current Level of Proficiency						Future Importance — How important is this competency for future success?		
		None	Very Little	Limited	Consistent	Advanced	Exceptional			
Facilitates sales peer team interviews and candidate testing— Prepares candidates for end-point management and sales team interviews; facilitates behavioral or sales simulation interview scenarios that emulate real-world requirements; co-interviews candidates to ensure all critical position requirements are addressed (for example, compensation package, base and commission payout formulas, and relocation expenses); where warranted, facilitates in candidate testing; debriefs candidates and end-point sales interviewees to assess match, determine fit, and make recommendations; and advises interviewers on human resources, legal, and compliance requirements.	□ YES □ NO	0	1	2	3	4	5	1	2	3
Generates offers and conducts negotiations with sales stakeholders to closure— Develops and communicates offer letters to candidates; conducts negotiations with candidates and end-point management to close outstanding gaps (for example, raise benefits and modify requirements); identifies area of mutual hiring acceptance and brokers key compromises; monitors candidates' bargaining behavior and claims to ensure veracity, integrity and overall fit; and resolves outstanding issues.	□ YES □ NO	0	1	2	3	4	5	1	2	3

Supports on-boarding—Develops appropriate on-boarding plan; briefs new hire on next steps and works with human resources to implement seamless hand-off to orientation; maintains contact with new hire to troubleshoot problems and ensure on-boarding success; and, where warranted by new hires that do not assimilate successfully, works with end-point management to refill position.	☐ YES ☐ NO	0	1	2	3	4	5	1	2	3

Worksheet B3. Summary of Results

Section A: Obtaining Average Scores

Use tables B3-1 through B3-14 to summarize and analyze the results of your data collection.

Simply follow these easy steps:

1. Each competency in tables B3-1 through B3-14 has two rows for entering data. In the top row, enter the assessment scores that you received for your current level of proficiency (0-5). In the bottom row, enter the assessment scores for the future importance of the competency (1-3).
2. For each current level row, write in all of the scores that you received from your direct reports in the cell provided. Do the same for your self-assessment scores, your peers' scores, and your supervisor's scores.
3. Add all the scores together and write the total in the appropriate cell.
4. Divide the total by the number of responses that you received to calculate the average. Write the average in the appropriate cell.
5. Repeat steps 1–4 for the future importance scores for each competency.

Figure B3-1 shows an example of a completed data analysis table.

Figure B3-1. Example of a Completed Analysis Table

Foundational Competencies		Direct Reports	Self	Peers	Supervisor	Totals	Average
Advances collaboration and positive relationships across organizational boundaries	Current	4, 5, 2	2	3, 4, 4	5	29	3.63
	Future	3, 2, 3	2	3, 3, 4	2	22	2.75

Table B3-1. Summary of Results, Foundational Competencies

Foundational Competencies		Direct Reports	Self	Peers	Supervisor	Totals	Average
Advances collaboration and positive relationships across organizational boundaries	Current						
	Future						
Recognizes and addresses gaps among personal, team, or organizational responsibilities	Current						
	Future						
Demonstrates active listening	Current						
	Future						
Achieves communication objectives	Current						
	Future						
Ensures responsive communication	Current						
	Future						
Attains persuasive communication	Current						
	Future						
Contributes to customer satisfaction	Current						
	Future						
Advocates for the customer	Current						
	Future						
Communicates expectations to all stakeholders	Current						
	Future						
Ensures clear understanding of responsibilities	Current						
	Future						

Understands and addresses potential obstacles to proposed solutions	Current							
	Future							
Determines optimum negotiation positions	Current							
	Future							
Addresses objections accordingly	Current							
	Future							
Builds consensus and commitment	Current							
	Future							
Actively nurtures positive relationships	Current							
	Future							
Protects and develops relationships to higher levels of trust and confidence	Current							
	Future							
Assesses resources accurately	Current							
	Future							
Balances risk with goal achievement when determining next steps	Current							
	Future							
Situates work meaningfully in terms of its relationship to other functions	Current							
	Future							
Contributes to the organization's success	Current							
	Future							
Develops and implements robust evaluations of solutions	Current							
	Future							

(continued on the next page)

Table B3-1. Summary of Results, Foundational Competencies (continued)

Foundational Competencies		Direct Reports	Self	Peers	Supervisor	Totals	Average
Communicates performance in terms of the organization's key performance drivers	Current						
	Future						
Determines the range, type, and scope of information needed	Current						
	Future						
Applies the most appropriate tools and strategies to gather needed information	Current						
	Future						
Develops sources of ongoing information	Current						
	Future						
Thoroughly diagnoses needs to identify their true nature	Current						
	Future						
Prioritizes the most critical causes as a basis for proceeding	Current						
	Future						
Explores the scope of possible solutions	Current						
	Future						
Approaches option assessment creatively	Current						
	Future						
Surveys the impact of all alternatives for selecting and prioritizing the best option	Current						
	Future						
Commits to action	Current						
	Future						
Identifies critical business metrics	Current						
	Future						

	Current / Future						
Builds the value justifications required to commit resources	Current						
	Future						
Clearly identifies the business or financial benefits to be realized by investments	Current						
	Future						
Advocates change and its benefits	Current						
	Future						
Manages change effectively	Current						
	Future						
Approaches work with a proactive attitude	Current						
	Future						
Secures appropriate commitment	Current						
	Future						
Appropriately communicates agreements	Current						
	Future						
Documents agreements	Current						
	Future						
Actively monitors situations for potential problems	Current						
	Future						
Monitors implementation or deployment to ensure success	Current						
	Future						
Acts as a focal point of escalation to expedite problem resolution	Current						
	Future						

(continued on the next page)

Table B3-1. Summary of Results, Foundational Competencies (continued)

Foundational Competencies		Direct Reports	Self	Peers	Supervisor	Totals	Average
Organizes and manages work systematically	Current						
	Future						
Organizes and manages resources effectively	Current						
	Future						
Adaptively applies methods as needed to achieve goals	Current						
	Future						
Leverages success through active promotion	Current						
	Future						
Documents and communicates best practices	Current						
	Future						
Ensures that criteria for decision making are shared and addressed	Current						
	Future						
Adapts and tailors messages as required	Current						
	Future						
Confirms validity of the proposed solution	Current						
	Future						
Incorporates business and industry acumen into work	Current						
	Future						
Exhibits business-oriented perspective in assessing needs	Current						
	Future						
Incorporates legal and contractual requirements into work	Current						
	Future						

Incorporates financial understanding into work	Current					
	Future					
Approaches challenges creatively	Current					
	Future					
Crosses disciplines to frame or address challenges	Current					
	Future					
Demonstrates respect for others	Current					
	Future					
Acclimates to diverse work settings	Current					
	Future					
Harnesses diversity to create workplace synergies	Current					
	Future					
Demonstrates personal integrity	Current					
	Future					
Incorporates quality considerations into decision making	Current					
	Future					
Provides proactive knowledge transfer	Current					
	Future					
Ensures that communication tools and processes advance information storage and transfer	Current					
	Future					
Maintains understanding of technical innovations	Current					
	Future					

(continued on the next page)

Table B3-1. Summary of Results, Foundational Competencies (continued)

Foundational Competencies		Direct Reports	Self	Peers	Supervisor	Totals	Average
Uses information technology to align and expedite work	Current						
	Future						
Improves personal productivity technology	Current						
	Future						
Takes personal responsibility for development	Current						
	Future						
Demonstrates agility in addressing development need	Current						
	Future						
Leverages information to change behavior	Current						
	Future						
Develops plans that clearly actualize strategy	Current						
	Future						
Builds commitment to plan	Current						
	Future						
Executes to plan, yet adapts to emergent circumstances	Current						
	Future						
Delivers to plan	Current						
	Future						
Incorporates a strategic perspective in activity planning	Current						
	Future						
Practices time management	Current						
	Future						

Aligns and relates work to sales success	Current						
	Future						
Incorporates selling sensibilities into work execution	Current						
	Future						
Demonstrates a systemic understanding of sales	Current						
	Future						
Ensures that work helps to advance sales	Current						
	Future						

Table B3-2. Summary of Results, Area of Expertise: Creating and Closing Opportunities

Creating and Closing Opportunities		Direct Reports	Self	Peers	Supervisor	Totals	Average
Researches and targets prospects	Current						
	Future						
Conducts interest building calls (cold calls) when applicable	Current						
	Future						
Identifies, follows up on, and manages sales leads	Current						
	Future						
Gains interest	Current						
	Future						
Qualifies opportunities	Current						
	Future						
Develops winning proposals	Current						
	Future						
Builds business justification cases	Current						
	Future						
Orchestrates support for negotiations	Current						
	Future						
Maintains opportunity momentum to expand sales	Current						
	Future						

Table B3-3. Summary of Results, Area of Expertise: Protecting Accounts

Protecting Accounts		Direct Reports	Self	Peers	Supervisor	Totals	Average
Gathers and monitors account intelligence	Current						
	Future						
Documents account plans and sales forecasts	Current						
	Future						
Builds client executive business relationships	Current						
	Future						
Cultivates and develops trusted advisor status	Current						
	Future						
Protects and expands accounts	Current						
	Future						
Manages deployment readiness and resource alignment	Current						
	Future						

Table B3-4. Summary of Results, Area of Expertise: Defining and Positioning Solutions

Defining and Positioning Solutions		Direct Reports	Self	Peers	Supervisor	Totals	Average
Performs technical qualifications	Current						
	Future						
Designs solutions	Current						
	Future						
Customizes standard products or services	Current						
	Future						
Conducts technical demonstrations and benchmarks	Current						
	Future						
Contributes to solution sizing and modification	Current						
	Future						
Articulates solution designs	Current						
	Future						

Table B3-5. Summary of Results, Area of Expertise: Supporting Indirect Selling

Supporting Indirect Selling		Direct Reports	Self	Peers	Supervisor	Totals	Average
Assesses and helps develop partner's sales force	Current						
	Future						
Drives partner sales planning or forecasting	Current						
	Future						
Motivates and educates partners	Current						
	Future						
Cultivates partner business relationships	Current						
	Future						
Facilitates inventory balancing or clearance	Current						
	Future						
Tracks investments in partner selling to determine business impact	Current						
	Future						
Facilitates partner transformation	Current						
	Future						
Monitors and manages contract fulfillment	Current						
	Future						
Troubleshoots partner sales crediting	Current						
	Future						
Collaborates on team selling and positioning	Current						
	Future						

Table B3-6. Summary of Results, Area of Expertise: Setting Sales Strategy

Setting Sales Strategy		Direct Reports	Self	Peers	Supervisor	Totals	Average
Identifies and articulates innovative sales practices	Current						
	Future						
Creates strategic plans that guide organizational, technical, process, or practice planning and implementation	Current						
	Future						
Builds business and partner alliances to increase sales	Current						
	Future						
Provides leadership to accelerate strategy diffusion	Current						
	Future						
Configures and aligns sales territories for maximum effectiveness	Current						
	Future						

Table B3-7. Summary of Results, Area of Expertise: Managing within the Sales Ecosystem

Managing within the Sales Ecosystem		Direct Reports	Self	Peers	Supervisor	Totals	Average
Aligns tactical activities to support strategic sales plans	Current						
	Future						
Establishes, monitors, and controls costs that affect sales margins	Current						
	Future						
Aligns resources with opportunities	Current						
	Future						
Screens administrative demands and troubleshoots back-office operations to minimize sale disruptions	Current						
	Future						
Ensures accurate forecasting while monitoring performance to metrics	Current						
	Future						
Hires, promotes, and terminates to improve sales performance and address capability gaps	Current						
	Future						
Aligns reward and recognition strategies to performance goals	Current						
	Future						

Table B3-8. Summary of Results, Area of Expertise: Developing Sales Force Capability

Developing Sales Force Capability		Direct Reports	Self	Peers	Supervisor	Totals	Average
Determines competencies required to achieve sales strategy	Current						
	Future						
Conducts sales-related needs assessments	Current						
	Future						
Designs and develops sales development programs, curricula, or learning solutions	Current						
	Future						
Uses learning management systems	Current						
	Future						
Ties learning strategy to organizational capacity	Current						
	Future						
Evaluates learning program or solution effectiveness	Current						
	Future						
Reports results to organizational stakeholders	Current						
	Future						

Table B3-9. Summary of Results, Area of Expertise: Delivering Sales Training

Delivering Sales Training		Direct Reports	Self	Peers	Supervisor	Totals	Average
Reviews and supplements learning	Current						
	Future						
Motivates participants	Current						
	Future						
Manages instructional delivery	Current						
	Future						
Administers tests	Current						
	Future						

Table B3-10. Summary of Results, Area of Expertise: Coaching for Sales Results

Coaching for Sales Results		Direct Reports	Self	Peers	Supervisor	Totals	Average
Observes salesperson behavior to identify strengths, weaknesses, and opportunities for improvement	Current						
	Future						
Balances corrective with positive feedback to ensure optimum guidance and performance improvement	Current						
	Future						
Leverages motivation as a key enabler of sales performance	Current						
	Future						
Links expected behaviors to strategic outcomes	Current						
	Future						
Demonstrates and mentors expected sales behaviors	Current						
	Future						
Establishes support programs to expand and enrich new learning	Current						
	Future						

Table B3-11. Summary of Results, Area of Expertise: Building Sales Infrastructure

Building Sales Infrastructure		Direct Reports	Self	Peers	Supervisor	Totals	Average
Monitors current business processes and sales productivity tools for adequacy	Current						
	Future						
Develops and drives strategic infrastructure planning	Current						
	Future						
Manages infrastructure upkeep or revision	Current						
	Future						
Drives or supports infrastructure change and alignment	Current						
	Future						
Pilots and evaluates infrastructure programs	Current						
	Future						

Table B3-12. Summary of Results, Area of Expertise: Designing Compensation

Designing Compensation		Direct Reports	Self	Peers	Supervisor	Totals	Average
Assesses current compensation against best practices and innovative sales compensation options	Current						
	Future						
Aligns compensation with business requirements and appropriate sales behavior and metrics	Current						
	Future						
Develops and enlists support for sales compensation models and plans	Current						
	Future						
Drives sales compensation acceptance	Current						
	Future						

Table B3-13. Summary of Results, Area of Expertise: Maintaining Accounts

Maintaining Accounts		Direct Reports	Self	Peers	Supervisor	Totals	Average
Prepares standard and ad hoc reports on account status	Current						
	Future						
Provides agile task substitution assistance to facilitate sales	Current						
	Future						
Crafts contracts and statements of work	Current						
	Future						
Troubleshoots customer operational issues	Current						
	Future						
Tracks and administers contracts	Current						
	Future						

Table B3-14. Summary of Results, Area of Expertise: Recruiting Sales Talent

Recruiting Sales Talent		Direct Reports	Self	Peers	Supervisor	Totals	Average
Aligns and modifies sales job profiles	Current						
	Future						
Ensures valid compensation package	Current						
	Future						
Monitors and maintains sales candidate pipeline	Current						
	Future						
Sources sales candidates	Current						
	Future						
Solicits, screens, and profiles candidates and determines person-job fit	Current						
	Future						
Facilitates sales peer team interviews and candidate testing	Current						
	Future						
Generates offers and conducts negotiations with sales stakeholders to closure	Current						
	Future						
Supports on-boarding	Current						
	Future						

Worksheet B3. Summary of Results

Section B: Interpreting the Scores

Based on your own competency assessment, the competency assessments performed by others familiar with your work, and an examination of the previous summary, interpret your scores and their meaning for your career, by following these cues.

Answer each of the following questions. There are no "right" or "wrong" answers. Add paper as needed.

1. What are your key strengths, as identified in the competency assessments?

2. What are your key developmental areas, as identified in the competency assessments?

3. What additional feedback would you like to seek from others?

4. Consider your responses to questions 1–3 and then create a list of objectives that would move you toward greater expertise in important competency areas. Use more paper as needed:

Objective 1: _____

Objective 2: _____

Objective 3: _____

Objective 4: _____

Worksheet B4. Development Planning Tool

There are many ways to build new competencies, and many resources are available to help in that process.

The following is a brief review of potential resources:

- Talk to other sales professionals, especially those you perceive as being especially successful.
- Develop a relationship with a professional coach.
- Observe and imitate role models.
- Participate in informal learning groups or communities of practice.
- Attend college courses.
- Pursue training online.
- Search the Internet for topics related to professional selling.
- Attend continuing-education seminars and conferences.
- Participate in professional associations.
- Use networks (online or interpersonal).
- Read periodicals, journals, and newsletters.
- Read books.
- Watch videotapes or DVDs.
- Listen to audiocassettes, CDs, and podcasts.
- Use software or multimedia-based learning methods.
- Request new project assignments or positions that include the targeted competency.

Use the development planning tool in table B4-1 to generate ideas on how to develop the competencies that are necessary for success in the sales profession.

Follow these steps:

1. List a competency that you need to develop and consider how to use the suggestions listed in the left column.
2. Make notes in the right column about ways to implement the suggestions to build proficiency.
3. Remember there are no "right" or "wrong" answers.
4. Make additional copies of table B4-1 or use more paper if needed. Figure B4-1 presents an examples of a completed development planning tool.

Figure B4-1. Example of a Completed Development Planning Tool

Competency: Motivates Participants

Ways to build the competency	Ideas on how to implement suggestions
• Talk to other people	• Get with Bob to see how he does it
• Get coaching from someone	• Have Jennifer ride along with me on a sales call with a salesperson I am coaching
• Observe and imitate role models	• Watch Tim as he motivates the team at the next all-staff meeting.
• Participate in formal or informal learning groups	• Attend a webinar on sales coaching at www.SalesTrainingDrivers.org
• Use networks (online or interpersonal)	• Solicit help from social networking sites regarding motivating sales team members
• Read books	• Read a book on motivating or coaching the sales team

Table B4-1. Development Planning Tool

Competency: _____

Ways to build the competency	Ideas on how to implement suggestions
• Talk to other people	• • •
• Get coaching from someone	• • •
• Observe and imitate role models	• • •
• Participate in formal or informal learning groups	• • •
• Attend college courses	• • •
• Participate in online courses	• • •
• Search the Internet on topics that are related to learning technologies	• • •

Ways to build the competency	Ideas on how to implement suggestions
• Attend nondegree continuing-education seminars	• • •
• Participate in professional associations	• • •
• Use networks (online or interpersonal)	• • •
• Read periodicals, journals, or newsletters	• • •
• Read books	• • •
• Watch videotapes or DVDs	• • •
• Listen to audiocassettes, CDs, or podcasts	• • •
• Use software or multimedia-based learning methods	• • •
• Attend conferences	• • •
• Request new project assignments or positions that include the targeted competency	• • •

Worksheet B5. Learning Contract

The idea behind a learning contract is to formalize your objectives into a plan of action. This can be a valuable tool for gaining the support of your supervisor, your co-workers, and your organization. It also will help you to track your progress toward your goals. To complete this learning contract, follow these steps:

1. In table B5-1, fill in your first objective (transfer your objectives from worksheet B3, section B, question 4) for bridging the gaps between your current competencies and the competencies that you need for future success. You will need a separate copy of table B5-1 for each objective.
2. Fill in every activity that you believe will be needed to accomplish this objective.
3. Estimate the amount of time each activity will take, the projected completion date, what the deliverable will be (output), what evaluation criteria will be used, who will evaluate it, what resources will be needed, and what obstacles you may encounter.
4. When you have completed one copy of table B5-1 for each objective, make an appointment to discuss them with your supervisor.
5. Negotiate the terms of the learning contract with your supervisor, update the document, and get all parties involved to sign and date the document. Figure B5-1 shows an example of a completed learning contract.

Figure B5-1. Example of a Completed Learning Contract

Activities	Date/Number	Deliverable	Evaluation	Evaluator	Resources	Obstacles
Attended online sales training session on prospecting	11/12	Filled out ideal client profile worksheet	Showed filled out ideal client profile worksheet to co-worker and supervisor	John	Product catalog, pricing worksheets, scripted call sheet	Continued use
Product training on XYZ product	12/15	Filled out satisfaction survey at end of session	Level of satisfaction with content	Marketing department	New product brochures, new feature sheets, value proposition changes	Ability to articulate the benefits and value to customers

Table B5-1. Learning Contract

Objective: _____

Activities	Date/Number	Deliverable	Evaluation	Evaluator	Resources	Obstacles

Employee's Signature: _____ Date:_____

Supervisor's Signature: _____ Date:_____

Worksheet B6. Sales Team Analysis Tool

Leveraging this sales team analysis tool, sales trainers, sales managers, and sales executives will improve efficiency and manage sales team development processes more effectively within a strategic context.

This sales development analysis tool offers a structured way to identify, prioritize, and implement sales training solutions. Because the tool takes a systems approach, it can help sales teams align with the buying organization, focus on ratcheting up performance, and address immediate problems while keeping an eye on the longer term. With the help of the tool, sales trainers, sales managers, and sales executives can approach each sales training action with ready information about the selling organization, the buying organization, and the relationship between them.

The model presented in figure B6-1 is a recurring cycle. The model's five phases are

1. Identify: determine desired outcome(s) required to achieve the overall sales strategy.
2. Examine: determine gaps in achieving the desired outcomes.
3. Enable: develop specific recommendations and solutions for success.
4. Execute: create a comprehensive plan and get buy-in from stakeholders.
5. Evaluate: collect feedback and measure against the expected outcomes.

Figure B6-1. The ASTD Sales Analysis Tool

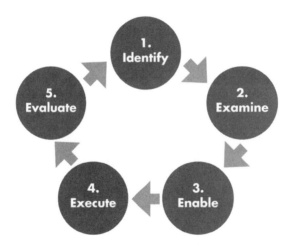

As your organization begins to think about sales development needs within a phased, cyclical process, you will be better equipped to adopt a holistic approach to sales force recruiting, retention, and engagement that includes talent management and leadership development—building a path toward improved sales team performance.

Table B6-1 shows an example of the tool in use. It can help your organization understand the alignment of areas of expertise in relation to long-term sales goals. By answering the questions outlined under each step of the sales development analysis tool, you can begin to see how each phase builds upon the one before and how specific skills and knowledge are developed. It will help you set the stage within your organization to effect the paradigm shift from "sales training" to "sales development and performance" and will guide your efforts to make the business case for this shift as well as tie it to desired business outcomes. By adopting this approach, you can ensure that your sales organization is knowledgeable, engaged, and equipped to work with even the most demanding buyers to ensure your company's future growth and profitability.

Table B6-1. The ASTD Sales Analysis Tool in Action

Step 1. Identify Determine outcome(s) required to achieve the overall sales strategy or identify competencies	Step 2. Examine Determine gaps in achieving the desired outcome(s)	Step 3. Enable Develop specific recommendations and solutions for success	Step 4. Execute Execute a comprehensive plan and get buy-in from key stakeholders	Step 5. Evaluate Collect feedback and measure against the expected outcome(s)
Based on the alignment with your strategic customer's needs, what sales competencies (knowledge, skills, and attitudes) are needed in the organization?	How many of your entire sales group (catalysts, developers, and enablers) will be exiting the organization in the next one to two years? How much of the current levels of selling knowledge, skill, and ability will leave?	Decide upon an enabling strategy. Will your organization a) hire for an already developed competency, b) develop competency internally, c) manage the gaps through outsourcing, or d) blend all three approaches?	Create a sales-wide learning plan to address competency gaps; manage resource deployment; and measure outcomes for sales catalysts, developers, and enablers.	Measure sales team member progress on the learning plans against individual and organizational goals. Measure progress before and after learning takes place, including the impact on
With your organization's sales strategies and business functions in mind, what sales competencies are needed now and into the future?	Identify the current gap between existing content areas tailored to the sales learning gap and missing content areas. Are there unique sales learning needs by role, function, industry, or geography?	Set baseline measures by documenting every sale team member's current competencies (including catalysts, developers, and enablers) via assessments.	Select appropriate delivery modes for learning opportunities: instructor-led classroom, online instruction, guided on-the-job experience, informal learning, or a combination of methods.	• leading inputs (i.e., length of sales cycle, closing rate, etc.) • lagging outputs (i.e., sales results by channel, product, team, etc.) • behavior change (i.e., observable increases or decreases in targeted areas)
Assess the current competencies (knowledge, skills, and attitudes) of the sales team (from entry-level workers to senior executives) in relation to the requirements of the future state to define what gaps exist and do not exist.	How does your organization currently define sales training content? Does it address all necessary aspects of the sales profession, such as	Identify targets for closing the gap between current competency sets and those needed to support the future goals of the sales team as well as the overall organization.	In addition to guided learning methods (see above), include other opportunities to drive self-directed learning, such as • job rotation • tuition reimbursement • personal development reimbursement • professional association memberships.	• knowledge transfer (i.e., measured retention of knowledge pre-, post-, and 90 days later) • customer satisfaction.
Determine the priority of sales competencies needed—what are the most critical and necessary for sales team members to possess to be successful now?	• "catalyst competencies" (e.g., those competencies critical to quota-carrying team members) • "development competencies" (e.g., those competencies directly responsible for developing sales capability in your sales force)	Did you address how quickly you need to develop competencies, the availability of required resources and time, and how you will measure the effectiveness of the development initiative?	Create a development map for every sales team member (catalysts, developers, and enablers). Ensure it is meaningful to sales team leaders by mapping competencies to job function within the sales team, area of expertise, or job role. Is the map robust enough to be used for both individual development as well as an indicator of organization development?	Report results to all stakeholders in the organization. Test for senior leadership's awareness of any progress in building needed sales competency and challenge the continuation of noncontributing "learning" activities.
Define the sales team's "future state" in relation to the sales learning mix identified—these are the competencies each sales team member must have (in the next one to three years, for example) to meet business goals.	• "enablement competencies" (e.g., those competencies directly responsible for ensuring that customer relationships are both successful and profitable).	Set goals for internal communication and change management plans that will accompany the comprehensive action plan to address the entire sales team's competency gap.		Create or improve processes and methods for identifying potential high performers, recruiting new players, and retaining players with the key competency sets that the sales team and organization needs.
	Consider these questions: • Are the gaps more pronounced in specific employee groups? • Are the gaps geographically-based?	Develop a separate communication and change management strategy for sales managers. Include sales managers in every step of the strategy.		

235

Sales Team Competency and Organizational Capacity

Maximizing your organization's capacity to perform, while optimizing the competencies of the people on the sales team, will help your organization achieve sales results now and into the future. Table B6-1 focused on helping you move to a holistic, competency-based approach to sales training and development. Table B6-2 helps you bring your organization into alignment with those efforts. As you read each question, think about what conversations you need to have with key members of your organization. Begin to build a plan that increases the efficiency and effectiveness of the organization's capacity to support and align to the sales team members as they become more competent.

Table B6-2. Aligning Your Organization with a Competency-Based Approach to Sales Training and Development

Diagnostic Question	Thoughts, Ideas, Actions
What are the exact steps in your company's sales process? Can you (and your sales team members) as well as other customer-facing professionals repeat it from memory?	
How well do your company's sales process, compensation plan, and marketing messages align with the buyer's unique purchasing processes?	
How does your sales organization measure sales team productivity? Do you know how to use these measures to help roll out effective training solutions?	
What challenges are sales team members facing on a regular basis? How are key organizational linkages addressing these challenges?	
What is the number one complaint of your customers and your sales-team members?	
How does your sales training content help attain your organization's key strategies, goals, and objectives?	
Which training content helps sales team members? Which content doesn't help them? Which content requires the most attention to keep customers satisfied and engaged?	
How are your senior leaders measured? What is the relationship between their goals and the sales team's goals?	
What is your company's position in the market? In relation to that position, how adequate is each component of the sales training mix (product knowledge, selling skills, industry knowledge, and knowledge of your company)?	
How does your training program help sales team members differentiate themselves from your company's top competitors?	
How well does communication flow from your sales team to other important value-creating team members? How well does the communication flow help sales team members transfer relevant knowledge and co-create customized solutions?	
How well does your sales culture support training solutions that you believe to be important and relevant?	

Worksheet B7. Sales Training Diagnostic

There are literally dozens of knowledge areas, skills, and abilities (KSAs) that have a significant impact on sales team performance. Because today's selling environment is tough, your ability to equip and prepare sales team members is more critical than ever. To that end, everyone who has input into the design or delivery of sales training needs to know what salespeople must learn. They must understand the sales process and the attendant KSAs that are needed by each salesperson to improve his or her performance. Some examples of topics to include in sales training are

- ▲ asking effective or productive questions of customers
- ▲ becoming better listeners
- ▲ selling with the customer's best interest in mind
- ▲ making ethical decisions
- ▲ leveraging sales approaches that can be adapted from one situation to the next.

The seven-step sales process presented in figure B7-1 can serve as the foundation for your training program strategy. It is provided as an example of selling systems that have proven to be successful with many types of product or service selling systems. The seven-step sales process follows the chronological steps that occur as a seller interacts with a buyer and is purposely focused on the selling side of that interaction.

Figure B7-1. The Seven-Step Sales Process

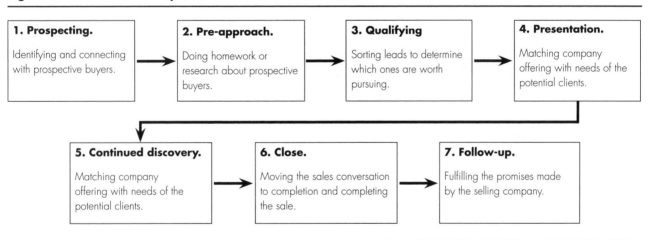

To achieve sales training excellence, sales trainers can design training solutions after you identify the elements of current training programs that work well and those that need work by focusing on those areas with the most room for improvement. You can use the seven-step sales process or your company's own sales process.

The rest of this worksheet illustrates how to use the seven steps of the sales process to provide information critical to designing and developing training for each step.

Directions

Rate your organization's content using the sales training rating tool in table B7-1. Using the scale provided, rate whether your sales training adequately covers the necessary content to deliver sales results in column 2. In column 3, rate the design and delivery effectiveness of your sales training. Then add up your ratings for coverage and for design and delivery. When completing the table, think about the impact of each of the content areas on the sales team. Is that content (and its delivery method) adequate to meet the needs of your buyers?

When you have completed rating your content using table B7-1, use table B7-2 to interpret your results.

Table B7-1. Sales Training Rating Tool

Scale:

Unacceptable	Weak	Acceptable	Very good	Excellent
1	2	3	4	5

Step 1. Prospecting		
Rate your sales training content related to...	The coverage is...	The design and delivery are...
Utilizing sales collateral resources		
Cold-calling sales techniques		
Customer-related vertical market or industry information resources		
Business-alliance building skills (client, third party, etc.)		
Business workshop facilitation and management skills		
Competitive information resources		
Technical trust-building and selling techniques		
Leveraging marketing programs to advance sales		
Translating competitive knowledge into relevant sales practices		
Step 2. Pre-approach		
Rate your sales training content related to...	The coverage is...	The design and delivery are...
Formal and ad hoc research strategies (systematic exploration, personal networking, website scanning)		
Resources (technical, pricing, legal, delivery, and fulfillment)		
Industry research engines and resources (Dun and Bradstreet, analyst reports)		
Customer-organization communications (websites, annual reports, press releases, position and white papers)		
Business health indicators such as ratios		
Solution configuration frameworks or templates		
Business environment for technical solutions		
Vertical industry solutions		
Interpreting and synthesizing information from multiple sources		
Implementing environmental scanning to ensure well-targeted sales messages		
Applying relevant account planning tools, templates, and procedures		
Applying funnel management practices, tools, metrics, and policies effectively to prioritize and manage selling		
Managing technical teams and integrating their contributions		

Step 3. Qualifying		
Rate your sales training content related to...	The coverage is...	The design and delivery are...
Lead management procedures		
Cost estimation and sizing techniques		
Sales cycle management skills		
Opportunity qualification skills		
Customer business and operations (reporting structures, decision makers)		
Business analysis methods		
Funnel management practices, tools, metrics, and policies		
Resource management strategies		
Requirements analysis and management techniques		
Solution sizing criteria		
Leveraging vertical market and industry knowledge in product or service positioning		
Leading business analysis discussions		
Determining how customer organizations are organized and how they make purchasing decisions		
Summarizing salient content from customer communication sources		
Determining business health and viability using key business ratios		
Accurately mapping customer's product or service operating environment		
Step 4. Presentation		
Rate your sales training content related to...	The coverage is...	The design and delivery are...
Personal engagement and interest-generation strategies		
Business-analysis metrics and procedures (health ratios, balance sheet analysis)		
Supply chain knowledge (lead times, response rates, fulfillment processes)		
Product or service or solution technology (concepts, uses)		
Solution technical foundations		
Solution design procedures and communication conventions (written or graphic)		
Solution design methodologies, best practices, and trends		
Oral and written communication skills (sufficient for ensuring that technical concepts are meaningful to nontechnical audiences)		
Customer-facing skills		
Technical team leadership		
Creating compelling sales presentations		
Communicating product or service benefits and features in a compelling manner		
Communicating features and benefits of solution-related tools or packages		
Effectively communicating technical solutions		

(continued on the next page)

Table B7-1. Sales Training Rating Tool (continued)

Step 5. Continued discovery		
Rate your sales training content related to...	The coverage is...	The design and delivery are...
Sales negotiation and closing methods		
Return-on-investment and total cost of ownership techniques		
Objection-handling techniques		
Accurately estimating costs and sizing appropriate solutions		
Calculating business metrics and translating product or service features into value propositions		
Countering competitor product or service feature-and-benefit messages		
Translating solution designs into meaningful customer benefits, differentiating them by stakeholder needs		
Step 6. Close		
Rate your sales training content related to...	The coverage is...	The design and delivery are...
Proposal development, component integration, and management practices		
Formal sales negotiation and closing methods or strategies		
Transition-to-farming practices		
Deployment practices and back-office-administrative or order-entry procedures		
Solution deployment or delivery practices (expectation setting, quality checking)		
Determining buyer readiness from verbal and nonverbal cues		
Managing multiple or interrelated sales calls		
Managing leads and ensuring follow-up or follow-through		
Aligning sales activities with their respective points in the sales process		
Coordinating and aligning all account activities with the plan		
Setting accurate customer expectations for order fulfillment		
Ensuring cost-effective solution deployment and delivery practices		
Step 7. Follow-up		
Rate your sales training content related to...	The coverage is...	The design and delivery are...
Account history (prior investments, account relationships)		
Account-farming procedures or practices (check-ins, sponsoring market initiatives)		
Account-planning tools, templates, and procedures		
Account-related marketing plans		
Contract administration and renewal processes		

Step 7. Follow-up		
Rate your sales training content related to...	The coverage is...	The design and delivery are...
Standard contractual and service level agreement (SLA) terms, conditions, and milestone metrics		
Managing total customer satisfaction to optimize relationships		
Leveraging contract administration and renewal into up- or cross-selling opportunities		
Monitoring or managing contractual and service level agreement terms, conditions, and milestone metrics		
Developing trusted advisor status with customers based on technical acumen		
Total		

Table B7-2. Interpreting the Results of the Sales Training Rating Tool

Total	Recommendations for coverage	Recommendations for design and delivery
81–165: "Needs Work"	• Begin with interviewing your sales leadership team • Focus on the customer and determine the most appropriate content for your sales team	• Start with looking at how much time your sales team spends in front of customers, on the road, or in the office. The way you delivery the content should support their work habits and still get the content across.
166–245: "Acceptable"	• Your content is sufficient to meet the needs of your sales team	• Your delivery methodology is adequate but not optimal.
246–325: "Doing Great"	• Your content is contributing to your competitive advantage	• Your delivery method synchronizes with how salespeople learn within the constraints they have.
326–405: "Best Practice"	• Your content is helping the organization drive results	• Your delivery is helping your organization drive results.

Appendix C

A History of the ASTD Competency Models

ASTD has sponsored six studies of practitioner roles and competencies. These studies all attempted to identify what roles should be fulfilled and what competencies successful practitioners should demonstrate.

By looking back on these six models, workplace learning and performance (WLP) practitioners can see how the field has gradually moved away from a single area of focus (that is, training) to an emphasis on learning as a means to an end: improving individual and organizational performance. These studies have built a framework for thinking about the WLP field and have driven professional development and education curricula to prepare people to move into the profession or advance in it.

Each study reflects a major shift in thinking about the competencies essential for professionals' success. And each study is regarded as an evolutionary—and sometimes revolutionary—shift in defining the field and establishing expectations for practitioners and stakeholders. A brief description of each study follows.

2004: Mapping the Future: New Workplace Learning and Performance Competencies

Bernthal, et al. (2004) unveiled a new competency model that was designed to take WLP into the 21st century. The publication defines the profession in the context of its strategic contribution to organizational performance. The model was created with the participation of more than 2,000 ASTD members and other WLP practitioners who helped define the current and future state of the profession and identified the key trends that were shaping it.

Structured as a pyramid, the model includes three layers of knowledge and skill areas: competencies, areas of professional expertise, and roles. These three layers correlate to important drivers of the profession: foundation, focus, and successful execution. Inputs to model creation included a literature review, expert interviews, and special conference sessions. It was later validated through a survey that asked respondents to rate its features in terms of importance for effectiveness in their current jobs.

1999: ASTD Models for Workplace Learning and Performance

ASTD Models for Workplace Learning and Performance was driven by the desire to determine what competencies practitioners, senior practitioners, and line managers needed for success in the WLP field then and in the next five years. As in earlier ASTD studies, this report defines roles as "a grouping of competencies targeted to meet specific expectations of a job or function" and identified seven major WLP roles (Rothwell, Sanders, and Soper, 1999, p. xv).

The study used a three-fold methodology that compared the perceptions of a cross-cultural mix of practitioners, senior practitioners, and line managers to identify 52 competencies, understood in ASTD's tradition to mean "an area of knowledge or skill that is critical for producing key outputs . . . international capabilities that people bring to their jobs" (McLagan, 1989, p. 77). These competencies are classified into six groupings: analytical, technical, leadership, business, interpersonal, and technological.

1998: *ASTD Models for Learning Technologies*

This report examines the roles, competencies, and work outputs that human resource development (HRD) professionals need to implement learning technologies within their organizations (Piskurich and Sanders, 1998). (HRD is further defined in the 1989 study.) It also provides a classification system that relates instructional methods (for example, lectures, role plays, and simulations) to presentation methods (for example, computer-based training, electronic performance support systems, multimedia, and video) and distribution methods (for example, audiotape, CD-ROM, Internet, and videotape). Although this work enhances professionals' understanding of the issues surrounding learning technologies, it does not intend to describe the larger field within which training resides.

1996: *ASTD Models for Human Performance Improvement*

This report explores the roles, competencies, and outputs that human performance improvement professionals (performance consultants) need to effect meaningful changes within organizations (Rothwell, 1996). The report emphasizes that human performance improvement (HPI) is a process, not a discipline. A host of disciplines within WLP (for example, human resource development, human resources, performance consulting, ergonomic design, and line management) carry out the HPI process.

A key point of this study is that everyone in organizational settings plays an important part in improving performance and contributes to enhanced organizational competitiveness. Practitioners, line managers, employees, and others may perform HPI work; HRD professionals are not its sole practitioners. A second key point is that no one individual can play all the roles and master all the competencies described. Instead, the report supplies a menu of options for doing HPI work.

1989: *Models for HRD Practice*

This study was groundbreaking because it expanded the profession beyond training and development to include career development and organization development (McLagan, 1989). Naming the field human resource development (HRD), the report defines HRD as "the integrated use of training and development, organization development, and career development to improve individual, group, and organizational effectiveness," and positions HRD within the larger human resource field. It was an expansion of the 1983 study, which focused on training and development alone.

1983: *Models for Excellence*

In 1981, Patricia McLagan carried out a series of studies focused on training and development and the trainer's role that led to the publication of *Models for Excellence* in 1983 (McLagan and McCullough, 1983). This study represented the first modern attempt to define training and development. It also established the format for all later competency model studies. The report included a definition of training and development, a list of 34 future forces expected to affect the field, and 31 foundational competencies.

1978: A Study of Professional Training and Development Roles and Competencies

This study was the first published effort sponsored by ASTD (Pinto and Walker, 1978). The goal of the study was to investigate what training and development professionals really do and to "define the basic skills, knowledge, understanding, and other attributes required for professionals for effective performance of training and development activities."

To that end, six panels of ASTD chapter members and the Professional Development Committee of ASTD reviewed the study questionnaire. The final study questionnaires, containing 92 multiple-choice items, were mailed to more than 14,000 ASTD members worldwide. A total of 2,790 usable questionnaires were returned, for a response rate of nearly 20 percent.

The ensuing report revealed the following major areas for training and development practitioners:

- ▲ Analyzing and diagnosing needs
- ▲ Determining appropriate training approaches
- ▲ Designing and developing programs
- ▲ Developing material resources
- ▲ Managing internal resources
- ▲ Managing external resources
- ▲ Developing and counseling individuals
- ▲ Preparing job- or performance-related training
- ▲ Conducting classroom training
- ▲ Developing group and organization
- ▲ Conducting research on training
- ▲ Managing working relationships with managers and clients
- ▲ Managing the training and development function
- ▲ Managing professional self-development.

What's Next

All ASTD competency studies, including those that informed *World-Class Selling: New Sales Competencies,* use a systematic approach to determine what it takes to be a successful practitioner in the field. The approach used in the ASTD 2008 World-Class Sales Competency Study is described in Appendix D. To obtain copies of any of the reports mentioned in this section, or to license the World-Class Sales Competency Model, contact ASTD at 703.683.8100.

Appendix D

Research Methodology

Purpose

The purpose of this research project was to develop a valid set of roles, competencies, and sales areas of expertise (AOEs) relevant for sales team members. The roles, competencies, and AOEs were intended to be comprehensive enough to address both emerging and current responsibilities. To that end, the final model was developed based on a multi-perspective and multi-method approach to avoid bias from any single information source.

Although the model is intended to be comprehensive, it must be specific enough to identify the particular skills, knowledge, and outputs necessary to achieve world-class selling excellence. The model's ultimate effectiveness is defined by how it will be used (for example, workforce planning, guiding professional development, providing personnel selection criteria, determining eligibility for leadership development programs, and assessing the impact of training).

All of the competencies in the model are important for success, but an individual might perform only one role or multiple roles, depending on his or her position, tenure in the profession, and size and maturity of the sales organization. If practitioners effectively demonstrate all the competencies in the model, they should be considered highly valuable for organizations that hope to promote sales professionalism in the workplace.

Approach

To create the ASTD World-Class Sales Competency Model, the project team followed a four-phase process: data collection, model development, validation, and refinement and confirmation. See Figure D-1 for a graphic representation of the basic development process.

Phase 1: Needs Assessment and Data Collection

The objective of this phase was to finalize project requirements and define a solid research plan that replicated the high standards and past successes of ASTD competency modeling efforts (see Appendix C for a history of these efforts). The project also leveraged a solid partnership with Productivity Dynamics, which possesses a proven methodology that follows best practices in competency modeling for numerous sales-specific roles.

The first phase consisted of three parts: expert interviews, literature review, and a review of existing competency models. One of the goals of the research was to build an international model. Every effort was made to ensure a global perspective: The literature review included international sources, the expert interviews were conducted with a worldwide sample, focus groups were conducted in multiple countries, and advisory panel members were drawn from around the world.

Figure D-1. Process Used to Create the World-Class Sales Competency Model

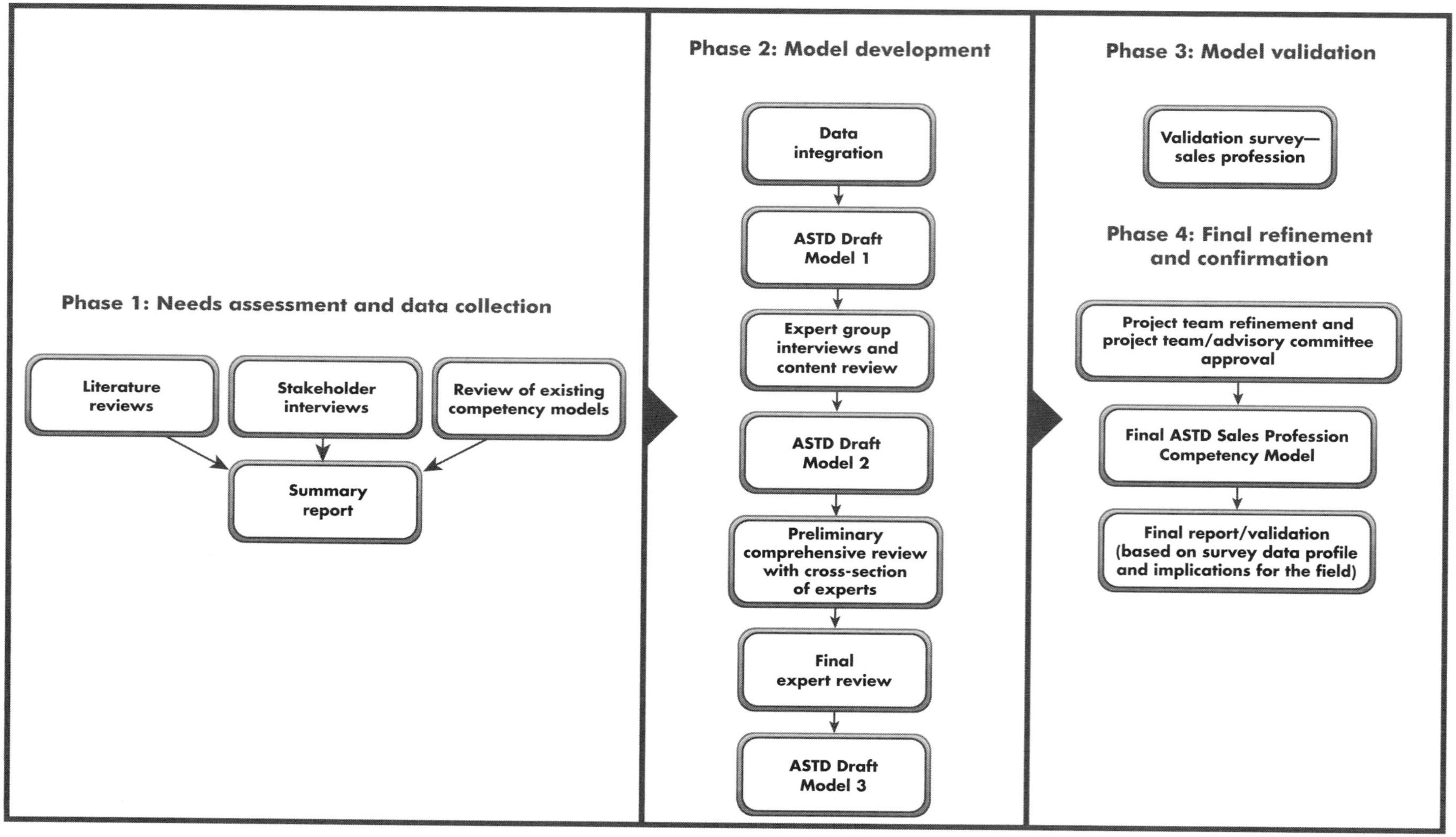

Phase 1: Needs assessment and data collection

- Literature reviews
- Stakeholder interviews
- Review of existing competency models
- Summary report

Phase 2: Model development

- Data integration
- ASTD Draft Model 1
- Expert group interviews and content review
- ASTD Draft Model 2
- Preliminary comprehensive review with cross-section of experts
- Final expert review
- ASTD Draft Model 3

Phase 3: Model validation

- Validation survey—sales profession

Phase 4: Final refinement and confirmation

- Project team refinement and project team/advisory committee approval
- Final ASTD Sales Profession Competency Model
- Final report/validation (based on survey data profile and implications for the field)

Expert Interviews

Analysts gathered information from job incumbents, executives, and thought leaders regarding current and future job competencies and role requirements. This approach focused on the strategic direction of sales jobs within the context of trends affecting the profession.

Most input was gathered from the World-Class Sales Competency Advisory Panel, a group of leading sales experts whose role was to provide wisdom and guidance to the project research team. Advisory Panel members represented

- companies engaged in business-to-business selling
- direct, indirect, and technical selling activities
- multiple industries engaged in business-to-business selling (financial services, information technology, telecommunications, pharmaceutical, public sector and education, and management consulting)
- sales team members, sales operations members, sales managers, and sales trainers or consultants.

Advisory panel members were asked the following questions:

- What are the major tasks and categories of work performed by sales profession role representatives?
- What are the outputs produced?
- What are the quality indicators for these outputs?
- What competencies are needed to complete the tasks or work?
- What are the necessary skills and knowledge domains that support the competencies?
- What trends and forces are currently shaping the sales profession?
- What forces or issues are pertinent and "front of mind" for professionals in each role category (that is, performance, ethics, globalization, and talent management)?

Literature Review

Analysts conducted a search of current international publications, studies, and websites to ensure an adequate analysis of competencies, roles, and areas of expertise. They conducted an environmental scan and literature review to determine major trends and forces shaping the sales profession as well as current best practices in sales competency modeling and worked to identify pivotal roles in the sales profession.

Review of Existing Competency Models

Analysts obtained and reviewed existing sales competency models, skills inventories, and related documents from various organizations, associations, and public sources.

At the conclusion of Phase 1, a summary report was drafted, presenting the findings. This report became the major input for phase 2, model development.

Phase 2: Model Development

The objective of this phase was to create a draft of the competency model for the sales profession that covered pivotal sales roles. This information was garnered through a series of in-depth interviews with subject matter experts—people with exemplary performance as sales professionals who represented

- top performers and managers in multiple roles within each of the role categories identified
- business-to-business sales efforts

- ▲ direct selling, indirect selling, technical selling, and sales management functions
- ▲ multiple industries (financial services, information technology, telecommunications, pharmaceutical, public sector and education, and management consulting).

Phase 2 comprised the following steps: data integration, expert group interviews and content review, creation of a Draft 2 Model, a special session at the 2008 ASTD International Conference and Exposition, final expert review, and the creation of a Draft Model 3.

Data Integration

The data integration step was conducted over a three-month period. A team of analysts focused on identifying best practices in sales competency modeling as well as existing models and relevant literature on the topic. Activities in this step included

- ▲ reviewing existing competency models and related documents to extract information related to sales exemplary performance, sales competencies, trends, and forces that shape the sales profession
- ▲ conducting interviews and facilitating meetings with advisory panel members
- ▲ defining an architecture for the sales competency model
- ▲ populating the model with existing competencies.

Simultaneously with integrating the feedback of subject matter experts on pivotal sales roles, analysts worked to define the sales competency model architecture. Their goal was to develop a straw model that was shaped by the steps in phase 1, as well as input from advisory panel members. The roles and competencies were defined as fully and as clearly as possible using sample outputs. The competencies included a brief definition and key actions.

Individual competencies in the model were specifically mapped to at least five other major competency studies. This approach ensured that the competencies identified were derived from consistent and powerful trends in findings across multiple publications and studies. In some cases, analysts reviewed existing competency models from other organizations. From these inputs, the first draft model was created.

Expert Group Interviews and Content Review

Two consultants conducted one-on-one interviews with 115 participants, each lasting between 30 and 50 minutes, covering the following set of core questions (with opportunities for follow-up questioning):

- ▲ Does the list of competencies address all of the major competencies required for people working in the sales profession? If not, what competencies should be added? Why?
- ▲ Should any of the competencies be removed, combined, or subdivided?
- ▲ Are they sufficiently discrete? What should be changed? Why?
- ▲ What specific edits do you have for competency titles, definitions, or key actions?
- ▲ Does the list of roles cover all of the major roles for the sales profession? If not, what roles should be added?
- ▲ Should any of the roles be removed, combined, or subdivided? Are they sufficiently discrete? What should be changed? Why?
- ▲ What specific edits do you have for role titles, definitions, or representative actions?
- ▲ Does the list of areas of expertise address most of the major specialty areas in the sales profession? If not, what AOE should be added? Why?

- Should any of the AOEs be removed, combined, or subdivided? Are they sufficiently discrete? What should be changed? Why?
- Please address one or two of the AOEs in which you have expertise. For each AOE you are reviewing, what specific edits do you have for titles, definitions, key knowledge areas, or key actions?
- Are the key knowledge areas comprehensive? Would you suggest any additions, deletions, or edits?
- Are the key actions comprehensive? Would you suggest any additions, deletions, or edits?
- Please list some of the common outputs a person would produce when using the knowledge and skills associated with each competency.
- What are the quality indicators for these outputs?
- What trends and forces are currently shaping the sales profession?
- What forces or issues are front-of-mind for professionals in each role category?

Draft Model 2

The objective of this step was to define a complete model. Activities included

- using qualitative data analysis techniques to analyze the results of interviews and defining a set of core competencies for the sales profession
- populating the architecture and straw model developed in the first step of phase 2 and preparing a comprehensive next iteration (Draft 2) of the model
- sharing Draft 2 of the model with stakeholders and members of the advisory panel to obtain feedback
- revising the model iteratively as feedback was received from reviewers
- finalizing Draft 2 of the model.

ASTD 2008 International Conference and Exposition Special Session

In a special session at the ASTD 2008 International Conference and Exposition in May 2008, attendees were shown the draft model and then broken into subject matter teams to discuss specific sales areas of expertise. They were asked to share their thoughts on each AOE and to identify any missing information or unclear terminology. Each AOE had an advisory panel member available to discuss methodology and content. Comments were compiled and summarized by analysts within two weeks.

Final Expert Review and Draft Model 3

The goals of this step were to validate Draft Model 2 and the data collected in the first and second phases of the project and to determine the relative importance of the competencies across the various roles. The third draft of the model was created by validating the model through 20 virtual and face-to-face focus groups in multiple countries and locations.

Analysts conducted interviews with a total of about 200 people who reviewed the existing model content. Participants were given 30 minutes to review the model for accuracy and provide suggestions for refinement in their areas of content expertise. A partial list of these experts and others who contributed to the study can be found in Appendix F.

Participants were selected to provide broad expertise in selling, sales operations, sales training and development, and sales management. They were asked open-ended questions designed to determine whether the core competencies, roles, and areas of expertise described in the model were comprehensive, accurate, and understandable. They were also asked to review the key knowledge areas and key actions associated with each competency and role, to list the common outputs and quality indicators for sales team members, and to identify the major trends and issues facing the sales profession. These inputs were used to create Draft Model 3.

Phase 3: Model Validation

The objective of this step was to use a quantitative research approach to further validate the model and determine the relative importance of the sales profession AOEs and competencies for various roles and job titles. Activities in this step included

- developing a survey to align the emerging competency model with the pivotal roles
- identifying appropriate demographics and related variables (role, industry, and tenure) to stratify, then select the sample
- implementing the survey leveraging ASTD resources
- utilizing quantitative data analysis techniques to analyze the results and capture the relative importance of the competencies and AOEs for various roles and job titles.

A survey instrument enabled the team to collect background information from participants and ask them to indicate relevance and desired proficiency level of behavioral indicators for each competency using five-point Likert scales. The results from this survey can be found in Appendix E.

Analysts administered the survey on a website using third-party software. The survey mirrored the structure of the ASTD competency model and its content. Survey items were designed to address a list of critical questions posed by the research team, such as the relative importance of the competencies and time spent performing each AOE.

All survey participants were asked to rate roles and competencies in terms of importance and frequency of use. Participants were also asked to indicate their primary area of expertise and then were prompted to rate content appropriate for their expertise. The competencies, roles, and AOEs presented in the survey were based on the refined model developed from the information gathered in phases 1 and 2. Copies of the survey are on file at ASTD.

The final sample size included 2,128 responses, representing 5.9 percent of the targeted population.

Demographics from this sample are similar to the demographics of ASTD's actual membership. The margin of error for conclusions is +/- 5 percent. This means that if the survey were to be conducted again, there is an extremely high probability that the results would be exactly the same. The margin of error for this study is in line with commonly accepted standards for survey research. Demographics of the survey respondents can be found in Appendix E.

Phase 4: Final Refinement and Confirmation

Project Team Refinement and Advisory Panel Approval

Using information collected from the survey results, analysts from Productivity Dynamics created a final model for approval by the ASTD project team and advisory committee, which was the same as the final draft model presented to survey respondents. Analysts reviewed survey responses using specialized software to determine if any content should be dropped from the final model due to invalid responses or a lack of data. No content was dropped from the final model.

Creation of the Final Model

The final draft of the model was presented to the project team and advisory committee in December 2008. No revisions were suggested. After the model was finalized, the project team began to draft the structure and content of this report.

Validation and Final Report

The objectives of this step were to finalize the competency model and to prepare and issue the final report. Activities in this step included

- ▲ developing the validation survey based on role-specific and job-specific competency priorities and cross-role and cross-job similarities
- ▲ administering the validation survey and collecting the results
- ▲ preparing this final report, which includes the methodology and results of the validation survey.

Using information collected from the survey results, ASTD created a final model for approval by the ASTD project team and advisory committee. It included slight modifications made in response to a content analysis of written comments from survey respondents. Each written comment was evaluated in terms of its relationship to the model and how frequently it was mentioned. Changes were reviewed in a group setting and approved by subject matter experts when appropriate. Usually, any revisions represented clear omissions from the model. These revisions included clarifying words for particular key actions or key knowledge areas. All of these revisions are reflected in the Competency Dictionary in Appendix A. Copies of the final revisions are on file at ASTD.

A meeting was held with the ASTD project team and advisory committee to review the final competency model structure, gather feedback, and suggest revisions. Minor revisions were made to the model graphic. After the model was finalized, the project team began to draft the structure and content of this report. The end product represents the systematic development and phased process for creating a well-constructed and validated sales profession competency model.

Appendix E

Demographics and Summary of Survey Responses

Demographics

The following tables include demographics of the 2,108 respondents to the World-Class Sales Competency Model survey.

In which region of the world are you based?

Regions	%
Asia/Pacific (including China, SE Asia, India, and Australia/New Zealand)	3.4%
Europe (including EU and Russia)	4.7%
Middle East/Africa	2.3%
Central and Latin America	1.4%
North America (including Canada and US)	88.2%

Which of the following roles best characterizes your current job (regardless of the title you currently hold)? If more than one of the following characterizes your job, please pick your primary role.

Job title	%
Selling	
Sales executive (senior level sales management and oversight of selling organization and associated resources)	12.5%
Sales manager (management of salespeople and budget, resource and personnel alignment, etc.)	9.1%
Sales representative (account manager, territory manager, account executive)	20.6%
Sales specialist (selling aligned with specific product or service or sales support)	6.7%
Pre-sales consultant (aligned with sales as a technical consultant or solution designer)	1.6%
Sales Enablement	
Operations manager (operations manager, compensation manager, recruitment manager, etc.)	2.2%
Operations executive (director or vice president of operations, compensation, etc.)	1.9%
Sales compensation planner	0.6%
Sales operations infrastructure developer	0.5%

(continued on the next page)

Which of the following roles best characterizes your current job (regardless of the title you currently hold)? If more than one of the following characterizes your job, please pick your primary role (continued).

Job title	%
Sales Enablement (continued)	
Sales operations account researcher or analyst	0.1%
Sales Recruiter	0.7%
Sales Training and Development	
Sales training manager	10.7%
Sales training executive (director, vice president)	7.1%
Sales trainer (sales instructor, facilitator, sales consultant, sales coach)	12.5%
Sales training designer and developer	4.5%
Sales researcher	3.0%
Sales professor or academic	5.8%

How many years have you been in this current role?

Years	%
Less than 1 year	7.0%
Between 1 and 3 years	19.8%
Between 3 and 5 years	21.1%
Between 6 and 10 years	18.5%
Between 11 and 15 years	10.0%
More than 15 years	23.6%

Which industry is your organization part of?

Industry	%
Construction	3.4%
Consulting	6.8%
Education	4.3%
Energy	1.3%
Financial services	10.3%
Government (nonmilitary, noneducational)	0.6%
Healthcare	6.3%
Manufacturing	11.5%
Military	0.2%
Nonprofit	0.9%
Raw material production	0.3%

(continued on the next page)

Which industry is your organization part of (continued)?

Industry	%
Real estate	3.8%
Retail	11.3%
Technology	13.3%
Training-and-development-related products and services	4.2%
Other	21.2%
Don't know	0.3%

Into which of the following ranges does your age fall into?

Age Range	%
29 or less	9.1%
30–39	25.5%
40–49	27.0%
50–59	27.3%
60 or above	11.0%

Gender

Gender	%
Male	61.9%
Female	38.1%

Are you a member of ASTD?

ASTD	%
Yes	22.4%
No	77.6%

Do you consider yourself to be part of the sales profession?

Sales Profession	%
Yes	89.4%
No	10.6%

Do you consider yourself to be part of the training and development profession?

Training Profession	%
Yes	61.2%
No	38.8%

Summary

The following tables contain the importance ratings provided by 2,108 respondents to the World-Class Sales Competency Model survey. In some cases, ratings were made using the following five-point scale:

- ▲ Essential (5)
- ▲ Very important (4)
- ▲ Moderately important (3)
- ▲ Slightly important (2)
- ▲ Unnecessary (1).

The percentage of responses is given in the first five columns and the average score is given in the last column. For importance ratings, any average score was considered to be meaningful when it equaled or exceeded 3.0.

Roles

Please rate the importance of the "hats" (roles) to your success at your current job by stating whether each role is essential, very important, moderately important, slightly important, or unnecessary to your current job.

	Essential (5)	Very important (4)	Moderately important (3)	Slightly important (2)	Unnecessary (1)	Average Rating
Administrator	21.0%	27.5%	28.8%	14.1%	8.6%	**3.38**
Analyst	19.1%	38.5%	25.7%	10.7%	5.9%	**3.54**
Consultant	34.3%	37.8%	19.2%	5.9%	2.9%	**3.95**
Developer	30.8%	36.8%	20.0%	7.8%	4.6%	**3.81**
Manager	29.2%	32.0%	18.9%	9.9%	10.1%	**3.60**
Strategist	35.6%	34.6%	20.2%	6.7%	3.1%	**3.93**

Sales Areas of Expertise (AOEs)

Please rate the importance of the following areas of expertise as they pertain to your success at your current job, as you perform it.

	Essential (5)	Very important (4)	Moderately important (3)	Slightly important (2)	Unnecessary (1)	Average Rating
Creating and Closing Opportunities	48.5%	27.2%	11.9%	5.7%	6.7%	**4.05**
Protecting Accounts	47.2%	28.2%	14.3%	4.1%	6.2%	**4.06**
Defining and Positioning Solutions	22.8%	31.8%	26.6%	9.1%	9.7%	**3.49**
Supporting Indirect Selling	20.1%	30.4%	25.5%	12.2%	11.8%	**3.35**
Setting Sales Strategy	33.4%	34.0%	17.8%	7.2%	7.6%	**3.78**

(continued on the next page)

Please rate the importance of the following areas of expertise as they pertain to your success at your current job, as you perform it (continued).

	Essential (5)	Very important (4)	Moderately important (3)	Slightly important (2)	Unnecessary (1)	Average Rating
Managing within the Sales Ecosystem	17.7%	30.9%	26.1%	11.6%	13.7%	**3.27**
Developing Sales Force Capability	32.0%	29.8%	20.7%	8.5%	9.0%	**3.67**
Delivering Sales Training	31.2%	28.0%	21.4%	9.7%	9.7%	**3.61**
Coaching for Sales Results	33.1%	30.5%	18.6%	8.7%	9.2%	**3.70**
Building Sales Infrastructure	26.7%	35.5%	21.1%	9.0%	7.7%	**3.65**
Designing Compensation	16.1%	25.9%	21.6%	14.9%	21.5%	**3.00**
Maintaining Accounts	33.7%	31.5%	18.5%	7.4%	8.8%	**3.74**
Recruiting Sales Talent	21.9%	24.5%	19.7%	13.9%	20.0%	**3.15**

Please identify the top three areas of expertise (AOEs) where you spend the most time.

Area of Expertise	%
Creating and Closing Opportunities	19.1%
Maintaining Accounts	11.9%
Protecting Accounts	11.7%

Cross-Tabulation of AOE Importance by Job Title

	Creating and Closing Opportunities	Protecting Accounts	Defining and Positioning Solutions	Supporting Indirect Selling	Setting Sales Strategy	Managing within the Sales Ecosystem	Developing Sales Force Capability	Delivering Sales Training	Coaching for Sales Results	Building Sales Infrastructure	Designing Compensation	Maintaining Accounts	Recruiting Sales Talent
Sales													
Sales Executive	23.3%	11.0%	7.4%	4.0%	15.4%	5.1%	4.7%	1.6%	5.8%	6.5%	0.7%	11.4%	3.1%
Sales Manager	17.1%	7.9%	6.2%	1.8%	15.3%	8.5%	9.4%	3.2%	10.0%	5.3%	1.5%	10.0%	3.8%
Sales Representative	27.9%	20.1%	7.3%	4.6%	8.3%	2.0%	1.2%	1.6%	1.6%	3.6%	0.5%	20.4%	0.8%
Sales Specialist	26.2%	15.6%	7.2%	5.1%	9.7%	2.1%	2.5%	1.7%	4.2%	3.8%	0.4%	20.3%	1.3%
Pre-Sales Consultant	16.7%	12.5%	18.8%	6.3%	6.3%	6.3%	4.2%	6.3%	4.2%	8.3%	0.0%	8.3%	2.1%
Sales Enablement													
Operations Manager	18.6%	10.0%	7.1%	10.0%	7.1%	8.6%	4.3%	1.4%	11.4%	4.3%	0.0%	10.0%	7.1%
Operations Executive	11.4%	11.4%	12.7%	5.1%	8.9%	7.6%	3.8%	7.6%	8.9%	11.4%	1.3%	7.6%	2.5%
Sales Compensation Planner	0.0%	11.8%	5.9%	0.0%	17.6%	5.9%	5.9%	0.0%	11.8%	5.9%	17.6%	17.6%	0.0%
Sales Operations Infrastructure Developer	13.3%	6.7%	0.0%	6.7%	20.0%	6.7%	13.3%	0.0%	0.0%	13.3%	6.7%	6.7%	6.7%
Sales Operations Account Researcher/Analyst	0.0%	0.0%	0.0%	33.3%	33.3%	0.0%	33.3%	0.0%	0.0%	0.0%	0.0%	0.0%	0.0%
Sales Recruiter	18.5%	7.4%	11.1%	7.4%	14.8%	3.7%	3.7%	0.0%	3.7%	11.1%	3.7%	3.7%	11.1%

Sales Development													
Sales Training Manager	11.5%	7.4%	6.1%	3.7%	6.9%	2.7%	15.2%	18.4%	14.3%	3.7%	1.0%	6.4%	2.7%
Sales Training Executive	12.6%	6.7%	8.0%	3.4%	13.9%	3.4%	11.8%	11.8%	11.3%	5.0%	0.8%	7.1%	4.2%
Sales Trainer	14.6%	7.3%	5.6%	4.4%	6.3%	1.5%	10.9%	16.5%	17.8%	4.4%	0.7%	6.8%	3.2%
Sales Training Designer and Developer	10.3%	6.9%	6.2%	4.1%	10.3%	3.4%	13.1%	20.7%	16.6%	4.1%	1.4%	2.8%	0.0%
Sales Researcher	19.1%	16.2%	0.0%	8.8%	2.9%	4.4%	4.4%	4.4%	4.4%	13.2%	1.5%	20.6%	0.0%
Sales Professor/ Academic	16.0%	11.1%	7.6%	3.5%	11.8%	2.8%	7.6%	12.5%	9.0%	5.6%	1.4%	9.0%	2.1%

Key Actions

AOE1: Creating and Closing Opportunities

How important are each of the following key actions for effective performance in the Creating and Closing Opportunities area of expertise?

	Essential (5)	Very important (4)	Moderately important (3)	Slightly important (2)	Unnecessary (1)	Average Rating
Researching and targeting prospects for sales pursuit	44.8%	39.2%	13.4%	2.0%	0.5%	**4.26**
Conducting interest building calls (cold calls) when applicable	35.8%	37.0%	18.0%	6.8%	2.4%	**3.97**
Identifying, following up on, and managing sales leads	57.0%	33.3%	8.3%	1.2%	0.2%	**4.46**
Gaining interest (through marketing materials and discussion)	35.1%	40.4%	20.2%	3.9%	0.3%	**4.06**
Qualifying opportunities	49.9%	35.0%	11.7%	2.4%	1.0%	**4.30**
Developing winning proposals	46.3%	37.7%	12.1%	3.1%	0.8%	**4.26**
Building business justification cases	22.9%	37.7%	27.3%	8.3%	3.7%	**3.68**
Orchestrating the support of specialists in negotiations	22.6%	34.1%	26.7%	10.5%	6.1%	**3.57**
Maintaining the momentum of sales wins to expand selling to the customer	41.3%	40.6%	14.6%	2.5%	1.0%	**4.19**

AOE 2: Protecting Accounts

How important are each of the following key actions for effective performance in the Protecting Accounts area of expertise?

	Essential (5)	Very important (4)	Moderately important (3)	Slightly important (2)	Unnecessary (1)	Average Rating
Gathering account intelligence and monitoring customer business activities	36.9%	43.1%	16.4%	3.1%	0.6%	**4.13**
Documenting account plans and sales forecasts	26.1%	33.1%	29.2%	9.7%	1.9%	**3.72**
Building business relationships with customer executives	63.6%	27.2%	6.4%	1.9%	0.8%	**4.51**
Cultivating and developing trusted advisor status	48.1%	34.2%	12.8%	3.3%	1.7%	**4.24**
Protecting and expanding accounts	60.3%	33.9%	4.7%	0.8%	0.3%	**4.53**
Managing the readiness of solutions for deployment and the alignment of needed resources	28.1%	39.4%	22.5%	6.9%	3.1%	**3.83**

AOE 3: Defining and Positioning Solutions

How important are each of the following key actions *for effective performance in the Defining and Positioning Solutions area of expertise?*

	Essential (5)	Very important (4)	Moderately important (3)	Slightly important (2)	Unnecessary (1)	Average Rating
Performing technical qualifications	16.3%	38.8%	27.8%	9.1%	8.1%	**3.46**
Designing solutions	38.3%	41.1%	15.3%	4.8%	0.5%	**4.12**
Customizing standard products or services to align with customer need	39.2%	37.3%	18.2%	3.8%	1.4%	**4.09**
Conducting technical demonstrations and benchmark testing	21.5%	34.4%	26.3%	11.5%	6.2%	**3.54**
Contributing to solution sizing and modification to meet all customer requirements	25.4%	40.2%	24.9%	6.7%	2.9%	**3.78**
Articulating solution designs (effectively communicating the strategy to both technical and business stakeholders)	45.9%	33.0%	17.7%	2.9%	0.5%	**4.21**

AOE 4: Supporting Indirect Selling

How important are each of the following key actions *for effective performance in the Supporting Indirect Selling area of expertise?*

	Essential (5)	Very important (4)	Moderately important (3)	Slightly important (2)	Unnecessary (1)	Average Rating
Assessing and helping develop partner's sales force	27.3%	31.4%	28.9%	4.1%	8.3%	**3.65**
Driving partner sales planning and forecasting	19.0%	36.4%	29.8%	9.9%	5.0%	**3.55**
Motivating partner to sell more and educating them on products or services	39.7%	33.1%	16.5%	7.4%	3.3%	**3.98**
Developing positive partner business relationships	45.5%	32.2%	17.4%	2.5%	2.5%	**4.16**
Helping partner achieve optimum product inventory balance and sell-through to end customers	24.8%	37.2%	24.8%	7.4%	5.8%	**3.68**
Tracking investments on behalf of partner selling to determine business impact and return	17.4%	30.6%	26.4%	15.7%	9.9%	**3.30**

(continued on the next page)

AOE 4: Supporting Indirect Selling (continued)

How important are each of the following key actions for effective performance in the Supporting Indirect Selling area of expertise?

	Essential (5)	Very important (4)	Moderately important (3)	Slightly important (2)	Unnecessary (1)	Average Rating
Facilitating partner transformation (introducing effective selling strategies, identifying market opportunities, etc.)	23.1%	40.5%	25.6%	5.8%	5.0%	**3.71**
Monitoring and managing partner's fulfillment of contractual sales obligations to company	25.6%	27.3%	26.4%	14.0%	6.6%	**3.51**
Troubleshooting operational obstacles to the accurate or quick crediting of partner's sales	26.4%	35.5%	25.6%	8.3%	4.1%	**3.72**
Collaborating with partners to co-sell and position solutions to customers	30.6%	42.1%	19.0%	5.0%	3.3%	**3.92**

AOE 5: Setting Sales Strategy

How important are each of the following key actions for effective performance in the Setting Sales Strategy area of expertise?

	Essential (5)	Very important (4)	Moderately important (3)	Slightly important (2)	Unnecessary (1)	Average Rating
Identifying and communicating innovative sales practices, procedures, models, and organizational structures	37.1%	42.9%	16.1%	2.9%	1.0%	**4.12**
Developing strategic plans to guide the development of a more effective sales organization	49.4%	33.9%	12.6%	2.3%	1.9%	**4.26**
Building business and partner alliances to extend the sales reach of the organization	36.5%	40.0%	17.1%	4.8%	1.6%	**4.05**
Driving the acceptance and incorporation of sales innovations by the organization	28.1%	47.4%	18.7%	3.2%	2.6%	**3.95**
Configuring and aligning sales territories for maximum effectiveness	26.8%	35.5%	25.2%	7.4%	5.2%	**3.71**

AOE 6: Managing within the Sales Ecosystem

How important are each of the following key actions for effective performance in the Managing within the Sales Ecosystem area of expertise?

	Essential (5)	Very important (4)	Moderately important (3)	Slightly important (2)	Unnecessary (1)	Average Rating
Aligning tactical activities to larger organizational strategies (setting priorities, measuring progress to plan)	30.6%	50.0%	18.5%	0.9%	0.0%	**4.10**
Establishing, monitoring, and controlling costs that affect sales margins	31.5%	41.7%	24.1%	2.8%	0.0%	**4.02**
Aligning resources with opportunities	36.1%	50.0%	12.0%	1.9%	0.0%	**4.20**
Screening administrative demands and troubleshooting back-office operations to minimize disruptions to sales representatives	21.3%	51.9%	17.6%	8.3%	0.9%	**3.84**
Ensuring accurate forecasting while monitoring performance to metrics	33.3%	42.6%	23.1%	0.9%	0.0%	**4.08**
Hiring, promoting, and terminating to improve sales performance and address capability gaps	26.9%	41.7%	25.9%	2.8%	2.8%	**3.87**
Aligning reward and recognition strategies to performance goals	30.6%	39.8%	25.0%	3.7%	0.9%	**3.95**

AOE 7: Developing Sales Force Capability

How important are each of the following key actions *for effective performance in the Developing Sales Force Capability area of expertise?*

	Essential (5)	Very important (4)	Moderately important (3)	Slightly important (2)	Unnecessary (1)	Average Rating
Determining competencies required to achieve sales strategy	50.7%	36.3%	9.0%	2.7%	1.3%	**4.32**
Conducting sales-related needs assessments	35.0%	46.6%	14.8%	2.7%	0.9%	**4.12**
Designing and developing sales development programs, curricula, or learning solutions	47.5%	33.2%	13.9%	4.0%	1.3%	**4.22**
Using learning management systems	18.8%	36.8%	28.3%	11.7%	4.5%	**3.54**
Tying learning strategy to organizational capacity	38.6%	34.1%	19.3%	5.4%	2.7%	**4.00**
Evaluating learning program or learning solution effectiveness	39.5%	36.8%	17.0%	4.9%	1.8%	**4.07**
Reporting learning results to organizational stakeholders	28.3%	35.4%	25.6%	7.2%	3.6%	**3.78**

AOE 8: Delivering Sales Training

How important are each of the following key actions *for effective performance in the Delivering Sales Training area of expertise?*

	Essential (5)	Very important (4)	Moderately important (3)	Slightly important (2)	Unnecessary (1)	Average Rating
Reviewing and enhancing learning materials to ensure their effectiveness	53.2%	38.0%	6.3%	1.7%	0.8%	**4.41**
Motivating participants to stimulate their interest, maintain attention, and advance learning	66.7%	27.4%	2.5%	2.5%	0.8%	**4.57**
Managing instructional delivery and an environment conducive to learning	54.9%	35.4%	7.2%	2.1%	0.4%	**4.42**
Administering tests	13.9%	23.2%	34.2%	17.7%	11.0%	**3.11**

AOE 9: Coaching for Sales Results

How important are each of the following key actions for effective performance in the Coaching for Sales Results area of expertise?

	Essential (5)	Very important (4)	Moderately important (3)	Slightly important (2)	Unnecessary (1)	Average Rating
Observing sales behavior to identify strengths, weaknesses, and opportunities for improvement	56.3%	33.8%	9.2%	0.7%	0.0%	**4.46**
Balancing corrective with positive feedback to ensure optimum guidance and performance improvement	50.4%	36.4%	12.1%	1.1%	0.0%	**4.36**
Motivating individuals to enable sales performance	52.2%	37.5%	8.5%	1.5%	0.4%	**4.40**
Linking expected behaviors to strategic sales-related outcomes	47.4%	36.8%	11.8%	2.9%	1.1%	**4.26**
Demonstrating expected sales behaviors and mentoring individuals on how to achieve these	53.3%	34.6%	9.6%	1.1%	1.5%	**4.37**
Identifying support programs or training (formally and informally) to expand and enrich new learning	36.8%	46.0%	15.8%	1.1%	0.4%	**4.18**

AOE 10: Building Sales Infrastructure

How important are each of the following key actions for effective performance in the Building Sales Infrastructure area of expertise?

	Essential (5)	Very important (4)	Moderately important (3)	Slightly important (2)	Unnecessary (1)	Average Rating
Monitoring current business processes and sales productivity tools for adequacy	31.9%	46.8%	17.0%	3.5%	0.7%	**4.06**
Developing and driving strategic infrastructure planning	36.9%	40.4%	17.7%	5.0%	0.0%	**4.09**
Managing infrastructure upkeep or revision	30.5%	36.9%	24.1%	8.5%	0.0%	**3.89**
Driving or supporting infrastructure change and alignment	30.5%	38.3%	24.8%	5.0%	1.4%	**3.91**
Piloting and evaluating infrastructure programs	22.0%	41.1%	25.5%	9.9%	1.4%	**3.72**

AOE 11: Designing Compensation

How important are each of the following key actions *for effective performance in the Designing Compensation area of expertise?*

	Essential (5)	Very important (4)	Moderately important (3)	Slightly important (2)	Unnecessary (1)	Average Rating
Assessing current compensation against best practices and innovative sales compensation options	28.6%	35.7%	28.6%	3.6%	3.6%	**3.82**
Aligning compensation with business requirements and appropriate sales behaviors and metrics	32.1%	39.3%	21.4%	0.0%	7.1%	**3.89**
Developing and enlisting support for sales compensation models and plans	32.1%	46.4%	17.9%	3.6%	0.0%	**4.07**
Driving organizational acceptance of sales compensation strategies and plans	35.7%	35.7%	25.0%	0.0%	3.6%	**4.00**

AOE 12: Maintaining Accounts

How important are each of the following key actions *for effective performance in the Maintaining Accounts area of expertise?*

	Essential (5)	Very important (4)	Moderately important (3)	Slightly important (2)	Unnecessary (1)	Average Rating
Preparing standard and ad hoc reports on account status	17.5%	31.8%	32.3%	10.4%	7.9%	**3.41**
Providing task substitution assistance to facilitate sales	23.8%	35.1%	27.1%	9.6%	4.4%	**3.64**
Crafting standard contracts and statements of work	20.8%	32.9%	26.0%	12.9%	7.4%	**3.47**
Troubleshooting customer operational issues	43.6%	38.9%	11.5%	4.4%	1.6%	**4.18**
Tracking and administering contracts	29.0%	38.4%	19.7%	7.7%	5.2%	**3.87**

AOE 13: Recruiting Sales Talent

How important are each of the following key actions for effective performance in the Recruiting Sales Talent area of expertise?

	Essential (5)	Very important (4)	Moderately important (3)	Slightly important (2)	Unnecessary (1)	Average Rating
Aligning and modifying sales job profiles to ensure accuracy of requirements	30.4%	39.1%	21.7%	4.3%	4.3%	**3.87**
Ensuring valid compensation package (as measured by industry practices and metrics)	30.4%	31.9%	29.0%	5.8%	2.9%	**3.81**
Monitoring and maintaining sales candidate pipeline	31.9%	42.0%	21.7%	21.7%	2.9%	**3.99**
Conducting candidate searches using a variety of methods	23.2%	50.7%	18.8%	2.9%	4.3%	**3.86**
Soliciting, screening, and profiling individual candidates and determining person-job fit	42.0%	39.1%	14.5%	0.0%	4.3%	**4.14**
Facilitating group interviews and testing of prospective candidates	21.7%	39.1%	29.0%	7.2%	2.9%	**3.70**
Communicating offers, conducting negotiations with candidates, and filling the open position	34.8%	42.0%	17.4%	2.9%	2.9%	**4.03**
Supporting on-boarding activities (orientation, introductions)	31.9%	46.4%	15.9%	2.9%	2.9%	**4.01**

Key Knowledge Areas

AOE 1: Creating and Closing Opportunities

How important are each of the following key knowledge areas *for effective performance in the Creating and Closing Opportunities area of expertise?*

	Essential (5)	Very important (4)	Moderately important (3)	Slightly important (2)	Unnecessary (1)	Average Rating
Product or service features, benefits, and value propositions	50.7%	34.9%	12.0%	1.1%	1.4%	**4.32**
Sales collateral resources	22.2%	41.8%	23.2%	10.1%	2.6%	**3.71**
Cold-calling sales techniques	41.2%	28.6%	20.4%	7.1%	2.7%	**3.98**
Customer-related vertical market or industry information resources	29.6%	39.5%	21.0%	6.8%	3.1%	**3.86**
Sales negotiation and closing methods	61.7%	29.8%	7.4%	1.2%	0.0%	**4.52**
Formal and ad hoc research strategies (e.g., systematic exploration, personal networking, website scanning)	20.2%	36.0%	27.6%	8.4%	7.7%	**3.53**
Lead management procedures	29.9%	39.6%	21.1%	6.9%	2.5%	**3.87**
Cost-estimation and sizing techniques	32.2%	38.4%	18.6%	6.5%	4.2%	**3.88**
Personal engagement and interest-generation strategies	39.5%	42.4%	15.1%	2.3%	0.7%	**4.18**
Business alliance building skills (e.g., client, third party, and so forth)	33.6%	40.8%	19.4%	3.8%	2.4%	**3.99**
Business analysis metrics and procedures (e.g., health ratios, balance sheet analysis)	18.5%	31.5%	26.5%	12.3%	11.2%	**3.34**
Return-on-investment and total cost of ownership techniques (ROI, TCO)	30.8%	33.9%	21.2%	6.8%	7.2%	**3.74**
Business workshop facilitation and management skills	17.4%	37.7%	26.3%	11.7%	6.8%	**3.47**
Sales cycle management skills	32.5%	40.2%	19.6%	5.6%	2.1%	**3.95**
Proposal development, component integration, and management practices	33.1%	43.6%	16.1%	4.3%	3.0%	**4.00**
Formal sales negotiation and closing methods or strategies	46.9%	38.4%	10.7%	3.6%	0.3%	**4.28**
Objection-handling techniques	49.7%	36.4%	12.4%	0.3%	1.2%	**4.33**
Opportunity qualification skills	39.2%	38.9%	16.0%	4.8%	1.0%	**4.11**
Resource knowledge (technical, pricing, legal, delivery and fulfillment)	37.8%	42.2%	15.2%	3.7%	1.0%	**4.12**

AOE 2: Protecting Accounts

How important are each of the following key knowledge areas for effective performance in the Protecting Accounts area of expertise?

	Essential (5)	Very important (4)	Moderately important (3)	Slightly important (2)	Unnecessary (1)	Average Rating
Customer business and operations (e.g., reporting structures, decision makers)	31.8%	40.3%	19.4%	3.8%	4.7%	**3.91**
Account history (prior investments, account relationships)	38.2%	34.3%	20.8%	4.3%	2.4%	**4.01**
Account farming procedures or practices (e.g., check-ins, sponsoring marketing initiatives)	25.5%	29.9%	27.5%	11.3%	5.9%	**3.58**
Transition-to-farming practices	12.7%	23.6%	29.7%	16.0%	17.9%	**2.97**
Business analysis methods	22.3%	31.4%	27.3%	12.3%	6.9%	**3.50**
Industry research engines and resources (e.g., Dun and Bradstreet, analysts reports)	19.0%	19.5%	31.7%	17.1%	12.7%	**3.15**
Customer organizational communication resources (websites, annual reports, press releases, position and white papers)	22.0%	34.5%	23.0%	8.5%	12.0%	**3.46**
Customer business health indictors (e.g., ratios)	25.2%	31.6%	24.3%	11.7%	7.3%	**3.56**
Account planning tools, templates, and procedures	23.3%	36.1%	26.5%	11.0%	3.2%	**3.65**
Account-related marketing plans	28.4%	36.6%	23.2%	6.2%	5.7%	**3.76**
Supply chain knowledge (lead times, response rates, fulfillment processes)	28.4%	36.5%	23.1%	7.2%	4.8%	**3.76**
Funnel management practices, tools, metrics, and policies	18.9%	30.6%	28.1%	14.8%	7.7%	**3.38**
Deployment practices and back-office administrative or order-entry procedures	25.8%	26.8%	30.1%	9.6%	7.7%	**3.54**
Competitive information resources	36.3%	38.7%	17.6%	4.4%	2.9%	**4.01**
Contract administration and renewal processes	22.1%	38.7%	22.6%	8.8%	7.8%	**3.59**
Standard contractual and service level agreement (SLA) terms, conditions, and milestone metrics	19.0%	32.7%	24.9%	9.3%	14.1%	**3.33**
Resource management strategies	20.2%	35.2%	27.5%	11.9%	5.2%	**3.53**

AOE 3: Defining and Positioning Solutions

How important are each of the following key knowledge areas for effective performance in the Defining and Positioning Solutions area of expertise?

	Essential (5)	Very important (4)	Moderately important (3)	Slightly important (2)	Unnecessary (1)	Average Rating
Product or service or solution technology (e.g., concepts, uses)	39.0%	37.6%	20.6%	2.8%	0.0%	**4.13**
Solution technical foundation	16.9%	39.6%	31.2%	9.1%	3.2%	**3.58**
Solution configuration frameworks or templates	22.1%	32.9%	33.6%	7.1%	4.3%	**3.61**
Requirements analysis and management techniques	25.9%	43.4%	28.0%	2.1%	0.7%	**3.92**
Solution design procedures and communication conventions (written or graphical)	21.5%	47.7%	22.1%	5.4%	3.4%	**3.79**
Solution design methodologies, best practices, and trends	29.3%	45.7%	20.0%	5.0%	0.0%	**3.99**
Oral and written communication skills (sufficient for ensuring that technical concepts are meaningful to nontechnical audiences)	46.0%	42.0%	10.7%	0.7%	0.7%	**4.32**
Customer-facing skills	50.7%	36.7%	8.0%	4.0%	0.7%	**4.33**
Technical trust building and selling	38.7%	36.6%	20.4%	2.1%	2.1%	**4.08**
Business context of technical solution knowledge	33.8%	44.1%	18.4%	2.9%	0.7%	**4.07**
Solution-sizing criteria	24.0%	36.7%	29.3%	7.3%	2.7%	**3.72**
Technical team leadership	20.9%	36.5%	30.4%	8.1%	4.1%	**3.62**
Vertical industry solutions	19.1%	46.8%	21.7%	8.6%	3.9%	**3.68**
Solution deployment or delivery practices (expectation setting, quality checking)	29.6%	43.0%	21.5%	5.2%	0.7%	**3.96**

AOE 4: Supporting Indirect Selling

How important are each of the following key knowledge areas for effective performance in the Supporting Indirect Selling area of expertise?

	Essential (5)	Very important (4)	Moderately important (3)	Slightly important (2)	Unnecessary (1)	Average Rating
Partner types and functions (distributors, resellers)	25.0%	36.1%	27.8%	8.3%	2.8%	**3.72**
Company indirect sales motion, strategy, and direction	29.7%	40.5%	21.6%	4.1%	4.1%	**3.88**
Marketing promotional programs and initiatives	25.3%	46.7%	20.0%	5.3%	2.7%	**3.87**
Partner incentive programs	28.2%	32.4%	22.5%	9.9%	7.0%	**3.65**
Partner business model and financial health	22.2%	30.2%	30.2%	7.9%	9.5%	**3.48**
Partner market niche and product or service alignment model	20.6%	39.7%	31.7%	0.0%	7.9%	**3.65**
Partner loyalty and commitment-building techniques	36.1%	27.8%	26.4%	5.6%	4.2%	**3.86**
Partner issues escalation and resolution procedures	21.2%	37.9%	25.8%	9.1%	6.1%	**3.59**
Sell-with, sell-through, sell-for techniques	32.2%	37.3%	22.0%	5.1%	3.4%	**3.90**
Business planning	30.2%	41.3%	19.0%	6.3%	3.2%	**3.89**
Business or influencing methods	33.8%	36.9%	27.7%	0.0%	1.5%	**4.02**
Product or service information resources	40.3%	32.8%	20.9%	3.0%	3.0%	**4.04**
Partner sales crediting processes and tools	19.5%	33.8%	29.9%	9.1%	7.8%	**3.48**
Partner scorecard metrics	10.4%	26.9%	38.8%	11.9%	11.9%	**3.12**
Sales forecasting and metrics management skills	21.3%	37.3%	32.0%	2.7%	6.7%	**3.64**
Knowledge transfer and communication skills	39.1%	37.7%	18.8%	1.4%	2.9%	**4.09**
Vendor requirements and certification processes	29.2%	30.6%	25.0%	9.7%	5.6%	**3.68**

AOE 5: Setting Sales Strategy

How important are each of the following key knowledge areas for effective performance in the Setting Sales Strategy area of expertise?

	Essential (5)	Very important (4)	Moderately important (3)	Slightly important (2)	Unnecessary (1)	Average Rating
Emerging market and sales trend knowledge	37.2%	40.2%	15.9%	4.9%	1.8%	**4.06**
Company business plans, strategic direction, and goals	44.0%	34.5%	19.0%	1.8%	0.6%	**4.20**
Company sales and competitive policies	34.6%	41.4%	18.5%	4.3%	1.2%	**4.04**
Company market position and market performance information	34.7%	44.3%	15.6%	3.6%	1.8%	**4.07**
Cultural and market segment diversity	26.1%	35.2%	30.3%	6.7%	1.8%	**3.77**
Market dynamics (general and product- or service-specific trends)	35.0%	43.7%	16.9%	2.2%	2.2%	**4.07**
Risk management and mitigation strategies	23.9%	37.5%	29.3%	7.1%	2.2%	**3.74**
Competitive knowledge and best practices	49.1%	40.7%	9.6%	0.6%	0.0%	**4.38**
Situational leadership methods	33.5%	38.4%	22.0%	3.7%	2.4%	**3.97**
Sales best practice and industry sales benchmarking resources	34.4%	45.0%	17.5%	2.5%	0.6%	**4.10**
Companywide organizational and value-chain information	27.0%	40.3%	23.3%	5.7%	3.8%	**3.81**
Systemic change, diffusion, and management methods	21.5%	37.3%	28.5%	8.9%	3.8%	**3.64**
Program management and measurement methods	28.4%	32.5%	29.0%	8.3%	1.8%	**3.78**
Sales metrics and measurement methods	36.3%	34.5%	21.4%	6.5%	1.2%	**3.98**
Sales system or tool or process automation information	28.7%	46.1%	18.6%	5.4%	1.2%	**3.96**
Workforce planning concepts	20.9%	39.9%	31.3%	5.5%	2.5%	**3.71**
Regulatory environment resources (global)	13.6%	38.5%	33.7%	5.3%	8.9%	**3.43**
Executive relationship-building strategies	42.2%	37.0%	15.6%	2.9%	2.3%	**4.14**

AOE 6: Managing within the Sales Ecosystem

How important are each of the following key knowledge areas for effective performance in the Managing within the Sales Ecosystem area of expertise?

	Essential (5)	Very important (4)	Moderately important (3)	Slightly important (2)	Unnecessary (1)	Average Rating
Company business or sales targets and metrics	31.5%	55.6%	13.0%	0.0%	0.0%	**4.19**
Performance measurement and management processes and tools	40.5%	38.1%	21.4%	0.0%	0.0%	**4.19**
Human resources policies and procedures	31.3%	31.3%	29.2%	8.3%	0.0%	**3.85**
Financial concepts and spread-sheet tools	18.2%	59.1%	20.5%	2.3%	0.0%	**3.93**
Forecasting and aggregation methods or tools	23.8%	47.6%	28.6%	0.0%	0.0%	**3.95**
Funnel management and aggregation methods or tools	14.6%	54.2%	27.1%	4.2%	0.0%	**3.79**
Supply chain or order fulfillment processes and procedures	22.8%	29.8%	43.9%	1.8%	1.8%	**3.70**
Competitive sales management tactics	28.6%	57.1%	11.9%	2.4%	0.0%	**4.12**
Workforce planning methods	25.0%	41.7%	29.2%	0.0%	4.2%	**3.83**
Capability gap analysis methods	13.2%	47.4%	31.6%	5.3%	2.6%	**3.63**
Career counseling methods	15.3%	44.1%	25.4%	10.2%	5.1%	**3.54**
Behavioral interview methods	17.8%	46.7%	26.7%	6.7%	2.2%	**3.71**
Business organizational culture	34.5%	37.9%	24.1%	0.0%	3.4%	**4.00**
Organization and operations	32.1%	50.0%	17.9%	0.0%	0.0%	**4.14**
High-performance or team-building methods	34.0%	49.1%	15.1%	0.0%	1.9%	**4.13**
Risk assessment and management methods	24.5%	37.7%	32.1%	5.7%	0.0%	**3.81**
Business development methods	21.2%	59.6%	15.4%	3.8%	0.0%	**3.98**
Contract administration and vendor management methods	22.4%	42.9%	22.4%	8.2%	4.1%	**3.71**
Legal or regulatory requirements	23.4%	27.7%	34.0%	12.8%	2.1%	**3.57**
Profit and loss (P&L) management methods	23.1%	53.8%	20.5%	2.6%	0.0%	**3.97**
Cost-center management methods	16.3%	58.1%	18.6%	4.7%	2.3%	**3.81**
Business standards of conduct and ethical guidelines	39.5%	32.6%	14.0%	11.6%	2.3%	**3.95**

Appendix E

AOE 7: Developing Sales Force Capability

How important are each of the following key knowledge areas for effective performance in the Developing Sales Force Capability area of expertise?

	Essential (5)	Very important (4)	Moderately important (3)	Slightly important (2)	Unnecessary (1)	Average Rating
Rapid instructional design methods	19.4%	33.8%	31.9%	8.1%	6.9%	**3.51**
Sales operations and fulfillment processes	26.3%	39.4%	25.6%	6.9%	1.9%	**3.81**
Audience learning style and preferences (individual, cultural)	29.0%	38.1%	27.7%	3.9%	1.3%	**3.90**
Test development (item construction and validation)	17.9%	31.4%	34.6%	11.5%	4.5%	**3.47**
Learning delivery systems and media	19.0%	35.6%	35.6%	5.5%	4.3%	**3.60**
Learning program evaluation methods (formative, summative, transfer, business impact, ROI)	23.3%	45.4%	28.2%	1.8%	1.2%	**3.88**
Human performance improvement concepts	31.1%	41.7%	23.8%	2.0%	1.3%	**3.99**
Performance analysis methods	25.0%	43.1%	24.4%	4.4%	3.1%	**3.83**
Business direction and goals	50.7%	35.0%	11.4%	1.4%	1.4%	**4.32**
Sales cycle components and stage-specific milestones	29.0%	42.0%	20.4%	6.2%	2.5%	**3.89**
Learning delivery systems and media	15.9%	39.0%	32.9%	7.3%	4.9%	**3.54**
Blended learning techniques	29.0%	36.8%	27.1%	5.2%	1.9%	**3.86**
Experiential learning methods (work-based learning and on-the-job development techniques—mentoring, job rotation, sabbatical)	42.6%	35.8%	15.5%	4.1%	2.0%	**4.13**
Learning management systems	15.3%	35.0%	32.5%	10.4%	6.7%	**3.42**

276

AOE 8: Delivering Sales Training

How important are each of the following key knowledge areas for effective performance in the Delivering Sales Training area of expertise?

	Essential (5)	Very important (4)	Moderately important (3)	Slightly important (2)	Unnecessary (1)	Average Rating
Platform training methods or strategies	36.9%	40.8%	18.4%	2.8%	1.1%	**4.09**
Sales cycle and challenges	37.3%	46.2%	14.2%	1.8%	0.6%	**4.18**
Rapport-building techniques	46.1%	38.9%	10.2%	4.2%	0.6%	**4.26**
Sales operations and fulfillment processes	26.3%	37.4%	23.4%	9.9%	2.9%	**3.74**
Audience learning style and preferences	45.8%	34.1%	16.2%	2.8%	1.1%	**4.21**
Test monitoring or proctoring methods	17.4%	21.1%	29.8%	11.8%	9.9%	**3.34**
Certification processes and requirements	17.9%	31.8%	29.1%	15.9%	5.3%	**3.41**
Learning delivery systems and media utilization strategies	26.7%	39.4%	23.0%	5.5%	5.5%	**3.76**
Instructor-led delivery techniques	45.7%	37.2%	11.6%	3.7%	1.8%	**4.21**
Learning management systems	14.1%	35.9%	32.9%	11.8%	5.3%	**3.42**
Online (virtual) delivery techniques	20.2%	38.2%	26.6%	8.7%	6.4%	**3.57**
Classroom management techniques	42.9%	36.8%	16.0%	3.1%	1.2%	**4.17**
Small group discussion techniques	34.8%	45.7%	17.1%	2.4%	0.0%	**4.13**
Questioning techniques	55.5%	34.1%	8.5%	1.2%	0.6%	**4.43**

AOE 9: Coaching for Sales Results

How important are each of the following key knowledge areas for effective performance in the Coaching for Sales Results area of expertise?

	Essential (5)	Very important (4)	Moderately important (3)	Slightly important (2)	Unnecessary (1)	Average Rating
Motivation methods	49.8%	40.1%	6.4%	3.0%	0.7%	**4.35**
Performance observation techniques	46.8%	38.6%	12.0%	1.9%	0.7%	**4.29**
Listening and feedback methods	63.7%	28.1%	6.4%	1.9%	0.0%	**4.54**
Coaching methodology and techniques	56.2%	37.5%	5.2%	1.1%	0.0%	**4.49**
Organization and business strategy	35.2%	45.3%	16.5%	3.0%	0.0%	**4.13**
Performance review instruments and administration methods	28.5%	44.2%	21.3%	4.1%	1.9%	**3.93**
Counseling methods	39.7%	44.2%	12.7%	3.0%	0.4%	**4.20**
Business standards of conduct and ethical guidelines	43.1%	38.6%	13.1%	3.7%	1.5%	**4.18**

AOE 10: Building Sales Infrastructure

How important are each of the following key knowledge areas for effective performance in the Building Sales Infrastructure area of expertise?

	Essential (5)	Very important (4)	Moderately important (3)	Slightly important (2)	Unnecessary (1)	Average Rating
Sales operations-related tools and technologies	32.3%	35.4%	27.6%	3.1%	1.6%	**3.94**
Requirements definition techniques	19.8%	38.1%	29.4%	8.7%	4.0%	**3.61**
Technical prototyping testing strategies	15.2%	39.2%	24.8%	16.0%	4.8%	**3.44**
Strategic planning methods	26.2%	47.5%	19.7%	5.7%	0.8%	**3.93**
Data analysis methods	19.5%	37.3%	34.7%	6.8%	1.7%	**3.66**
Process analysis and planning methods	24.2%	38.3%	26.7%	10.8%	0.0%	**3.76**
Sales stakeholder requirements (e.g., business planners, sales management, sales force, partners)	26.4%	35.5%	32.2%	5.0%	0.8%	**3.82**
Sales operations functions and processes	34.1%	43.7%	18.3%	4.0%	0.0%	**4.08**

(continued on the next page)

AOE 10: Building Sales Infrastructure (continued)

How important are each of the following **key knowledge areas** *for effective performance in the Building Sales Infrastructure area of expertise?*

	Essential (5)	Very important (4)	Moderately important (3)	Slightly important (2)	Unnecessary (1)	Average Rating
Sales operations best practices (order entry and fulfillment, value chain maintenance)	33.9%	39.5%	17.7%	7.3%	1.6%	**3.97**
ROI calculation methods	20.0%	35.0%	35.8%	7.5%	1.7%	**3.64**
Change management methodologies	20.7%	38.0%	28.1%	9.1%	4.1%	**3.62**

AOE 11: Designing Compensation

How important are each of the following **key knowledge areas** *for effective performance in the Designing Compensation area of expertise?*

	Essential (5)	Very important (4)	Moderately important (3)	Slightly important (2)	Unnecessary (1)	Average Rating
Research methods	4.0%	48.0%	24.0%	16.0%	8.0%	**3.24**
Industry benchmarking sources	10.0%	45.0%	30.0%	5.0%	10.0%	**3.40**
Payout processes, key milestones, ratios, and formulas	20.0%	36.0%	36.0%	4.0%	4.0%	**3.64**
Sales force motivators	38.5%	34.6%	15.4%	7.7%	3.8%	**3.96**
Financial compensation vehicles and metrics	16.7%	37.5%	37.5%	8.3%	0.0%	**3.63**
Financial modeling methods	27.3%	22.7%	45.5%	4.5%	0.0%	**3.73**
Business analysis methods	18.2%	45.5%	22.7%	9.1%	4.5%	**3.64**
Program planning and management skills	8.0%	60.0%	28.0%	0.0%	4.0%	**3.68**
Change management requirements	0.0%	47.8%	43.5%	4.3%	4.3%	**3.35**
Sales culture	9.5%	61.9%	23.8%	4.8%	0.0%	**3.76**
Local, regional, and/or country-level regulatory requirements	4.8%	47.6%	14.3%	23.8%	9.5%	**3.14**
Business performance resources	0.0%	57.7%	30.8%	7.7%	3.8%	**3.42**

AOE 12: Maintaining Accounts

How important are each of the following **key knowledge areas** *for effective performance in the Maintaining Accounts area of expertise?*

	Essential (5)	Very important (4)	Moderately important (3)	Slightly important (2)	Unnecessary (1)	Average Rating
Sales system or tools	38.7%	38.3%	19.7%	1.8%	1.5%	**4.11**
Sales-related databases (e.g., what they contain, how to access)	37.2%	35.7%	21.6%	3.0%	2.6%	**4.02**
Sales process	53.2%	33.6%	11.1%	1.4%	0.7%	**4.37**
Sales culture	28.7%	43.3%	20.7%	5.7%	1.5%	**3.92**
Pricing or costing formulas	42.4%	33.6%	19.9%	2.6%	1.5%	**4.13**
Account management processes	39.3%	40.0%	16.5%	2.8%	1.4%	**4.13**
Order entry and fulfillment processes	35.7%	34.3%	19.9%	6.6%	3.5%	**3.92**
Funnel management administration	19.0%	30.8%	31.5%	9.7%	9.0%	**3.41**
Contractual terms and conditions (standard)	30.4%	39.2%	20.1%	5.5%	4.8%	**3.85**
Report templates	16.4%	30.2%	29.1%	14.2%	10.1%	**3.29**
Supply chain (e.g., components, strategy, processes, key contacts)	30.4%	34.3%	23.3%	7.1%	4.9%	**3.78**
Customer satisfaction requirements	65.8%	28.4%	5.0%	0.7%	0.0%	**4.59**
Process improvement methods	25.6%	43.2%	23.1%	4.8%	3.3%	**3.83**

AOE 13: Recruiting Sales Talent

How important are each of the following **key knowledge areas** *for effective performance in the Recruiting Sales Talent area of expertise?*

	Essential (5)	Very important (4)	Moderately important (3)	Slightly important (2)	Unnecessary (1)	Average Rating
Psychometric tests (uses and output)	10.9%	23.9%	43.5%	13.0%	8.7%	**3.15**
Industry recruitment practices	12.5%	47.5%	25.0%	7.5%	7.5%	**3.50**
Industry networking methods	24.0%	40.0%	28.0%	4.0%	4.0%	**3.76**
Sales organization or company compensation structure and practices	31.7%	46.3%	22.0%	0.0%	0.0%	**4.10**
Sales or organization culture and personality variables	28.6%	45.2%	21.4%	2.4%	2.4%	**3.95**

(continued on the next page)

AOE 13: Recruiting Sales Talent (continued)

How important are each of the following key knowledge areas for effective performance in the Recruiting Sales Talent area of expertise?

	Essential (5)	Very important (4)	Moderately important (3)	Slightly important (2)	Unnecessary (1)	Average Rating
Sales interviewing methods	33.3%	55.6%	8.3%	0.0%	2.8%	**4.17**
Job or position analysis methods	13.5%	54.1%	21.6%	8.1%	2.7%	**3.68**
Human resources recruitment policies, compliance requirements, and procedures	20.8%	45.8%	25.0%	2.1%	6.3%	**3.73**
Human resources operational policies (including diversity and harassment policies)	20.0%	44.4%	28.9%	4.4%	2.2%	**3.76**
Products or services or solutions (target markets and customers)	32.5%	42.5%	20.0%	0.0%	5.0%	**3.98**
Industry vertical selling requirements	15.9%	45.5%	34.1%	4.5%	0.0%	**3.73**
Candidate pipeline management tools	12.5%	50.0%	25.0%	8.3%	4.2%	**3.58**
Local, regional, country-level labor laws	18.6%	34.9%	32.6%	9.3%	4.7%	**3.53**
Interviewing methods and strategies (behavioral based, probing techniques)	31.7%	53.7%	12.2%	0.0%	2.4%	**4.12**
Company mission, vision, and goals	37.2%	39.5%	23.3%	0.0%	0.0%	**4.14**
Negotiation methods	27.8%	41.7%	25.0%	0.0%	5.6%	**3.86**

Key Skills

AOE 1: Creating and Closing Opportunities

How important are each of the following abilities for effective performance in the Creating and Closing Opportunities area of expertise?

	Essential (5)	Very important (4)	Moderately important (3)	Slightly important (2)	Unnecessary (1)	Average Rating
Create compelling sales presentations	45.0%	38.9%	14.0%	1.5%	0.6%	**4.26**
Interpret and synthesize information from multiple sources (e.g., databases, online resources, colleagues)	25.7%	39.4%	25.7%	7.0%	2.2%	**3.80**
Compellingly communicate product or service benefits and features	49.9%	34.8%	12.5%	1.9%	0.8%	**4.31**
Determine buyer readiness from verbal and nonverbal cues	50.4%	36.8%	11.6%	0.9%	0.2%	**4.36**
Manage multiple or interrelated sales calls	34.8%	43.0%	16.5%	2.2%	3.5%	**4.03**
Implement environmental scanning to ensure well-targeted sales messages	21.4%	38.6%	24.1%	7.8%	8.2%	**3.57**
Manage leads and ensure follow-up or follow-through	53.2%	34.8%	10.4%	1.5%	0.0%	**4.40**
Accurately estimate costs and size solutions	38.7%	36.6%	18.1%	4.8%	1.7%	**4.06**
Calculate business metrics and translate product or service features meaningfully into value propositions	27.8%	37.6%	24.3%	6.5%	3.8%	**3.79**
Leverage vertical market and industry knowledge in product or service positioning	26.8%	43.1%	21.9%	4.5%	3.7%	**3.85**
Align sales activities with their respective point in the sales process	34.9%	40.6%	20.0%	2.8%	1.7%	**4.04**
Lead business analysis discussions	23.1%	35.0%	29.1%	7.7%	5.1%	**3.63**

AOE 2: Protecting Accounts

How important are each of the following abilities for effective performance in the Protecting Accounts area of expertise?

	Essential (5)	Very important (4)	Moderately important (3)	Slightly important (2)	Unnecessary (1)	Average Rating
Manage total customer satisfaction to optimize relationships	56.6%	32.9%	8.0%	1.4%	1.0%	**4.43**
Coordinate and align all account activities with overarching plan	26.9%	36.4%	25.1%	8.4%	3.3%	**3.75**
Determine how customers are organized and how they make purchasing decisions	48.4%	31.6%	15.3%	2.5%	2.2%	**4.21**
Leverage marketing programs to advance sales	29.3%	35.7%	24.4%	5.7%	4.9%	**3.79**
Summarize salient content from customer communication sources (websites, annual reports, press releases, position and white papers)	23.1%	28.1%	29.2%	12.5%	7.1%	**3.48**
Determine business health and viability using key business ratios	24.8%	31.5%	28.7%	7.0%	8.0%	**3.58**
Apply relevant account planning tools, templates, and procedures	22.7%	35.4%	27.1%	9.3%	5.5%	**3.60**
Apply funnel management practices, tools, metrics, and policies effectively to prioritize and manage selling	21.9%	36.1%	25.3%	10.1%	6.6%	**3.57**
Translate competitive knowledge into relevant sales practices	39.9%	38.4%	16.7%	2.9%	2.2%	**4.11**
Leverage contract administration and renewal into up- or cross-selling opportunities	24.4%	40.8%	23.7%	4.9%	6.3%	**3.72**
Monitor and manage contractual and service level agreement terms, conditions, and milestone metrics	25.9%	35.5%	26.6%	5.0%	7.1%	**3.68**
Set accurate customer expectations for order fulfillment (e.g., lead times, response rates, fulfillment processes)	49.3%	36.8%	10.0%	3.2%	0.7%	**4.31**

AOE 3: Defining and Positioning Solutions

How important are each of the following abilities for effective performance in the Defining and Positioning Solutions area of expertise?

	Essential (5)	Very important (4)	Moderately important (3)	Slightly important (2)	Unnecessary (1)	Average Rating
Counter competitor product or service feature and benefit messages	32.3%	43.4%	19.2%	3.5%	1.5%	**4.02**
Communicate features and benefits of solution-related tools or packages	44.9%	34.3%	15.7%	4.0%	1.0%	**4.18**
Accurately map customer's product or service operating environment	28.8%	40.4%	20.7%	6.6%	3.5%	**3.84**
Effectively communicate technical solutions	40.4%	37.4%	16.2%	4.0%	2.0%	**4.10**
Translate solution designs into meaningful customer benefits, and differentiate these by stakeholder needs	50.0%	36.4%	10.6%	2.0%	1.0%	**4.32**
Develop trusted advisor status with customers based on technical acumen	42.9%	40.9%	13.1%	2.5%	0.5%	**4.23**
Ensure cost-effective solution deployment and delivery practices	32.3%	42.4%	20.7%	2.5%	2.0%	**4.01**
Manage technical teams and integrate their contributions	20.7%	42.4%	20.2%	9.1%	7.6%	**3.60**

AOE 4: Supporting Indirect Selling

How important are each of the following abilities *for effective performance in the Supporting Indirect Selling area of expertise?*

	Essential (5)	Very important (4)	Moderately important (3)	Slightly important (2)	Unnecessary (1)	Average Rating
Build personal relationships with partners to advance mind-share	43.6%	31.6%	17.9%	4.3%	2.6%	**4.09**
Leverage marketing programs and initiatives to advance partner selling	24.8%	39.3%	25.6%	6.0%	4.3%	**3.74**
Influence operations to ensure timely and accurate payout to partners	25.6%	30.8%	27.4%	6.8%	9.4%	**3.56**
Ensure timely and accurate product or service updates to partners based on the most appropriate communication method (e.g., web portals, telecommunications)	35.9%	41.0%	16.2%	3.4%	3.4%	**4.03**
Implement partner performance assessments and evaluations impartially	24.8%	28.2%	27.4%	13.7%	6.0%	**3.52**
Ensure partner compliance with product or service certification requirements	29.1%	36.8%	23.1%	6.0%	5.1%	**3.79**

AOE 5: Setting Sales Strategy

How important are each of the following abilities *for effective performance in the Setting Sales Strategy area of expertise?*

	Essential (5)	Very important (4)	Moderately important (3)	Slightly important (2)	Unnecessary (1)	Average Rating
Synthesize industry or market knowledge toward the creation of sales force requirements	26.5%	47.7%	20.5%	3.4%	2.0%	**3.93**
Identify areas of risk and their probability and develop appropriate contingency plans	28.2%	42.3%	21.5%	5.7%	2.3%	**3.88**
Leverage and diffuse best practices in selling within the organization (industry and competitive)	35.2%	40.3%	18.8%	3.4%	2.3%	**4.03**

(continued on the next page)

AOE 5: Setting Sales Strategy (continued)

How important are each of the following abilities for effective performance in the Setting Sales Strategy area of expertise?

	Essential (5)	Very important (4)	Moderately important (3)	Slightly important (2)	Unnecessary (1)	Average Rating
Manage complex change or transformation programs (e.g., design, develop, implement, and evaluate) to preserve innovation while ensuring compliance with company policy	30.5%	38.3%	23.2%	5.4%	2.7%	**3.89**
Divide and allocate sales territories for maximum impact on company growth objectives	29.5%	36.2%	20.5%	7.0%	6.7%	**3.75**
Build executive sponsorship at the highest levels of the company	34.6%	39.6%	19.8%	2.7%	3.4%	**3.99**

AOE 6: Managing within the Sales Ecosystem

How important are each of the following abilities for effective performance in the Managing within the Sales Ecosystem area of expertise?

	Essential (5)	Very important (4)	Moderately important (3)	Slightly important (2)	Unnecessary (1)	Average Rating
Convert company targets and metrics into action	30.4%	46.1%	21.6%	2.0%	0.0%	**4.05**
Assess individual or team strengths and weaknesses	36.3%	43.1%	17.6%	2.0%	1.0%	**4.12**
Ensure compliance with applicable local, national, and international laws	33.3%	34.3%	29.4%	2.0%	1.0%	**3.97**
Manage operations to ensure cost-effectiveness	29.4%	55.9%	13.7%	1.0%	0.0%	**4.14**
Manage business forecasts to ensure accuracy	27.5%	48.0%	23.5%	1.0%	0.0%	**4.02**
Build strategies for counteracting competitive tactics	32.4%	49.0%	18.6%	0.0%	0.0%	**4.14**
Identify and address workforce gaps (e.g., training, hiring)	28.4%	44.1%	24.5%	2.9%	0.0%	**3.98**
Manage operations to minimize costs or maximize profits	31.4%	42.2%	26.5%	0.0%	0.0%	**4.05**
Ensure workforce compliance with standards of conduct, ethical guidelines, and specific human resources policies	33.3%	37.3%	27.5%	1.0%	1.0%	**4.01**

AOE 7: Developing Sales Force Capability

How important are each of the following abilities for effective performance in the Developing Sales Force Capability area of expertise?

	Essential (5)	Very important (4)	Moderately important (3)	Slightly important (2)	Unnecessary (1)	Average Rating
Translate business requirements or performance gaps into relevant learning improvements	48.4%	33.3%	11.7%	4.2%	2.3%	**4.21**
Apply appropriate approaches to learning to best meet the needs of target audiences	39.0%	40.8%	15.5%	2.8%	1.9%	**4.12**
Apply rapid instructional design methods to ensure responsiveness to performance challenges	20.2%	43.2%	25.8%	8.0%	2.8%	**3.70**
Build learning solutions sensitive to learning styles or cultural norms	30.5%	44.6%	17.4%	4.2%	3.3%	**3.95**
Leverage workplace opportunities to advance experiential learning (e.g., mentoring, cognitive apprenticeship, peer-to-peer tutoring)	40.4%	38.5%	15.5%	3.8%	1.9%	**4.12**
Construct valid and reliable tests	14.6%	39.4%	30.0%	11.3%	4.7%	**3.48**
Balance cost, target audience requirements, and content demands to select the most appropriate learning delivery systems and media	30.0%	43.2%	18.3%	5.6%	2.8%	**3.92**
Implement learning program evaluation systematically to establish a value chain that clearly connects interventions to business results (e.g., formative, summative)	29.6%	40.8%	21.1%	5.6%	2.8%	**3.89**

AOE 8: Delivering Sales Training

How important are each of the following abilities for effective performance in the Delivering Sales Training area of expertise?

	Essential (5)	Very important (4)	Moderately important (3)	Slightly important (2)	Unnecessary (1)	Average Rating
Apply platform skills, methods, and tactics effectively to advance learning	47.8%	34.5%	14.2%	1.8%	1.8%	**4.25**
Adapt instructional methods to target audience requirements	52.2%	33.6%	11.1%	2.7%	0.4%	**4.35**
Use personal style, management techniques, and media to optimize the conditions of learning	48.7%	40.7%	8.0%	1.8%	0.9%	**4.35**
Administer testing fairly and in a way that accurately assesses skill or knowledge acquisition	27.9%	36.7%	22.1%	6.6%	6.6%	**3.73**
Interpret attendance tracking and performance system data accurately	16.4%	34.1%	31.9%	11.5%	6.2%	**3.43**
Identify and recommend supplemental learning strategies that will reinforce and extend classroom learning	42.5%	37.6%	14.2%	3.5%	2.2%	**4.15**
Match experiential learning methods to appropriate content	44.2%	41.2%	10.6%	3.1%	0.9%	**4.25**

AOE 9: Coaching for Sales Results

How important are each of the following abilities for effective performance in the Coaching for Sales Results area of expertise?

	Essential (5)	Very important (4)	Moderately important (3)	Slightly important (2)	Unnecessary (1)	Average Rating
Assess performance objectively	54.9%	36.4%	6.4%	1.1%	1.1%	**4.43**
Assume various roles as needed in role-play to maximize learning (e.g., sales person, customer, sales manager, technical support)	36.7%	48.1%	12.5%	1.1%	1.5%	**4.17**
Employ observation to gather the most accurate depiction of performance data	42.8%	41.7%	12.1%	1.9%	1.5%	**4.22**
Identify "teachable moments" and use these as intervention points to improve performance	51.5%	37.5%	9.8%	0.4%	0.8%	**4.39**
Balance performance improvement objectives with a recipient's need for a healthy self-concept	35.6%	43.6%	15.5%	4.2%	1.1%	**4.08**

AOE 10: Building Sales Infrastructure

How important are each of the following abilities for effective performance in the Building Sales Infrastructure area of expertise?

	Essential (5)	Very important (4)	Moderately important (3)	Slightly important (2)	Unnecessary (1)	Average Rating
Establish valid requirement feeds from all key stakeholders	29.1%	36.6%	23.1%	6.7%	4.5%	**3.79**
Depict key value chain process inputs, milestones, and outputs	29.1%	35.8%	23.1%	9.0%	3.0%	**3.79**
Build comprehensive models depicting all stakeholder interfaces	21.6%	38.1%	23.1%	13.4%	3.7%	**3.60**
Assess current processes and tools for gaps or inefficiencies	30.6%	42.5%	17.9%	6.0%	3.0%	**3.92**

AOE 11: Designing Compensation

How important are each of the following abilities for effective performance in the Designing Compensation area of expertise?

	Essential (5)	Very important (4)	Moderately important (3)	Slightly important (2)	Unnecessary (1)	Average Rating
Synthesize data from a variety of sources and make valid inferences	25.0%	28.6%	32.1%	10.7%	3.6%	**3.61**
Determine competitive yet feasible compensation metrics	21.4%	32.1%	35.7%	7.1%	3.6%	**3.61**
Supplement base payout with innovative reward strategies	21.4%	28.6%	35.7%	7.1%	7.1%	**3.50**
Identify and incorporate market competitive practices in compensation	17.9%	39.3%	32.1%	7.1%	3.6%	**3.61**
Generate stakeholder buy-in	14.3%	39.3%	32.1%	7.1%	7.1%	**3.46**
Identify the impact of current and proposed compensation policies on company health and sales force retention or recruiting	17.9%	28.6%	46.4%	0.0%	7.1%	**3.50**

AOE 12: Maintaining Accounts

How important are each of the following abilities for effective performance in the Maintaining Accounts area of expertise?

	Essential (5)	Very important (4)	Moderately important (3)	Slightly important (2)	Unnecessary (1)	Average Rating
Collaborate effectively with account managers to meet customer needs	43.9%	38.5%	11.7%	2.8%	3.1%	**4.17**
Apply standard contractual terms and pricing appropriately and escalate for nonstandard conditions, where needed	30.5%	38.7%	21.7%	4.3%	4.8%	**3.86**
Identify account performance trends and key milestones	34.2%	39.9%	19.1%	4.6%	2.3%	**3.99**
Prioritize and fulfill customer requests with an appropriate sense of urgency	59.0%	33.9%	5.1%	1.7%	0.3%	**4.50**

AOE 13: Recruiting Sales Talent

How important are each of the following abilities for effective performance in the Recruiting Sales Talent area of expertise?

	Essential (5)	Very important (4)	Moderately important (3)	Slightly important (2)	Unnecessary (1)	Average Rating
Build and maintain professional industry and professional contacts	28.8%	50.0%	15.2%	1.5%	4.5%	**3.97**
Influence the definition of job and salary requirements to ensure logical alignment	19.7%	42.4%	25.8%	6.1%	6.1%	**3.64**
Accurately interpret psychometric test output	16.7%	37.9%	30.3%	4.5%	10.6%	**3.45**
Validate tacit impressions of a candidate through questioning techniques	21.2%	50.0%	22.7%	1.5%	4.5%	**3.82**
Establish candidate relationships based on trust	37.9%	43.9%	12.1%	1.5%	4.5%	**4.09**
Assess emerging information against prior information for consistency	25.8%	43.9%	21.2%	3.0%	6.1%	**3.80**
Protect the interests of company stakeholders during negotiations	31.8%	39.4%	21.2%	3.0%	4.5%	**3.91**

Foundational Competencies

Partnering Competencies

Spanning Boundaries

How important are each of the following key actions for effective performance in your job?

	Essential (5)	Very important (4)	Moderately important (3)	Slightly important (2)	Unnecessary (1)	Average Rating
Advancing collaboration and positive relationships across organizational boundaries	41.2%	36.7%	16.6%	3.8%	1.7%	**4.12**
Addressing coverage gaps to ensure success of the total endeavor	30.6%	42.5%	21.4%	3.5%	2.1%	**3.96**

Communicating Effectively

How important are each of the following key actions for effective performance in your job?

	Essential (5)	Very important (4)	Moderately important (3)	Slightly important (2)	Unnecessary (1)	Average Rating
Demonstrating active listening	62.1%	28.1%	8.1%	1.0%	0.6%	**4.50**
Achieving communication objectives	43.7%	41.4%	12.4%	1.5%	1.0%	**4.25**
Ensuring responsive communication	49.2%	38.4%	9.9%	1.6%	0.9%	**4.34**
Communicating persuasively	55.0%	35.0%	8.6%	0.7%	0.7%	**4.43**

Aligning to Customers

How important are each of the following key actions for effective performance in your job?

	Essential (5)	Very important (4)	Moderately important (3)	Slightly important (2)	Unnecessary (1)	Average Rating
Contributing to customer satisfaction	60.5%	29.5%	8.3%	1.3%	0.3%	**4.49**
Advocating for the customer	43.4%	41.3%	11.8%	2.8%	0.7%	**4.24**

Setting Expectations

How important are each of the following key actions for effective performance in your job?

	Essential (5)	Very important (4)	Moderately important (3)	Slightly important (2)	Unnecessary (1)	Average Rating
Communicating expectations to all stakeholders	43.2%	36.5%	14.5%	2.7%	3.2%	**4.14**
Ensuring that all stakeholders clearly understand what they are accountable for	41.2%	35.8%	16.7%	3.3%	3.0%	**4.09**
Understanding and addressing potential obstacles to proposed solutions	46.6%	38.4%	12.2%	2.3%	0.5%	**4.28**

Negotiating Positions

How important are each of the following key actions for effective performance in your job?

	Essential (5)	Very important (4)	Moderately important (3)	Slightly important (2)	Unnecessary (1)	Average Rating
Determining optimum negotiation positions	33.2%	40.2%	19.2%	4.1%	3.3%	**3.96**
Addressing objections accurately and professionally	54.4%	32.4%	11.1%	1.5%	0.5%	**4.39**
Building consensus and commitment	43.2%	40.3%	13.3%	2.2%	1.0%	**4.23**

Building Relationships

How important are each of the following key actions for effective performance in your job?

	Essential (5)	Very important (4)	Moderately important (3)	Slightly important (2)	Unnecessary (1)	Average Rating
Actively nurturing positive relationships	53.2%	35.2%	9.0%	1.7%	0.9%	**4.38**
Developing relationships based on trust and confidence	61.4%	29.0%	6.9%	2.0%	0.7%	**4.49**

Insight Competencies

Analyzing Organizational Capacity

How important are each of the following key actions for effective performance in your job?

	Essential (5)	Very important (4)	Moderately important (3)	Slightly important (2)	Unnecessary (1)	Average Rating
Accurately assessing resource requirements	28.4%	45.9%	18.6%	3.8%	3.4%	**3.92**
Balancing risk with potential advantage when determining next steps	25.0%	45.6%	20.6%	5.8%	3.1%	**3.84**

Understanding the Business Context

How important are each of the following key actions for effective performance in your job?

	Essential (5)	Very important (4)	Moderately important (3)	Slightly important (2)	Unnecessary (1)	Average Rating
Situating work meaningfully in terms of its relationship to other functions	26.6%	41.3%	22.9%	6.4%	2.8%	**3.83**
Ensuring that work meaningfully contributes to the organization's success	38.8%	40.6%	17.1%	1.8%	1.8%	**4.13**

Evaluating Customer Experiences

How important are each of the following key actions for effective performance in your job?

	Essential (5)	Very important (4)	Moderately important (3)	Slightly important (2)	Unnecessary (1)	Average Rating
Evaluating solutions to ensure that they work as planned	35.8%	45.3%	14.2%	3.8%	0.9%	**4.11**
Communicating performance in terms of bottom-line business metrics of benefit to stakeholders	30.2%	42.5%	18.5%	4.2%	4.6%	**3.90**

Gathering Intelligence

How important are each of the following key actions for effective performance in your job?

	Essential (5)	Very important (4)	Moderately important (3)	Slightly important (2)	Unnecessary (1)	Average Rating
Determining the range, type, and scope of information needed to address challenges	30.9%	43.6%	19.3%	4.4%	1.8%	**3.97**
Applying the most appropriate tools and strategies to gather needed information	32.5%	47.3%	16.8%	2.2%	1.2%	**4.08**
Tapping into information sources best suited to speak to the problem at hand	30.7%	42.3%	18.3%	5.2%	3.5%	**3.92**

Prioritizing Stakeholders Needs

How important are each of the following key actions for effective performance in your job?

	Essential (5)	Very important (4)	Moderately important (3)	Slightly important (2)	Unnecessary (1)	Average Rating
Thoroughly diagnosing problems to identify their true nature	39.9%	39.0%	14.9%	4.7%	1.6%	**4.11**
Prioritizing needs as a means for building strategies and allocating resources	35.7%	40.8%	16.9%	3.8%	2.8%	**4.03**

Identifying Options

How important are each of the following key actions for effective performance in your job?

	Essential (5)	Very important (4)	Moderately important (3)	Slightly important (2)	Unnecessary (1)	Average Rating
Exploring alternative solutions for feasibility before committing to action	28.5%	45.1%	20.0%	3.5%	3.0%	**3.93**
Applying creative problem solving to enhance the likelihood of innovative solutions	36.2%	45.5%	15.7%	1.6%	1.0%	**4.14**
Actively soliciting the input of all stakeholders to ensure solution effectiveness	28.8%	42.7%	20.0%	4.8%	3.6%	**3.88**
Determining an appropriate strategy and committing to a course of action	39.2%	44.1%	12.9%	2.1%	1.7%	**4.17**

Building a Business Case

How important are each of the following key actions for effective performance in your job?

	Essential (5)	Very important (4)	Moderately important (3)	Slightly important (2)	Unnecessary (1)	Average Rating
Using important business metrics to guide the development and evaluation of solutions	24.7%	43.5%	21.8%	7.1%	2.9%	**3.80**
Building the value justifications required to enlist support and ensure the commitment of resources	30.6%	39.1%	22.7%	4.3%	3.3%	**3.90**
Clearly identifying the business or financial benefits to be realized by investments	33.0%	41.1%	18.2%	4.2%	3.5%	**3.96**

Appendix E

Solution Competencies

Facilitating Change

How important are each of the following key actions for effective performance in your job?

	Essential (5)	Very important (4)	Moderately important (3)	Slightly important (2)	Unnecessary (1)	Average Rating
Encouraging others to embrace change as an opportunity rather than an obstacle	38.4%	39.3%	18.6%	1.6%	2.1%	**4.10**
Managing change effectively	42.4%	40.2%	14.7%	2.1%	0.5%	**4.22**
Approaching work with a proactive attitude	57.7%	32.7%	7.8%	1.2%	0.5%	**4.46**

Formalizing Agreements

How important are each of the following key actions for effective performance in your job?

	Essential (5)	Very important (4)	Moderately important (3)	Slightly important (2)	Unnecessary (1)	Average Rating
Building commitment and support as a basis for formal agreements	39.2%	40.3%	16.7%	2.8%	1.0%	**4.14**
Ensuring that agreements are communicated in a timely fashion to expedite implementation	37.2%	41.1%	17.5%	3.0%	1.1%	**4.10**
Documenting all agreements to ensure an accurate record of decisions and commitments	34.9%	37.3%	22.2%	3.7%	1.9%	**3.99**

Resolving Issues

How important are each of the following key actions for effective performance in your job?

	Essential (5)	Very important (4)	Moderately important (3)	Slightly important (2)	Unnecessary (1)	Average Rating
Actively monitoring situations for potential problems	36.0%	42.8%	17.3%	3.2%	0.8%	**4.10**
Monitoring implementation to ensure achievement of milestones	34.6%	40.7%	18.8%	3.8%	2.1%	**4.02**
Acting as a focal point of escalation to expedite problem resolution	32.3%	37.9%	23.8%	4.8%	1.2%	**3.95**

Managing Projects

How important are each of the following key actions for effective performance in your job?

	Essential (5)	Very important (4)	Moderately important (3)	Slightly important (2)	Unnecessary (1)	Average Rating
Organizing and managing work systematically	39.3%	42.5%	15.6%	1.9%	0.7%	**4.18**
Organizing and managing resources effectively	38.1%	42.4%	16.3%	2.1%	1.1%	**4.14**
Adapting formal methods as needed to achieve goals	27.4%	39.5%	24.5%	6.8%	1.8%	**3.84**

Leveraging Success

How important are each of the following key actions for effective performance in your job?

	Essential (5)	Very important (4)	Moderately important (3)	Slightly important (2)	Unnecessary (1)	Average Rating
Using success to build confidence and leverage additional opportunities	41.2%	43.0%	12.7%	1.7%	1.4%	**4.21**
Documenting and communicating best practices	33.6%	39.6%	21.2%	4.0%	1.6%	**4.00**

Articulating Value

How important are each of the following key actions for effective performance in your job?

	Essential (5)	Very important (4)	Moderately important (3)	Slightly important (2)	Unnecessary (1)	Average Rating
Ensuring that criteria for decision making are shared and addressed	31.4%	43.2%	19.8%	3.5%	2.1%	**3.98**
Adapting and tailoring messages to meet the needs of different audiences	43.2%	37.7%	16.0%	2.4%	0.7%	**4.20**
Building consensus with stakeholders on the effectiveness of proposed solutions	31.3%	42.9%	17.3%	5.0%	3.6%	**3.93**

Appendix E

Effectiveness Competencies

Building Business Skill

How important are each of the following key actions for effective performance in your job?

	Essential (5)	Very important (4)	Moderately important (3)	Slightly important (2)	Unnecessary (1)	Average Rating
Incorporating understanding of business concepts and processing effectively in business communications	33.6%	43.3%	18.9%	2.6%	1.6%	**4.05**
Applying a business perspective in assessing needs and judging the validity of proposed solutions	33.2%	41.8%	20.7%	2.4%	1.9%	**4.02**
Incorporating understanding of legal or contractual concepts and processes in defining work and setting expectations	21.7%	37.5%	28.6%	7.9%	4.3%	**3.64**
Incorporating understanding of financial concepts and processes in determining the business value of solutions or the use of resources	25.2%	42.2%	23.3%	6.1%	3.1%	**3.80**

Solving Problems

How important are each of the following key actions for effective performance in your job?

	Essential (5)	Very important (4)	Moderately important (3)	Slightly important (2)	Unnecessary (1)	Average Rating
Approaching challenges from a fresh perspective that encourages effective innovation	35.9%	44.8%	15.5%	2.0%	1.8%	**4.11**
Creatively drawing from multiple disciplines to generate new approaches to problem solving	33.3%	39.9%	19.0%	5.6%	2.1%	**3.97**

Embracing Diversity

How important are each of the following key actions for effective performance in your job?

	Essential (5)	Very important (4)	Moderately important (3)	Slightly important (2)	Unnecessary (1)	Average Rating
Demonstrating respect for others	55.2%	32.0%	10.1%	1.8%	1.0%	**4.38**
Appreciating diverse perspectives and approaches to work and actively seeking to understand these perspectives	34.4%	38.4%	20.9%	4.6%	1.8%	**3.99**
Leveraging the experiences and worldviews of others to drive innovations and stimulate creativity	25.1%	43.8%	20.1%	8.2%	2.7%	**3.80**

Making Ethical Decisions

How important are each of the following key actions for effective performance in your job?

	Essential (5)	Very important (4)	Moderately important (3)	Slightly important (2)	Unnecessary (1)	Average Rating
Taking personal responsibility for ensuring that all actions contribute to the integrity of the company and workplace	51.5%	32.3%	13.3%	1.5%	1.3%	**4.31**
Incorporating understanding of quality processes, business rules, and best practices into work activities	30.3%	44.7%	18.9%	3.9%	2.2%	**3.97**

Managing Knowledge

How important are each of the following key actions for effective performance in your job?

	Essential (5)	Very important (4)	Moderately important (3)	Slightly important (2)	Unnecessary (1)	Average Rating
Valuing and actively circulating information to improve overall work performance and productivity	33.2%	39.9%	21.6%	2.8%	2.3%	**3.99**
Identifying and resolving obstacles to the effective communication of information	37.4%	42.1%	17.2%	2.2%	1.0%	**4.13**

Using Technology

How important are each of the following key actions for effective performance in your job?

	Essential (5)	Very important (4)	Moderately important (3)	Slightly important (2)	Unnecessary (1)	Average Rating
Building and maintaining understanding of technical innovations applicable to area of responsibility	28.3%	42.6%	23.0%	4.6%	1.5%	**3.92**
Using information technology to align and expedite work	26.9%	45.4%	22.4%	4.7%	0.5%	**3.94**
Improving personal productivity by actively learning about new technologies	38.2%	36.9%	18.2%	5.4%	1.3%	**4.05**

Accelerating Learning

How important are each of the following key actions for effective performance in your job?

	Essential (5)	Very important (4)	Moderately important (3)	Slightly important (2)	Unnecessary (1)	Average Rating
Taking personal responsibility for development	49.1%	35.3%	11.9%	2.4%	1.3%	**4.28**
Using multiple learning options to creatively maximize the time available for learning	32.0%	40.7%	20.9%	4.4%	2.1%	**3.96**
Taking advantage of available information and resources to continuously develop personal skills	35.9%	44.1%	17.3%	1.5%	1.2%	**4.12**

Executing Plans

How important are each of the following key actions for effective performance in your job?

	Essential (5)	Very important (4)	Moderately important (3)	Slightly important (2)	Unnecessary (1)	Average Rating
Developing plans that clearly communicate strategy and enable implementation	40.5%	40.5%	13.8%	3.9%	1.2%	**4.15**
Building commitment to plan	37.5%	41.9%	14.8%	3.4%	2.3%	**4.09**
Executing to plan, yet adapting to emergent circumstances	42.2%	37.0%	14.7%	3.1%	3.1%	**4.12**
Delivering to plan	45.9%	40.4%	11.5%	1.0%	1.3%	**4.29**

Maximizing Personal Time

How important are each of the following key actions for effective performance in your job?

	Essential (5)	Very important (4)	Moderately important (3)	Slightly important (2)	Unnecessary (1)	Average Rating
Incorporating a strategic perspective in activity planning	31.3%	43.3%	18.5%	4.4%	2.3%	**3.97**
Practicing time management	48.2%	35.3%	14.5%	1.3%	0.8%	**4.29**

Aligning to Sales Process

How important are each of the following key actions for effective performance in your job?

	Essential (5)	Very important (4)	Moderately important (3)	Slightly important (2)	Unnecessary (1)	Average Rating
Understanding how personal work contributes to effective selling	36.8%	43.5%	15.4%	2.6%	1.7%	**4.11**
Incorporating selling sensibilities into work execution	33.7%	43.6%	20.0%	2.0%	0.7%	**4.07**
Demonstrating a systemic understanding of sales	42.9%	36.3%	16.3%	2.6%	1.8%	**4.16**
Ensuring that work helps to advance sales	45.4%	39.9%	13.6%	1.1%	0.0%	**4.30**

Appendix F

Project Participants

ASTD would like to acknowledge the people and ASTD chapters listed on the following pages as well as all others whose help and input contributed to this study. The authors greatly appreciate their efforts.

Individuals

Warren Adams
Human Resource Manager
URAC, DC

Mike Ahearne
Professor, Marketing and Sales
University of Houston, TX

Peter Anscombe
Managing Director, Commercial Division
Marsh Limited, UK

Kirk Arrowood
Director, Strategic Alliances
Quantum Corporation, NY

Paul Auchincloss
Vice President and Managing Director, Sales Association Financial Professionals, MD

Scott Barghaan
Sales Representative
EMC, VA

Richa Batra
Director of Sales
ASTD, VA

Stella M. Belich
Director Human Resource, Learning and Development
Kuehne + Nagel, NJ

Eva Bergenheim-Holmberg
Global Human Resource Director
Mercuri International, Sweden

Stephanie Biernbaum
Manager, Learning and Development Programs
Tiffany & Co., NY

Mark Bills
Chief Marketing Officer
Seamless NWS, CA

Jeff Bishop
Partner Development Manager
Exact Target, IN

Steve Boardman
Director, North American Sales
Align Technology, CA

Brad Bolnick
Vice President, Sales
Patni Computer Services, NY

Willem Boom
Sales Executive
Thomson Reuters, CA

Martin Brossman
President
Coaching Success, NC

Jeff Brown
Senior National Account Manager
Shell Lubricants, Canada

Natalie Buford-Young
CEO
Rainfield Group, VA

Suzanne Burgess
President
SalesBytes, South Africa

Greg Coleman
Sales Manager
OutStart, IL

R. Woody Daroca
Managing Director
Human Resource Solutions, CO

Jan Delory
President
Boston Professional Group, NC

Christopher Draven
Learning Delivery Supervisor
Prescription Solutions/UnitedHealth
Group, MO

Annette Dunlap, PHR
President
Jernigan-Hightower & Associates,
TX

Peter Eales
Sales and Marketing Consultant
OI solutions, UK

Joe Erfurt
Consultant
Erfurt Marketing, UK

Margaret Fiorenzo
Area Development Manager
Pitney Bowes, GA

John Flikeid
Senior Solutions Consultant
Ricoh Professional Services, VA

Tony Friday
President
Causing Excellence, CA

Dan Gibbs
National Account Manager
GeoLearning, IA

Brian Giese
CEO
IT Selling Bootcamp, VA

Ian Gilbert
CEO and Founder
Third Core, Canada

Desaray Granzow
Business Consultant
CareerBuilder, LLC, IL

Doris Greenwood
Sales Competency and Training
Evaluation Program Manager
The Hewlett-Packard Company, CA

Gerhard Gschwandtner
Publisher
Selling Power magazine, VA

Barry Gutwillig
Key Account Manager
AMICAS, MA

Marc Guyon
Competency and Development
Manager
Shell Oil, Malaysia

Chris Hall
Sales Director
Vizual, MD

Susan Hall
Sales Manager
Pitney Bowes, NC

Rob Harper
Sales Training
SAS, NC

Chuck Hayden
Sales Manager
Learning Tree, VA

John Heckbert
Senior Consultant
Auteur Group, Canada

Bob Heth
President
Kaizen Performance, TX

Sandy Hillmer
Sales Director
Krug, Canada

Shirley Hinton
President
TeachPath Training Group, NC

Mary Houston
Sales Manager Canadian Business
Anchor Hocking, Canada

John Huggart
Managing Director
Sales Positive, Sydney, Australia

Mark Hunter
Sales Trainer
MJH and Associates Consulting,
NE

Phil Janus
Chief Technical Officer
Sales Engineering, MA

Eli Jones
Director, Center for Sales Excellence
University of Houston, TX

Jason Jordan
Senior Consultant
Mercer Worldwide, DC

Jill Konrath
CEO and Chief Sales Officer
Selling to Big Companies, NY

Gil Laks
Vice President, International
Align Technology, CA

Andy Mank
District Manager
Fortify Software, NY

Marsha Marinich
President and CEO
Performance Interventions, Inc., VA

Jim Martin
President
Sales Architects, MD

Mark McCarthy
Director
Meta-Lucid, Ltd., UK

Ken Midtgaard
General Manager
Luxo ASA, Denmark

Michael Milbourn
Assistant Vice President, Marketing and Training
Ameritas Life Insurance, NE

Allan Mills
Project Manager
Perdue Farms, MD

Mark Moon
Professor
University of Tennessee Knoxville, TN

Kathryn Mundy
Global Sales and Training Consultant
SAS Institute, NC

Mark Myette
Director of Sales Center of Learning and Performance
Pitney Bowes, GA

Willis Newton
Consultant
Newton and Associates, Canada

Larry Noethlich
General Manager
ARS Business Solutions, IL

William Paullin
President
Selling Solutions, GA

Stone Payton
Director
The DeSai Group, GA

Al Pelham
Professor of Marketing
College of New Jersey, NJ

Rob Peterson
Professor
William Patterson University, NJ

Darin Phillips
Director, Customer Experience
Silver Hill Financial, FL

Tom Phillips
President
Sales University, VA

Marc Ramos
Director of Global Sales Training
Red Hat, NC

Jamie Robbins
Senior Director, Sales Operations
SAS Institute, NC

Duane Roemmich
Vice President, Consultant
My-Pipeline, MN

Orin Salas
Vice President, Sales
Herrmann International, NC

Mark Schermers
Sales Representative
SAP, TN

Jay Schippanoski
Key Account Manager
Shell Lubricants, Canada

Brian Schneider
Tracom Group, Inc., MA

Vaibhav Sharma
Chief Information Officer
Yaana Technologies, Bangalore, India

Barbra Sher
Curriculum Manager and Training Developer
The Hewlett-Packard Company, MA

Kevin Smith
Sales Manager
Pitney Bowes, SC

Reggie Smith
Division Sales Manager
Genentech, WA

Jonathan Sper
Sales Representative
Impact Channel, DC

Ken Spiller
Senior Manager, Sales Operations
Align Technology, CA

Aaron Steeves
Business Unit Manager
Ricoh Professional Services, VA

Caroline Tan
Learning and Development Manager for Sales and Sales Opportunities
Google, CA

Rick Tancreto
Sales Representative
Claritas, VA

Barbee Taylor
Sales Account Executive
Bell South, IL

Kevin Taylor
Sales Representative
Vizual, VA

Divakar Varadarajan
Sales Manager
LG-CNS, India

Michael Wade
National Special Markets Manager
AXIS Dental Corporation, TX

Alexander Williams
Manager Sales Training
Pitney Bowes Canada, Toronto

Gary Zimmermann
Sales Process Program Manager
Eaton Corporation/Electrical
Group, OH

ASTD Chapters

The following ASTD chapters circulated invitations to encourage participation. Individual members from chapters not listed above also contributed to the survey.

Greater Atlanta Chapter
Atlanta, GA

Orange County Chapter
Los Angeles, CA

Baton Rouge Chapter
Baton Rouge, LA

Midlands Chapter
Columbia, SC

Ft. Lauderdale Chapter
Ft. Lauderdale, FL

Long Island Chapter
New York, NY

Western Ohio Chapter
Dayton, OH

Glossary

A guide to key terms used in *World-Class Selling: New Sales Competencies.*

Area of expertise: the specific technical and professional skills and knowledge required for success in sales specialty areas.

Buyer facilitation: a customer-focused selling approach that begins with identifying the buyer's needs, proceeds through providing information and educating the buyer, then on to demonstrating the product's value and results. Emphasizes influence over manipulation.

Buying organization: any company, association, team, person, or entity that has been identified as needing to purchase a product or service. A buying organization can be a prospect, or a current or previous customer or client to the selling organization. The buying organization and the selling organization *can* be part of the same company, association, or entity, but not usually the same team or person.

Category management: a retailing concept in which the total range of products sold by a retailer is broken down into discrete groups of similar or related products; these groups are known as product categories.

Customer: a buying organization that (may) buy repeatedly, but is not actively engaged on a regular basis by the selling organization.

Client: a customer that is regularly and actively engaged by the selling organization.

Competency: a cluster of related knowledge, skills, abilities, and behaviors that affects a major part of one's job. A competency should correlate with performance on the job and have the ability to be measured.

Competency model: a structure designed to define the knowledge, skills, and abilities required for high performance that allows for a highly targeted training needs assessment and provides a roadmap to more objectively manage talent for competitive advantage.

Competency study: a rigorous, disciplined approach to defining exactly what members of a profession must know and be able to do to be successful.

Consultative selling: a sales approach that depends on a relationship between buyer and seller featuring trust, credibility, and mutual understanding; leverages the value proposition; and presents a compelling business case for the solution.

Leadership development: any activity that enhances the quality of leadership within an individual or organization and that focuses on developing the leadership abilities and attitudes of individuals.

Organizational performance: the outputs or results of an organization as measured against its goals and objectives.

Output: a tangible product that an individual delivers to others, especially colleagues, customers, or clients.

Result: a service that an employee renders to others.

Revenue generation system: a system for generating organizational profits through leveraging the subsystems of marketing, selling, infrastructure, and fulfillment.

Role: a broad area of responsibility. These are not job titles but different "hats" that people must wear to accomplish their jobs.

Sale: a unique transaction with deliverables and an exchange of money or its equivalent.

Sales process: a series of tactical and strategic steps that leads to the sales transaction.

Sales profession: the supportive business system and practices required to effectively develop, manage, enable, and execute a mutually beneficial, interpersonal exchange of goods or services for equitable value.

Sales stakeholders: anyone on the buying or selling side that is affected by the sale of a product or service.

Selling organization: any company, association, team, person, or entity that has defined and developed a product or service targeted to a specific market or markets.

Talent management: an organizational approach to leading people by building culture, engagement, capability, and capacity through integrated talent acquisition, development, and deployment processes that are aligned to business goals (ASTD, 2009).

Team selling: using the full resources of your company to sell an account through all of its relevant decision makers.

Workplace learning and performance: an organizational development approach defined by ASTD as the integrated use of learning and other solutions for the purpose of improving human performance and addressing individual and organizational needs. WLP uses a systematic process of analyzing and responding to individual, group, and organizational performance issues. WLP creates positive, progressive change within organizations by balancing human, ethical, technological, and operational considerations (Rothwell, Sanders, and Soper, 1999).

References

AMI (Andy Miller International). (2005). The 5 Most Dangerous Trends Facing VPs of Sales Today, Nightingale Conant. AMI whitepaper, www.andymillerinternational.com.

ASTD. (2008). Sales Training Perceptions. Unpublished ASTD market research study. Alexandria, VA.

———. (2009). The New Face of Talent Management: Making Sure That People Really Are Your Most Important Asset. ASTD white paper. Alexandria, VA: ASTD.

Bernthal, P., K. Colteryahn, P. Davis, J. Naughton, W. Rothwell, and R. Wellins. (2004). *ASTD 2004 Competency Study: Mapping the Future: New Workplace Learning and Performance Competencies.* Alexandria, VA: ASTD.

Boyatzis, R.E. (1982). *The Competent Manager: A Model for Effective Performance.* New York: Wiley.

Boyer, S.L., and B. Lambert. (2008). Take the Handcuffs Off the Sales Team with Self-Directed Learning. *T+D,* 62:62–66.

BPT Partners. (2006). The Future of Selling—Developing Customer Knowledge Competence & Leveraging the Sales Organization for Competitive Advantage, www.bptpartners.com/insight.aspx.

ChangingMinds.org. (2002–2009). Conscious and competence, http://changingminds.org/explanations/learning/consciousness_competence.htm.

Consultative Selling. http://sales-sense.com/ConsultativeSelling.htm.

Derven, M. (2008). Lessons Learned: Using Competency Models to Target Training Needs. *T+D,* 62(12):68–73.

Dickie, J., and B. Trailer. (2007). *Sales Performance Optimization 2007 Survey Results and Analysis Report.* Mill Valley, CA: CSO Insights.

Dubois, D., and W. Rothwell. (2000). *The Competency Toolkit.* Amherst, MA: HRD Press.

Friedman, W. (2004). *Birth of a Salesman: The Transformation of Selling in America.* Cambridge, MA: Harvard University Press.

Gist, E., and P. Mosher. (2004). *Changing Sales Force Behavior to Achieve High Performance.* New York: Accenture.

Hall, L.M. (1999). Invigorating Selling Skills with NLP. *Anchor Point,* http://www.nlpanchorpoint.com/HallSales.htm.

HR Chally. (2008). The World Class Sales Excellence Research Report: The Route to the Summit. Cleveland, OH.

Jones, E., C.G. Stevens, and L. Chonko. (2005). *Selling ASAP.* Mason, OH: South-Western Thomson Learning.

Lambert, B. (2007). *ASTD Sales Development & Performance Research.* Alexandria, VA: ASTD.

———. (2008). Is Your Sales Team Stuck in the 1890s? *T+D,* 62:42–47.

———. (2008). Selling with Competence: How Sales Teams Succeed. In *Sales Training Drivers: Owner's Manual for Sales Excellence,* ed. Brian Lambert. Alexandria, VA: ASTD Press.

Lambert, B., and G. Landvardt. (2008). So What's In It for the Sales Team? *T+D,* 62:38–41.

Lesser, E., and R. Rivera. (2006). *Closing the Generational Divide: Shifting Workforce Demographics and the Learning Function.* Somers, NY: IBM Global Business Services.

McLagan, P. (1980). Competency Models. *Training & Development Journal*, 34(12):22.

———. (1989). *Models for HRD Practice* [four volumes]. Alexandria, VA: ASTD.

———. (1996). Great Ideas Revisited. *Training & Development*, 50(1):60.

McLagan, P., and R. McCullough. (1983). *Models for Excellence: The Conclusions and Recommendations of the ASTD Training and Development Competency Study.* Alexandria, VA: ASTD.

McLagan, P., and D. Suhadolnik. (1991). *Models for HRD Practice: The Research Report.* Alexandria, VA: American Society for Training & Development.

Miller, A., and B. Lambert. (2008). Increased Capacity Brings Sales Results. *Learning Executive.* No. 4 (November), http://e-ditionsbyfry.com/Olive/AM3/LEX/Default.htm?href=LEX/2008/11/01.

Pelham, A. (2006). Sales Force Training: What Is Happening vs. What Is Needed. *Journal of Selling & Major Account Management,* Summer: 171–173.

Pinto, P., and J. Walker. (1978). *A Study of Professional Training and Development Role and Competencies.* Madison, WI: ASTD.

Piskurich, G., and E. Sanders. (1998). *ASTD Models for Learning Technologies: Roles, Competencies, and Outputs.* Alexandria, VA: ASTD.

Rothwell, W. (1996). *ASTD Models for Human Performance Improvement: Roles, Competencies, and Outputs.* Alexandria, VA: ASTD.

Rothwell, W., E. Sanders, and J. Soper. (1999). *ASTD Models for Workplace Learning and Performance: Roles, Competencies, and Outputs.* Alexandria, VA: ASTD.

Stevens, H., and T. Kinni. (2007). *Achieve Sales Excellence: The 7 Customer Rules for Becoming the New Sales Professional.* Avon, MA: Platinum Press.

Talent Shortage Survey Results: Global Results. (2007). Manpower, Inc.

Waterhouse Group. (2007). Team Selling Training, http://www.waterhousegroup.com/services/team-selling.html.

Additional Resources

Accenture. (2005). Achieving High Performance through Improved Sales Force Productivity. New York: Accenture.

Anderson, R. (1992). *Professional Selling.* Englewood Cliffs, NJ: Prentice Hall.

Artis, A.B., and E.G. Harris. (2007). Self-Directed Learning and Sales Force Performance: An Integrated Framework. *Journal of Personal Selling & Sales Management,* 27(1):9.

Attia, A.M., E.D. Honeycutt Jr., and M.P. Leach. (2005). A Three-Stage Model for Assessing and Improving Sales Force Training and Development. *Journal of Personal Selling & Sales Management,* 25(3):253–268.

Bloom, B.S. (1956). *Taxonomy of Educational Objectives—Handbook I: The Cognitive Domain.* New York: David McKay.

Blustain, H. (1992). Selling and Sales Management in Action—From Hot Boxes to Open Systems: The Changing World of Computer Salespeople. *Journal of Personal Selling & Sales Management,* 12(2):67.

Buskirk, R.H., and B.D. Buskirk. (1992). *Selling: Principles and Practices.* New York: McGraw-Hill.

CMO Council. (2007). *Marketing Outlook 2007.* Palo Alto, CA: CMO Council.

Coppett, J., and W.A. Staples. (1990). *Professional Selling: A Relationship Management Process.* Cincinnati, OH: South-Western.

Cross, J., S.W. Hartley, W. Rudelius, and M.J. Vassey. (2001). Sales Force Activities and Marketing Strategies in Industrial Firms: Relationships and Implications. *Journal of Personal Selling & Sales Management,* 21(3):199–206.

Davenport, T.O. (1999). Human Capital. *Management Review,* 88(11):37.

Deeter-Schmelz, D.R., and R. Ramsey. (1995). A Conceptualization of the Functions and Roles of Formalized Selling and Buying Teams. *Journal of Personal Selling & Sales Management,* 15(2):47.

Dillman, D. (2007). *Mail and Internet Surveys: The Tailored Design Method.* 2nd ed. Hoboken, NJ: John Wiley and Sons.

Dooley, K.E., J.R. Lindner, L.M. Dooley, and M. Alagaraja. (2004). Behaviorally Anchored Competencies: Evaluation Tool for Training via Distance. *Human Resource Development International,* 7(3):315.

Dubois, D., and W. Rothwell. (2004). *Competency-Based Human Resource Management.* Palo Alto, CA: Davies-Black.

Dweck, C.S. (1986). Motivational Processes Affecting Learning. *American Psychologist,* 41(10):1040–1048.

Futrell, C. (1988). *Sales Management.* New York: Dryden Press.

———. (1993). *Fundamentals of Selling.* Homewood, IL: Irwin.

Geiger, S., and D. Turley. (2006). The Perceived Impact of Information Technology on Salespeople's Relational Competencies. *Journal of Marketing Management,* 22(7/8):827–851.

Gordon, J., and B. Lowe. (2002). Employee Retention: Approaches for Achieving Performance Objectives. *Journal of American Academy of Business,* 1(2):201–205.

Gschwandtner, G. (2006). Selling Power 500: The Major Sales Forces. Selling Power.com, http://www.sellingpower .com/sp500/.

Gulati, R. (2007). Silo Busting: How to Execute on the Promise of Customer Focus. *Harvard Business Review,* http:// hbr.harvardbusiness.org/2007/05/silo-busting/ar/1.

Hawes, J.M., A.K. Rich, and S.M. Widmier. (2004). Assessing the Development of the Sales Profession. *Journal of Personal Selling & Sales Management,* 24(1):27.

Herring S., and A. Paradise. (2006). *State of the Industry Report.* Alexandria, VA: ASTD.

Ingram, T.N. (1996). Relationship Selling: Moving from Rhetoric to Reality. *Mid-American Journal of Business,* 11(1):5–13.

Jones, E., S.P. Brown, A.A. Zoltners, and B.A. Weitz. (2005). The Changing Environment of Selling and Sales Management. *Journal of Personal Selling & Sales Management,* 25(2):105.

Kofman, F.S., and P. Senge. (1993). Communities of Commitment: The Heart of Learning Organizations. *Organizational Dynamics,* 22:4.

Krathwohl, D., B. Bloom, and B. Masia. (1973). *Taxonomy of Educational Objectives, the Classification of Educational Goal—Handbook II: Affective Domain.* New York: David McKay.

Lysonski, S.J., and E.M. Johnson. (1983). The Sales Manager as a Boundary Spanner: A Role Theory Analysis. *Journal of Personal Selling & Sales Management,* 3(2):8.

Marshall, G., W. Moncrief, and F. Lassk. (1999). The Current State of Sales Force Activities. *Industrial Marketing Management,* 28:87–98.

McNeilis, K.S. (2002). Assessing Communication Competence in the Primary Care Medical Interview. *Communication Studies,* 53(4):400.

Meyer, T., and P. Semark. (1996). A Framework for the Use of Competencies for Achieving Competitive Advantage. *South African Journal of Business Management,* 27(4):96.

Mirabile, R.J. (1997). Everything You Wanted to Know about Competency Modeling. *Training & Development,* 51(8):73.

Moncrief, W.C. (1986). Selling Activity and Sales Position Taxonomies for Industrial Salesforces. *Journal of Marketing Research (JMR),* 23(3):261.

———. (1988). Five Types of Industrial Sales Jobs. *Industrial Marketing Management,* 17:161–167.

Moncrief, W.C., and G.W. Marshall. (2005). The Evolution of the Seven Steps of Selling. *Industrial Marketing Management,* 34(1):13.

Moncrief, W.C., G.W. Marshall, and F.G. Lassk. (2006). A Contemporary Taxonomy of Sales Positions. *Journal of Personal Selling & Sales Management,* 26(1):55–65.

Parry, S.B. (1998). Just What Is a Competency? (And Why Should You Care?). *Training,* 35(6):58.

Pelham, A. (2002). An Exploratory Model and Initial Test of the Influence of Firm Level Consulting-Oriented Sales Force Programs on Sales Force Performance. *Journal of Personal Selling & Sales Management,* 22(2):97–109.

———. (2006). Sales Force Involvement in Product Design: The Influence on the Relationships Between Consulting-Oriented Sales Management Programs and Performance. *Journal of Marketing Theory & Practice,* 14(1):37–55.

Randall, E.J., and C.H. Randall (2001). Current Review of Hiring Techniques for Sales Personnel: The First Step in the Sales Management Process. *Journal of Marketing Theory & Practice,* 9(2):70–83.

Rogers, B. (2007). *Rethinking Sales Management: A Strategic Guide for Practitioners.* West Sussex, UK: John Wiley & Sons, Ltd.

Rothwell, W., and H. Kazanas. (1998). *Mastering the Instructional Design Process: A Systematic Approach.* San Francisco: Jossey-Bass.

Rothwell, W., and J. Lindholm. (1999). Competency Identification, Modeling, and Assessment in the USA. *International Journal of Training & Development,* 3(2):90.

Rothwell, W., and R. Wellins. (2004). Mapping Your Future: Putting New Competencies to Work for You. *T+D,* 58(5):1–8.

Salas, E., and J.A. Cannon-Bowers. (2001). The Science of Training: A Decade of Progress. *Annual Review of Psychology,* 52(1):471.

Seonaid, F., and A.R. Hakstian. (2001). Improving Salesforce Performance: A Meta-analytic Investigation of the Effectiveness and Utility of Personnel Selection Procedures and Training Interventions. *Psychology & Marketing,* 18(3):281.

Sharma, V. (2001). Industrial and Organizational Salesforce Roles: A Relationship-Based Perspective. *Journal of Marketing Theory & Practice,* 9(3):44.

Shaw, D. (2007). Building Sales Competencies Through Service Learning. *Marketing Education Review,* 17(1):35–41.

Singh, J. (1998). Striking a Balance in Boundary-Spanning Positions: An Investigation of Some Unconventional Influences of Role Stressors and Job Characteristics on Job Outcomes of Sales People. *Journal of Marketing,* 62(3):69.

Snyder, D. (2001). *How to Mind Read Your Customer: Using Insights from Psychology to Increase Sales and Develop Better Business Relationships.* New York: AMACOM.

Spencer, L.M. (1997). Competency Assessment Methods. In *What Works: Assessment, Development, and Measurement.* Edited by L. Bassi and D. Russ-Eft. Alexandria, VA: American Society for Training & Development.

Spencer, L.M., and S.M. Spencer. (1993). *Competence at Work.* New York: John Wiley & Sons.

Stevens, H., and T. Kinni. (2006). *Achieve Sales Excellence: The 7 Customer Rules for Becoming the New Sales Professional.* Avon, MA: F&W Publications.

Strong, E.K. Jr. (1925). Theories of Selling. *Journal of Applied Psychology,* 9(1):75–86.

Sujan, H. (1986). Smarter Versus Harder: An Exploratory Attributional Analysis of Salespeople's Motivation. *Journal of Marketing Research (JMR),* 23(1):41.

Sujan, H., B.A. Weitz, and N. Kumar. (1994). Learning Orientation, Working Smart, and Effective Selling. *Journal of Marketing,* 58(3):39.

Tannenbaum, S.I., and G. Yukl. (1992). Training and Development in Work Organizations. *Annual Review of Psychology,* 43:399–441.

Thomas, B., S. Mitchell, and J. Del Rossa. (2007). *Sales: Strategic Partnership or Necessary Evil?* Pittsburgh, PA: DDI.

Twenge, J. (2006). *Generation Me: Why Today's Young Americans Are More Confident, Assertive, Entitled—and More Miserable Than Ever Before.* New York: Free Press.

VandeWalle, D., W.L. Cron, and J.W. Slocum Jr. (2001). The Role of Goal Orientation Following Performance Feedback. *Journal of Applied Psychology,* 86(4):629–640.

Varney, G.V. (1989). *Building Productive Teams.* San Francisco: Jossey-Bass.

Walker O. Jr., G. Churchill, and N. Ford. (1985). The Determinants of Salesperson Performance: A Meta-Analysis. *Journal of Marketing Research (JMR),* 22(2):103.

Walker, O.C. Jr., J.G.A. Churchill, and N.M. Ford. (1975). Organizational Determinants of the Industrial Salesman's Role Conflict and Ambiguity. *Journal of Marketing (pre-1986),* 39(1):32.

Weitz, B.A. (1978). Relationship Between Salesperson Performance and Understanding of Customer Decision Making. *Journal of Marketing Research (JMR),* 15(4):501.

———. (1981). Effectiveness in Sales Interactions: A Contingency Framework. *Journal of Marketing (pre-1986),* 45(1):85.

Weitz, B.A., and K.D. Bradford. (1999). Personal Selling and Sales Management: A Relationship Marketing Perspective. *Academy of Marketing Science. Journal,* 27(2):241.

Weitz, B.A., H. Sujan, and M. Sujan. (1986). Knowledge, Motivation, and Adaptive Behavior: A Framework for Improving Selling Effectiveness. *Journal of Marketing,* 50(4):174–191.

What Makes an Excellent Sales Force? (2007). Retrieved June 11, 2007, from http://www.esresearch.com/e/home/document.php?dA=Chally_1_Comp.

Wilson, D. (1995). An Integrated Model of Buyer-Seller Relationships. *Journal of the Academy of Marketing Science,* Fall:335–345.

Wilson, P.H., D. Strutton, and M.T. Farris II. (2002). Investigating the Perceptual Aspect of Sales Training. *Journal of Personal Selling & Sales Management,* 22(2):77–86.

Woodruffe, C. (1993). What Is Meant by a Competency? *Leadership & Organization Development Journal,* 14(1):29.

About the Authors

Brian W. Lambert

Brian W. Lambert is the director of ASTD's Sales Training Drivers, where he works with internal and external clients and ASTD members to create relevant content, tools, and resources for sales trainers, sales managers, and senior executives. Brian manages ASTD's sales competency modeling and sales training research and is a highly sought-after expert on delivering sales training, managing and developing high-performing sales talent, and improving salesperson performance.

Brian has 15 years of experience in all aspects of sales, sales management, and sales training. Before joining ASTD, Brian founded the United Professional Sales Association, where he oversaw the development of standards for salesperson performance worldwide. His work on salesperson competencies has helped thousands of sales team members around the world measure themselves against the standards of world-class selling. In 2006, Brian was recognized by *Sales & Marketing Management* as one of the most influential people in professional selling. Brian has a bachelor's degree from the University of Central Florida, a master's of science degree in administration and human resource management from Central Michigan University, and a doctorate from Capella University.

Tim Ohai

Tim Ohai is founder and president of Growth & Associates, a consulting association that focuses on the people dynamics of change, both organizationally and personally. Growth & Associates has created fit-for-purpose solutions for companies in a variety of industries, including ASTD, Shell Oil, and Wal-Mart. With more than a decade of learning and development experience, Tim brings a rare combination of high energy and real-life savvy to consulting on large, complex strategic issues, especially on the topics of key customer strategies, alignment, and organizational change. Tim's areas of expertise include sales performance, executive coaching, and developing the talent pipeline for emerging generations, but he also consults on key customer strategies, alignment, and organizational change. Tim has been recognized as a global coaching and sales expert, and his expertise has taken him to Latin America, Europe, Africa, Asia, and the Middle East.

Eric M. Kerkhoff

Eric M. Kerkhoff is account manager for Hewlett-Packard, where he is responsible for helping his clients leverage information technology to reduce cost, mitigate risk, and successfully respond to market conditions. Eric has more than 19 years of professional experience building diverse, high-performance sales and marketing teams. He is the author of *Sales Pro Success Secrets* as well as the first and second editions of *The Compendium of Professional Selling*. Eric has international speaking experience on a variety of sales and sales management topics. Before joining Hewlett-Packard, Eric developed and delivered the Business Development and Sales Certificate Program at The George Washington University's Center for Professional Development. He has consulted and trained sales and marketing teams in a variety of industry vertical markets.

2008 ASTD World-Class Sales Competency Advisory Panel

Jamie Barette
VP, North America
Mercuri International
TX

Eric Kerkhoff
Account Manager
Hewlett-Packard Company
VA

Tim Ohai
President
Growth and Associates
CA

Bonnie Brady
Global Sales Excellence Program
Manager
Hewlett-Packard Company
MA

Peter Korsos
General Manager
Luxo Lamp Ltd
Quebec, Canada

Richard Plank
Professor
Florida Polytechnic
FL

Tina Killough Busch
VP, Learning and Performance
Pitney Bowes, Inc.
GA

Brian Lambert
Director, ASTD Sales Training
ASTD
VA

Ian Platt
President
Trainique USA
Washington, DC

Sonia Clark
VP HR
Align Technology
CA

Guy Langvardt
Sales Executive
IBM Corporation
CA

Beth Rogers
Chairperson
University of Portsmouth and UK
Sales Board
UK

Kim Fletterman
National Sales Dev. Manager
Dimension Data
South Africa

Owen McManamon
Manager National Accounts
Shell
Ontario, Canada

Reza Sisakhti
Director, Learning Practice
Productivity Dynamics, Inc.
MA

David Hinson
Global Training and Development
Manager
SAS
Raleigh, NC

Andy Miller
President
Smguru.com
VA

Dave Stein
CEO
ES Research Group, Inc.
MA

Michelle Janecek
Global Relationship Manager
Acclivus R3 Solutions
TX

Pat Mustico
Sales Manager
Ricoh Professional
VA

Keith Stoneman
Group Sales Trainer
Ameritas Life Insurance Corp.
NE

Rande Neukam
Senior Consultant
Productivity Dynamics, Inc.
NH

Giles Watkins
Senior Manager
Shell
Jakarta, Indonesia

Chris Wellington
President
UPSA
NC

316

2008 ASTD World Class Sales Competency Project Team

ASTD
Tony Bingham
President, ASTD

Jennifer Homer
VP, External Relations

Brian Lambert
Director, Sales Training Drivers

Jennifer Naughton
Director, ASTD Competencies &
Credentialing

Jennifer Salopek
Contributing Editor

Productivity Dynamics
Reza Sisakhti
Director, Learning Practice
Productivity Dynamics, Inc.
MA

Rande Neukam
Senior Consultant
Productivity Dynamics, Inc.
NH

Joyce Nadeau
Project Manager
Productivity Dynamics, Inc.
NH

Growth & Associates
Tim Ohai
President

Index